Praise for

Third Base for Life

"A fun book to read. Berkowitz got it right. He is a great storyteller and the book moves at a nice pace . . . Berkowitz dug deep and shared so much about himself, his team and his family . . . He told it like it is."
—MLB Reports

"Endearing . . . the author is diplomatic (and amazingly patient) in dealing with his charges and owning up to his own shortcomings . . . honest sentiment trumps everything else."
—*New Jersey Jewish News*

"It's a heartfelt story about the bonds forged between kids who play America's National Pastime and the grown-up kids called parents who watch . . . Berkowitz has written about a game that packs anxiety, humor, and moral, if not outright, victories into nine innings and provides memorable life lessons at unexpected moments . . . Poignantly honest, *Third Base for Life* is about fathers and sons and moms and families and will touch any parent . . ."

—

"The book's got heart. And the stories Berkowitz shares are relevant to all parents."
—*Tablet*

"A uniquely Jewish story . . . The narrative made me

laugh out loud, and it brought tears to my eyes . . . It is as much a story about baseball as it is about a father's relationship with his son, and with his own father."

—Jewish Baseball News

"Josh describes the real-life quirky people so masterfully that you instantly feel for them . . . Josh weaves his story skillfully with both pleasant and sad twists that will keep you reading. And throughout the story he tactfully teaches kids and dads alike the importance of overcoming the fear that holds us back. If you love youth baseball and feel-good stories you will enjoy this true David vs. Goliath story about an all-Jewish youth-baseball team."

—*StatsDad*

"You get to know Josh . . . and his team, the Rashi Rams, and the community who loved and supported them, and you cannot help but feel for them as they live through this amazing experience of a lifetime . . . a lovely, inspirational baseball and family story, with a great message–perfect for any parent, grandparent, or young fan of the game."

—*Boston Red Thoughts*

Third Base
for Life

Third Base
for Life

A Memoir of Fathers, Sons, and Baseball

Joshua L. Berkowitz

San Diego

Third Base for Life

Quadrant Books

Published by arrangement with the author.

eISBN: 978-1-937868-26-0
ISBN: 978-1-937868-27-7

Library of Congress Control Number: 2013942364

Cover design by pintado.weebly.com.

Visit our website at:
www.endpaperspress.com

This memoir is based on actual events. Some names have been changed in order to preserve privacy, and certain details have been altered for narrative purposes.

Quadrant Books are published by Endpapers Press, a division of Author Coach, LLC.

The Quadrant Books logo featuring the "Q" with compass points is a trademark of Author Coach, LLC.

To Shani,
with all my love,
cross my fingers.

PROLOGUE

GABE TOED THE dirt anxiously with the tip of his cleat, watching the small clouds of dust that he created pool at his ankles. It was the beginning of summer, early June, and the sun was unusually strong on the back of his neck. He stood on the mound, rubbing the red stitching of the white baseball with two hands while his well-worn black Easton glove lay folded and tucked under his left armpit.

I looked closely at those hands—the very same that at two years old had formed small impressions in soft clay that, subsequently hardened, now hung in a picture frame on the wall of our kitchen back home. A mere seven years later, my son was growing into a young man. Slender and wiry, with long arms and a cherubic face, he filled out his red Cooperstown Dreams Park uniform nicely. His thick dark brown hair was cropped short and took up little room under his cap, which he preferred to pull down low over his eyes.

I could sense Gabe's anxiety as I watched him closely from the dugout. The batter in the on-deck circle was big for a ten-year-old, large and intimidating. He swung a massive aluminum bat with a blue doughnut weight on the end, but looked as if he could hit one over the fence with a toothpick if he needed to. But, of course, that was not surprising, considering we had found ourselves facing off against the best baseball talent in the country. We now knew what we were up against, although that had not always been the case.

The leadoff hitter finally stepped to the plate, staring down at my son with a hatred and hostility that was difficult for a father to witness. The green mountains of upstate New York that surrounded us suddenly lost their picturesque beauty. They weighed down on my chest, crushing the breath from my lungs. But now was not the time to assume the role of concerned father. It was a coach that my Gabriel needed, and a good one.

The dozens of spectators in the stands on either side of the field stood on their tiptoes in anticipation of our first pitch of the tournament. And as the umpire cried a deafening, "Play ball!" Gabe risked a quick glance over at the dugout, where our eyes met for an instant. I wiped all doubt from my face and gave him a half-smile and a firm nod.

"Go get 'em, kid!" I called. He smiled back and turned to face the imposing man-child standing at home plate.

Seemingly in slow motion, Gabe went into his windup. He pitched from the stretch, and his compact form reminded me of the grace and fluidity of a dancer. With a calm that belied the situation, he released the ball high overhead, sending it toward home plate straight and true.

As I held my breath, my eyes tracked the path of that random ball, chosen from some random box, which had been resting in a Dreams Park storage closet all winter. *What a crazy thing, that ball having so much riding on it,*

I thought, and while it was in midflight uttered a silent prayer to my old hero, Sandy Koufax.

"If there was ever a moment when a young Jewish pitcher needed your blessing, this is it," I muttered under my breath. The random ball quickly closed in on the batter, and as it approached home plate I wondered how in the world my son and I had arrived at such a time and such a place.

PART ONE

HOME

CHAPTER ONE

CRITICAL MINDS,

COMPASSIONATE HEARTS

"READY TO GO, Dad?"

I sat behind the wheel of our green Suzuki XL-7 in the school parking lot, my wife at my side and the kids behind us. It was the first day of school and the nervous anticipation emanating from the back seat was palpable. Not responding immediately, I stared at the modest cinder-block building with its large printed sign draped from one of the windows.

WELCOME TO RASHI, it proclaimed, with RASHI printed in bold teal letters on a white background. A private Jewish day school located outside of Boston in the suburb of Newton, Rashi was where we had chosen to educate our children for the past three years, and at no small expense. *Another year and thousands more dollars for each of the kids*, I thought to myself. *How could this possibly be worth it?*

"Ready, honey?" My wife's calm voice interrupted my silent accounting.

"Sure, Sher. Let's go, guys," I responded, rousing myself and shaking off the doubts. "Shani and Gabe, don't forget your lunch bags."

The four of us exited the car and walked toward the building as the parking lot began to fill up with the usual foreign-made SUVs. Gabe and Shani ran ahead while Sheryl and I followed behind, hauling their backpacks. I looked around to see much of the same—kids greeting one another and reuniting with enthusiasm after the long summer, while parents pulled up the rear with bags in tow. Doting mothers and fathers doing their children's work for them was the norm within the community to which I belonged.

I walked up to the second floor with Gabe, as Sheryl, trailing after Shani on the ground level, had found herself caught up in a conversation with another mother about an after-school playdate.

"Don't forget your backpack, honey!" I called to Gabe as he disappeared around the bend in the stairwell.

"Thanks, Dad," he said, running back down and taking it from my hands.

We arrived at Gabe's new classroom and he emptied into his locker the myriad of items he would need for the school day. While he was hard at work, I surveyed the hallway and, seeing Jeremy, motioned him over with a wave of my hand.

Jeremy Finkelstein stood about five foot seven, a couple inches shorter than I. His face was dominated by thick, bushy eyebrows and a warm, easy smile. A gray pinstriped suit and a yellow paisley tie rested on his trim frame. Jeremy was probably in the best physical condition of any father at the Rashi School. My friend had a passion for exercise that at times bordered on obsessive.

A private equity investor who commuted to and from Manhattan twice a week, Jeremy made money and lots of it, both for his company and for himself. A few lucky nonprofit organizations were also fortunate enough to be the recipients of his notable generosity. Our sons had met at preschool and had been inseparable ever since. The relationship between their fathers was not far behind.

Jeremy and I were different, however. He spent his life speeding down the highway at ninety miles per hour, while I chugged along at fifty-five. The time I spent in front of the television, he spent on the treadmill. He had an ambition and a drive that I could barely comprehend. But despite Jeremy's success and abundance, he remained grounded, something that I admired and appreciated. He respected me for my choices, as well. At least he made me think so, which was good enough for me.

"How was your summer, Josh?" he asked, slapping me hard on the shoulder.

"Not bad, not bad. How 'bout you?"

"Great. We just got back from a week in Jamaica. Weather was good, although the food wreaked havoc on Charlie's blood sugar."

Charlie Finkelstein, Jeremy's son and Gabe's close friend, had been diagnosed with diabetes the summer prior to kindergarten. The discovery had rocked the Finkelstein family to the core, but Jeremy and his wife rebounded quickly, shifting much of their seemingly boundless energy to care for Charlie and to treat his illness. His blood sugar was always in excellent control, partially due to the expensive high-tech pump he wore at his waist but also by virtue of his parents' incredible diligence.

"He looks no worse for the wear," I said, nodding in Charlie's direction as he and Gabe huddled near their new lockers, catching up on stories from the summer.

"He survived," Jeremy responded as he straightened his tie with one hand and smoothed his jet black hair with the other. "Listen, I've got to run. I have a plane to catch, but let's get together soon," he said, his voice already trailing away as he hustled down the hallway.

I waved good-bye and walked over to where the boys stood beside their lockers.

"Hey, Charlie, how was Jamaica?" I asked hesitantly.

"Great," he said. "The weather was awesome and we went swimming every day. I didn't get along with my little brother and sister, though. They were tough. Oh, and the food, it was amazing. Although I had trouble controlling my blood sugar . . ."

"Your dad told me," I interrupted. Charlie was a talker to say the least, and his tendency to ramble on meant that it was necessary to disrupt his monologues from time to time. "Well, it looks like you made it out okay. You looking forward to third grade?"

"Yeah, I am, Josh," he responded as he used one long arm to push a book into the back of his locker. He turned his tall, awkward frame back in my direction and I noticed that Charlie's parents had neglected to get him a back-to-school haircut. His head was covered with a dense and thick brown forest, rising a good two inches above his scalp.

"By the way," he continued, "Gabe and I were just talking. Is it okay if he leaves class and comes with me to the nurse to check my blood sugar during the day— same as last year? It's very important, Josh. If he doesn't come then, I'd have to ask someone else and I really don't want to do that . . ."

"No problem, guys," I said. "Have a great first day." Gabe kissed me good-bye without a care for who might be watching, and the boys headed for class.

I walked downstairs to look for my daughter, who was starting first grade that day. Shani stood in the hallway outside her classroom, waiting anxiously for the teacher to open the door.

"Shani! Give me a kiss good-bye, honey," I said as she walked over to me, scanning the vicinity to see if she was being observed by any of her friends.

"It's okay," I said. "Nobody's looking."

She gave me a quick hug around the neck and I squeezed her small body as hard as I dared.

"I love you, kiddo," I said.

"Cross my fingers, Dad," she whispered as she held up her hand and intertwined her index finger with the middle one. It was a tradition of ours, indicating how tight we were to one another. I responded in kind.

THAT AFTERNOON AT school, the third grade had recess outside. Rashi's playground consisted of a small, grassy area next to the parking lot, walled off by a chain-link fence. A jungle gym and swing set stood tucked in one corner, a broken-rimmed eight-foot basketball hoop in the other. Mismatched soccer goals on ei-

ther end of the grass rounded out the sports facilities
that were available for the three hundred kids who
called Rashi home from eight in the morning until three
in the afternoon.

With tuition being as high as it was, many of the families whose children attended the private school were
fairly well off; however, the institution had struggled to
find a permanent home with appropriate facilities. Although one heard the occasional whine or complaint, the
vast majority of Rashi's parents sent their children to
the school for the liberal Jewish education, community
spirit, and individual attention that was heaped upon
the students. Rashi's motto was, "Critical minds, com-
passionate hearts," and any focus on physical education
was an afterthought.

The forty or so third graders rushed out from the con-
fines of the building onto the grass. A handful immediately grabbed a soccer ball, some went right to the
climbing equipment, while others began walking the
fenced-in perimeter, perhaps searching for a mode of escape. A few teachers roamed among them, doing their
best to keep law and order.

Gabe and Charlie stood in the middle of the field with
their friend, Phil, tossing a tennis ball back and forth.
Phil Perlow had been born with many gifts. He was a
good-looking boy with a strong jaw, and even at his tender age of nine, his muscles showed some definition.
Those same muscles allowed him to excel on the athletic
field, at least among his peers at Rashi. He had a quick
mind and a knack for the game of chess. The Rashi chess
team, under Phil's leadership, had won the Massachu-

setts independent school state championship the previous year—no small accomplishment for Phil or his teammates. Unfortunately however, his many achievements on the sports field and at the chessboard occasionally gave Phil an overinflated sense of self that was well recognized by others in the third grade. While there was no doubt that his self-confidence would serve him well years down the road, at this point in his young life it was a social liability.

Despite his shortcomings, Gabe and Charlie appreciated Phil for his many strengths, and on this warm September afternoon, the three had plans to organize the school year's first game of pickle. The boys called over two more of their friends, as a minimum of five was needed to get a halfway decent game going.

"Rami! Jason! Get over here! I thought we were going to play some pickle," Gabe yelled.

"Coming, dude! Take it easy," Jason Armon responded from across the playground, trotting over with Rami Liebshutz close at his heels.

Jason was tall with dark skin, a stark contrast to most of his Jewish friends. His straight, silky black hair flowed down to cover both ears. He had been adopted as an infant, yet Jason's Mexican heritage was easy to recognize, and his undeniable good looks made him stand out in the Rashi crowd. Unfortunately, his striking appearance could not eclipse what Jason was truly famous for—a uniquely foul mouth. From the very first moment he opened it, Jason was uttering curses his parents didn't even recognize. How he came by such horrific language was a mystery, but it was suspected that God had simply placed him on Earth with the knowledge. It was unclear for what purpose.

Jason pulled up short as he approached Gabe, Charlie, and Phil. He stood eye to eye with Charlie but looked down upon the other two.

"Ready, dudes," he said. "Do you bitches have the ball?"

"Got it," said Gabe who was averse to swearing but had developed a thick skin when it came to his friend. He tossed the dirty yellow tennis ball to Rami, who came skidding to a stop in front of the group.

Rami Liebshutz was the shortest of the bunch, and in fact, shorter than every other kid in the grade. He had stringy light brown hair that came down almost to his shoulders and soft facial features that made him appear even younger than he was. Despite being vertically challenged, Rami carried himself with an air of confidence. He plucked the tennis ball in midflight and began bouncing it up and down on the instep of his foot.

"Forget pickle," he said in a high-pitched voice, "Let's play soccer. Did you guys hear what happened in the Arsenal game? It was unbelievable."

European-style football was almost as important as the Jewish religion in the Liebshutz home. Whereas most of the third grade boys discussed the Patriots or the Red Sox, Rami, the son of an English immigrant, spoke excitedly about the British Premier League and specifically his favorite team, Arsenal.

"We're not playing soccer, Ram," Jason responded. "And for the last time, there's no one on this playground except you that cares about friggin' Arsenal. We've been planning this game of pickle all morning."

"I'd like to hear about the Arsenal game," Charlie said.

"Not me," said Phil. "Let's play. I guess I should start out running since I'm the fastest."

The boys rolled their eyes at Phil, despite knowing that he spoke the truth. The group dispersed to either end, with Gabe and Charlie volunteering to start off as the catchers and the other three running between. They had no actual bases, so a sweatshirt and the plastic lid of the playground's garbage can would have to suffice.

"Here you go, Charlie," Gabe called as he tossed the ball in a long, slow arc, doing his best to tempt the runners. Random classmates walked across the playing field, barely paying attention to the pickle players.

"Back at you, Gabester!" Charlie called, heaving the ball high and deep. It sailed through the air and bounced off Gabe's hand, rolling toward the fence. Taking advantage of the opportunity, the runners took off, flaking up bits of grass and dirt with their sneakers.

Gabe gave chase and after tracking down the ball, momentarily hefted it before launching it back toward Charlie. His throw was strong, cutting through the air with enough velocity to keep Jason, Rami, and Phil from attempting to snag the extra base. But as Charlie reached out to grab it and put the catchers back in control of the game, a large hand appeared from nowhere, snatching the ball from his grasp. Simultaneously, Charlie felt a thump at his side and, losing his balance, tumbled to the ground.

"What did you do that for? You could have knocked out my pump!" Charlie hollered without looking, pulling himself onto his feet and immediately checking the life-saving device attached to his waist. After being reassured that everything was in its usual place, he spun around to see who had so rudely put him in harm's way. Fellow third-grader Sam Budd stood next to him, hands on hips. Charlie was tall but not tall enough to escape being looked down upon by the towering Sam Budd.

"I wanted to play," said Sam, dismissing Charlie with a brief wave. Sam proceeded to saunter down the pickle line, tennis ball in hand. Charlie, knowing his place in the social strata, stayed put, wisely deciding not to press the matter. The game came to a complete standstill as it was well known not to mess with Mr. Budd when he had a mind to put a stop to things.

Sam Budd stood close to five foot two, with curly brown hair and a dour face that made him an intimidating presence as he roamed the hallways of Rashi's second floor. His athletic accomplishments on the playground were legendary and would-be challengers shied away from him the way young lions will avoid the king of the pride. He had numerous followers among the third graders and the majority of Sam's classmates swore allegiance to him—the majority, but not all.

"What do you think you're doing, Sam? That's our ball!" Phil called, his inflated ego allowing him to muster the courage. Gabe, Rami, and Jason stared at Phil with horror but not shock. While it was considered unwise to challenge Sam Budd, they had seen their overly confident friend attempt it before.

Leaving a bruised and stunned Charlie behind, Sam approached the foursome.

"What's up, Sam? How you doin'?" Jason greeted him with more than a hint of anxiety in his voice. The two were friends but it was a tenuous relationship. Jason precariously straddled the line between being a member of the in-crowd, led by Sam, and actually enjoying his day by spending time with the second-tier group.

Sam however, had no interest in Jason at the moment. He ignored him completely, walking straight up to Phil Perlow and confronting his challenger. By this time, Sam's boorish behavior and the subsequent defiance had begun to garner some attention. The passersby who had previously ignored the game now turned to see what was happening.

"What do you mean, 'what am I doing?' I'm joining the game," Sam responded, looking down at Phil from inches away.

Phil stood, assessing the situation while tugging nervously on a wayward strand of hair. Anxiety crept over him as he second-guessed the spontaneous bravado that he had exhibited just moments before.

"Well . . . that's not . . . the way to go about it," he said hesitantly. "We were in the middle of the game."

"Were you? I didn't realize," Sam quipped sarcastically.

Phil hesitated, debating in his mind whether to pursue the matter. Thus distracted, he was oblivious to the fact that one of Sam's posse had used this opportunity to quietly sneak up behind him. Sam's popularity never failed to bring out those third graders looking to win his favor.

With a quick jerking motion, the nameless juvenile

delinquent yanked on Phil's shorts, pulling them to the knees and completely exposing his blue and white Jockeys to anyone on the playground who cared to look. Of course, everyone did.

The shorts-yanking offender screamed and howled in joy as he eyed Sam to see if his cowardly act had elicited the sought-after response. Sam looked on with surprise and managed a chuckle of nervous laughter, doing his best to keep up appearances, while apparently suspecting that the situation might have gone too far.

By this time anyone who was not already observing the scene finally turned to see what all the commotion was about. Eighty eyes turned toward Phil as he struggled to cover up, his heart racing with panic. Unbidden tears came to his face, which he held back by sheer force of will.

However, a good friend in a tight spot is ever a useful thing. Desperately thinking of any way to come to Phil's aid, Gabe quickly decided that he was in no position to physically challenge Sam Budd or any of his minions. However painful it might be, there was only one thing to do. He must create a distraction, drawing attention away from his friend and onto himself. And with the decision made in an instant, Gabe dropped his own shorts, exposing his plaid boxers to everyone on the playground. The spotlight immediately left Phil who, exhaling a tremendous sigh of relief, smiled heartily.

The two friends stood side by side, arms around each other's shoulders and exposed to their knees while forty of their classmates looked on in utter astonishment.

CHAPTER TWO

I KNOW WHAT YOU'RE THINKING

"...AND THEN CHARLIE was so upset about the whole thing that after it was over, his blood sugar dropped and we had to go see the nurse!"

Our family sat around the dinner table as Gabe finished telling the story of what happened that day at recess. The light outside the windows began to fade, with the sun, in typical New England fashion, setting noticeably earlier in September than in August. The four of us surrounded the antique dining room table that I had swiped from my mother's basement the previous year. Sheryl had cooked supper in celebration of the first day back to our school routine. Lasagna, garlic bread, and salad made their way around the table.

"Yeah, I heard about it," Shani piped in. "But I was told that they pulled down Phil's underwear, too." Apparently, it didn't take long for events taking place during third grade recess to find their way to the gossipmongers in the first grade.

"Nah, that's just a rumor. His underwear was still on and so was mine," Gabe corrected his little sister.

"Well, I'm extremely proud of you, Gabriel," Sheryl said. "It took incredible strength to stand up for your friend like that."

Gabe smiled in response.

"Yeah, unbelievable, Gabe," I chipped in. "I'm not sure I would've been able to do that." Staring out the window at the woods in the backyard, I wondered why my son was so much more courageous than me.

"Kenny called today," Sheryl said, changing the subject.

"Yeah? How's he doing?" I asked.

"Great. He wanted to let us know about the Cooperstown tournament they were at a few weeks ago."

Sheryl's older brother, Kenny, lived in Tallahassee, Florida. He called from time to time and occasionally would share stories of one of his three sons and their unique achievements on the sports field. They were all stellar athletes.

"Back in Cooperstown already, huh? Weren't they just there last summer?"

"Yeah, but this year it was Landon's turn. Anyway, apparently our nephew did quite well."

Kenny's boys were brilliant all-around athletes; however, their true passion was baseball. Over the years, I had heard numerous stories of their prowess on the diamonds of the Panhandle, and peppered among these were tales of Cooperstown.

Each of Kenny's sons had gone through a family rite of passage by participating in an exclusive youth baseball tournament located in a place called Cooperstown Dreams Park. The park ran weeklong tournaments all summer, and Kenny and I had spent a fair amount of time over the years discussing his boys' accomplishments in upstate New York.

"That's great. Do you know how his team fared?" I asked, taking the time to subtly remind my son that the primary focus of team sports should not be the individual.

"He said they placed in the top ten," Sheryl replied.

"That's impressive. Kenny says the competition is pretty tough there. They come from all across the country to play."

Sheryl and Gabe stole a glance at each other and she nodded in my direction.

"Go ahead, honey, ask him," she said to our son.

"You ask him, Mom," Gabe replied.

"No, it needs to come from you, honey."

"Well, somebody'd better ask me. What's going on with you two?"

Gabe looked at me sheepishly. "Dad, I'd like to play in Cooperstown."

"You *what?*" The surprise was evident on my face.

"When I'm old enough I would like to play there," he repeated.

Over the past year, Gabe had taken a keen interest in baseball. We had always enjoyed watching a good Red Sox game on TV together, but lately he had become infatuated. He had one season of Little League under his belt and that had lit the fire. Knowing what I knew about Cooperstown Dreams Park, I didn't want to raise my son's hopes.

"Gabe, sweetheart, I know that you're really getting interested in baseball, but from everything I hear, Cooperstown is an extremely tough place to play. Like I said, they have teams that travel from all over the country to compete there."

"I know, but I think I could do it."

"I'm sure you could, too, Gabe, but it may not be a great idea. I'm not even sure that I could find a team from the area that would be going, let alone get you on it."

Dejected, Gabe looked at the floor.

"Don't worry, honey," Sheryl said. "Dad and I will look into it. I promise." That brought hope to his eyes.

"If Gabe plays in Cooperstown, then I do, too!" Shani demanded. "Where is Cooperstown, anyway?"

"It's in New York," I said.

"What's so special about it?" she asked.

"Well, it's special to people who love baseball."

"Why?" she persisted.

"Because if baseball has a home, that's where it is," I explained. It seemed to satisfy her.

AT ELEVEN THAT night, I climbed into bed and placed my head on the pillow. It had been a long, exhausting day and I was looking forward to a peaceful night's sleep. Reaching over, I switched off the lamp that stood on the nightstand. The darkness quickly consumed me.

"Why did you tell Gabe that he couldn't go to Cooperstown?" The disembodied voice came out of the blackness.

Rolling over, I saw the outline of Sheryl's head poking out from under the covers next to me. I had a feeling that this was coming. One thing you did not do to my wife was disappoint her son. I briefly debated whether to just roll over and go to sleep but thinking better of it, decided to state my case.

"Because I think it's a really competitive tournament, and because I don't know if I could find a team for him, and because I don't know who they let in, and because I don't know if he's good enough. Are those enough reasons for you?" I asked the rhetorical question to which I knew the answer before it came out of her mouth.

"No, that's not even close to good enough. It sounds like I know more about this than you do. I already spoke with Kenny. They have a weeklong tournament for kids ten and under that takes place the first week of every summer. He could go a year from this coming June."

"Great, that's almost two years away. Why are you pestering me about it now?"

"Because I can't stand your negative attitude. Your son asks if he can do something challenging and your answer is, 'No, you can't'? What kind of lessons are you teaching him?"

"Lessons in real life," I said.

"Real life? How is he going to fare in real life if he's too afraid to try anything new? Are you kidding me? You teach your children to shoot for the stars. You teach them to go after their dreams. You don't teach them to give up before they even get started."

"And just what team do you think he would go with, anyway?"

"I already thought of that, too. You can organize a team from Rashi. Gabe's friends would love to do it."

I bolted upright in bed.

"Are you kidding me?" I practically screamed. "Do you think I'm suicidal? Take Gabe and his friends to Cooperstown? Do you realize how badly we would be destroyed? It would be humiliating. Besides there's no way they would let us in. They only take real teams."

"As always, you are coming up with reasons why not to do something," Sheryl said. "Stop letting your fear hold you back. Why not at least explore the option? Talk to the park. See what they say. Take a chance, for once in your life."

"I know what you're thinking," I said. "I know this isn't about Gabe going to Cooperstown.

"It's about that and a lot more."

She was right. I had always refused to take a chance, always been held back by my fears. My wife had seen it far too often, and so had I. Sheryl stopped talking and settled in for sleep. I looked over at her briefly. Things like this were so easy for her, but I was different. Staring at the ceiling, I drifted off as my mind began to wander.

"IS THAT A *boy . . . or a girl?" he said menacingly, his closely cropped blond hair giving him a confidence and swagger that I could not share.*

I was ten years old and sitting in Bill's House of Pizza in my hometown of Newton, Massachusetts. Harry Jacobson and Eli Fishman, two of my best friends, had stopped by the house earlier and we had walked into town for lunch.

Bill's was a favorite haunt of ours. It was a typical pizza joint, jammed in among a row of stores, between a pharmacy and a hair salon. The walls were covered with scenic photos of the Parthenon and the Mediterranean

Sea, interspersed with pictures of local Little League and soccer teams. A large chalkboard behind the counter listed Bill's ample selection of subs and pizzas. We made our way up to the front of the restaurant, where the owner's son greeted us with a familiar shrug.

"What can I get you guys?" he asked distractedly. Hulk was his name—at least to us. A burly twenty-something-year-old with a shock of brown hair that hung past his shoulders and with arms like lead pipes, it appeared that Hulk would have preferred to be pumping iron at the gym rather than helping his old man at the family restaurant.

"One large cheese pizza and three small Cokes, please," I said.

He nodded, jotted the order on a small white slip of paper, and turned his back on us. We grabbed our usual chairs and picked up our previous conversation on how the Red Sox might fare that summer. It was a beautiful spring day. The sun shining through Bill's front windows, along with the long stretch of weekend that lay ahead, combined to give us a peace of mind that felt as if it might last forever. It did not.

As so happened, three other boys our age were sitting at an adjacent table. Their attire was similar to ours, old shorts and T-shirts, with ripped sneakers covering feet that were too big for their bodies. I scanned their faces and did not recognize them, which was unusual given that we knew most of the kids in town. Their meddlesome behavior and defiant attitude was immediately noticeable as they horsed around, disrupting the typical peace that reigned over Bill's. Loud prepubescent voices filled the restaurant as they jostled and shoved each other whenever one felt that he had made a particularly good joke.

"Nudnicks," my grandfather would have called them in Yiddish, obnoxious and annoying. Harry, Eli, and I did our best to avoid eye contact but the nudnicks would have none of it. Before we had taken our first bites of pizza, one of them leaned over the table and stretched out his long, thin arm, pointing it directly at me.

"My friends and I want to know something," he shouted across the small restaurant. "Is that a boy . . . or a girl?"

Those were his exact words. I can hear his voice and see the look on his face even now, over thirty years later. Of course, I should have been mortified at the question and indeed it did not sit well. But truth be told, it wasn't an unfamiliar feeling. I had been dealing with similar humiliating moments for years.

My beloved mother didn't believe in frequent haircuts for her boys. Dark brown locks typically found the base of my pale neck before curling around and pointing back up toward the sky. My younger brother, Jonathan, struggled with the same challenge. Mom hadn't caught on to the fact that it was almost 1980 at the time, and as a result, her precious sons suffered a fair amount of pain and misery. Looking back, the true tragedy was the ease with which it could have been avoided. Just a few deft strokes of the scissors that lay unused in the vanity drawer beneath our bathroom sink, and my childhood might have been a vastly different experience.

Regardless, over the years I had hardened to it. Sure,

a few tears had been shed now and then under my blankets at night, but eventually I learned to stop caring about the poor souls who couldn't figure it out. Those who loved me knew the truth. I was a boy through and through—torn jeans from climbing trees in the backyard; an Atari 800 computer in my room with the game Centipede running nonstop; and Saturday mornings religiously set aside for my favorite cartoon, Thundarr the Barbarian. *Unfortunately, despite my gender security, I had neither the quick wit nor the courage to respond to my adversary. I stared at him blankly, which only served to further enrage him.*

"I asked what you are," he demanded with hostility, "a boy . . . or a girl?"

Stammering a little, I forced out an answer, albeit not one that would satisfy this particular nudnick.

"A boy," I whispered.

"Doesn't look like it to me," growled the ten-year-old, while walking up to us and placing both hands on our table in an intimidating show of force. His forearm muscles flexed as his eyes glared at me from under thin blond brows. I looked to Harry and Eli for assistance but we were friends for a reason and as such, we all stared at the floor.

"I'm waiting for a different answer," he said. "Like I told you, you don't look like a boy."

As the panic escalated, I chanced a glance up at the bully and at that very moment the look on his face changed. For an instant I thought perhaps it was because his victim had dared look him in the eye, but that was not the case. His expression of cruel joy rapidly trans-

formed into one of astonishment and it had nothing to do with me. Two very large hands had suddenly encircled his shoulders, quickly pinching down in a viselike grip. The hunter had become the hunted.

"Are you harassing our customers?" Hulk questioned. Apparently his devotion to the family business was stronger than I had initially presumed.

"No . . ., sir." The bully developed some manners with amazing speed.

"Do you have a problem with long hair?" Hulk asked, with barely hidden disgust.

"Nnnnnn . . . no . . . no, sir." I could hardly hear the feeble response.

"Good; then there is no problem here." And with that, he picked the kid up by the scruff of his neck and tossed him out the door. The remaining nudnicks *scrambled after their leader in haste.*

"Thanks," I said to Hulk, who nodded, as if his actions were a routine part of the job. I watched as he wandered off, repositioning himself behind the counter.

My friends and I finished our pizza, and after making sure the nudniks *were nowhere in sight, parted ways with an agreement to keep the story among ourselves.*

When I returned home that evening, I was greeted eagerly by my mother as she stood in our front hall. Our family lived in a moderate-size brick colonial on a street lined on either side by many more of the same. The lawns were small and well maintained. Each home had a free-standing garage in back and painted shutters hugged every window.

I ran in through the front door, letting the screen slam

behind me, happy to be back in my castle after surviving the dangers of the countryside.

"I'm glad you're finally home, honey," she said. "I've been wondering where you were."

A beautiful woman with long dark hair, my mother often had it pulled back from her face with one of many bandanas she had left over from a previous decade. She kissed my cheek softly and I basked in the security of home, ignoring the fact that the primary reason for the day's torment now stood before me.

"Hey, Mom," I said.

"You better hurry, Josh. I've been waiting for you to get back. Papa called this afternoon. He got Red Sox tickets for tonight's game and he's coming by to pick you up in twenty minutes."

"Great," I responded. "I'll get my glove."

Growing up in the Boston suburb of Newton, baseball was all I knew from April through September. Each summer as far back as I could remember, my grandfather would take me to Fenway Park to see our beloved Sox play. We would sit down by the first baseline and watch while Papa tested my knowledge of the game, asking question after question. In those days, Yastrzemski, Rice, Lynn, and Burleson were my heroes. While their performance and play was open for discussion, Papa also spent time filling my head with stories from the game's past. As for many boys growing up at Fenway, my memories of those hot summer nights would last a lifetime. Almost every evening that we went to the park was perfect. There was one moment, however, that I would just as soon have forgotten. It happened on that evening, dur-

ing that particular game.

Immediately after grabbing my baseball glove from under the bed, I heard the honk of Papa's car. Bounding down the stairs two at a time, I shouted good-bye to my mother and jumped into the front seat of the Ford station wagon.

"Hey, Papa," I said.

"Ready to go, Josh?" he asked, his twinkling eyes promising a night of fun.

"You bet." I looked over at him and smiled. He was spry for his age, slim and in good shape, with curly brown hair that was the envy of all his peers.

We drove down Commonwealth Avenue, a straight shot into Boston's Fenway area, and pulled the car into a small lot on a side street. The crowds were already thick as fans headed toward the park, and my feet quickened their step in anticipation. The smell of warm roasted peanuts and grilled sausages emanated from the vendors' carts to form an invisible ring of olfactory delight around the stadium.

Papa always managed to get good seats, and as we settled in a few rows behind the Red Sox dugout, he began immediately to partake of his favorite pastime. He started with questions probing my knowledge of the game and its terminology—"Josh, can you tell me what a Texas leaguer is?"—and ended with stories. His favorites were always those of Sandy Koufax.

"Did you know that Koufax was the greatest Jewish athlete of all time? He could throw a baseball by anybody. But it wasn't just his physical skill; the man also knew how to pitch. Do you understand what I mean, Josh? He

knew how to work the strike zone and how to adjust speeds. There is more to pitching than just throwing hard. And he had his priorities straight, I'll tell you. It's not an easy thing to announce to your teammates and fans that you won't pitch game one of the World Series because it's Yom Kippur." And on and on it went. I absorbed it all, loving every moment, and Sandy Koufax became my favorite player, even though I had never seen him take the mound.

The game went along as usual that night, the score going back and forth. I ate, drank, talked, and cheered, all the while refusing to remove the old Spaulding leather glove from my left hand for fear of missing that ever-elusive foul ball. It had always been my desperate desire to catch one. Game after game I waited, but despite the many long innings that Papa spent his hard-earned money on, I never got a chance. That night would be different.

It was early in the game, perhaps the third or fourth inning, although it could have been any other and the result would probably have been the same. Butch Hobson was at the plate. That I remember clearly. In between pitches I took just a moment to reach down below my seat searching for my Coke, which was resting on the ground beneath me. The drink eluded me however, and my hand brushed against some sticky pink gum stuck to the cement at my feet. Risking that I might miss some of the action, I took just a moment to look down.

Suddenly there came a loud "CRACK!" Jolting my head up, I saw a line drive, scorched off the bat of Hobson, coming directly at me. To my eyes it was hit hard, *harder than anything I had seen Butch hit before. It was a rocket and it was coming fast.*

There was but one brief moment in which to react, one chance to make the play. That moment somehow lasted a lifetime. An avalanche of emotions flooded over me— excitement, joy, hope—but unfortunately also, fear. What should I do? Stick my glove out and risk getting hurt but possibly come away with the prize that I had so hoped for all these years? Or watch the ball go by, not risking a thing but never knowing what could have been?

Looking back, I often wonder whether making a different choice would have changed me. Perhaps I would have learned right then and there that life is about taking chances. Maybe if I had caught that ball I would have come to understand that a life lived in fear is a life wasted. But I didn't catch it. I didn't even try. I watched it rip through the air, inches from my face and didn't move a muscle. It sailed right by me up into the stands and was gone, just like that. The entire unfortunate incident had taken only a heartbeat, a heartbeat that would stay with me for a very long time.

As I grew, the missed foul ball and others like it became familiar scenes that replayed themselves far too often in my life. Year after year went by and I was never able to take a chance. I had a pleasant life and I did what was expected of me—good grades, college, medical school, marriage and kids. But, my list of regrets mounted faster than I could keep track of. The late Frank Herbert summed it up well in one of the best science fiction novels of all time, Dune. *"Fear is the mind killer," he said. That accurately and succinctly described what held me back far too often—the mind killer, fear.*

I SAT UPRIGHT in bed and stared into the darkness, unsure whether I had been sleeping or awake. The silence permeating the bedroom was deafening, the only audible sound being Sheryl's soft, rhythmic breathing as she slept next to me. Moments passed. As I stared at the ceiling, a form slowly began to take shape. It was a face. I could just make out the lines and curves in the shadows. I recognized the man's smile and the dimple in his cheek. He wore a blue Dodgers cap on top of his head. Sandy Koufax was coming to visit. It was not the first time and I doubted it would be the last. Sandy stopped by now and again when I was in desperate need of advice.

"What do you say, Sandy? Should I agree to look into this?" I questioned him silently. It wouldn't do to wake Sheryl, to say nothing of letting her know that I had other consultants. Sandy stared at me blankly, silently, and I realized the counsel I was seeking would not be forthcoming. I had to figure this one out for myself. Should I agree to pursue this Cooperstown thing for Gabe? It would be a ton of work and I risked disappointing him and humiliating both of us. But of course, Sheryl was right. At some point I had to stop letting my fears hold me back. I lay in bed, and after spending an additional hour agonizing over the pros and cons, I felt I had reached a decision.

"Nope, it's not happening," I said aloud at two in the morning.

"Yes, it is," Sheryl responded, rolling over and falling

right back to sleep. *How was she able to do that?* I wondered.

AT LUNCHTIME THE following day, I sat in my office and stared at the slice of pizza and bottle of Sprite sitting on my desk. As usual, the practice was busy and my schedule was full. I loved working as a primary care doctor. Developing relationships with people and helping them with their problems was incredibly rewarding, but also incredibly time consuming. I had less than fifteen minutes to eat before my next patient was placed in the exam room.

I reached for the mouse on my desk and located the Cooperstown Dreams Park Website in a matter of seconds. It looked pleasant enough—pictures of boys in uniform and a couple of kids holding up a trophy filled my computer screen. I had no time to read through the details and so just honed in on what I needed—the off-season phone number. I dialed nine for an outside line and punched it in.

"Cooperstown Dreams Park," a young man answered.

"Yes, hi, I was thinking of bringing my son to play there and I have a few questions."

"Shoot."

"Um, how many players do you need on a team?"

"At least ten."

"And how many coaches?"

"Usually around four."

"How long does the tournament run?"

"One week."

"How many games?"

"At least eight. Seven regular and a minimum of one lay-off."

"Where do we stay?"

"Every team has its own bunkhouse."

"Okay, how do you get a spot to play in the tournament?"

"You just fill out the application."

"Does your team have to meet certain playing requirements?"

"Nope, you just need to send in the application with the fee."

"We don't have to have played in other tournaments or have won a certain number of games?"

"Nope."

"We don't need, like, a reference or something?"

"Nope."

"How do you decide who gets in?"

"Teams that have played here before get in."

"And teams that haven't?"

"Well, technically it's first come, first served, but hardly any new teams make the cut. If you want any chance at all, you'd better get that application in soon."

"No, I don't think you understand. I'm not talking about this coming summer. I'm talking about going over a year and a half from now."

"Sir, I think it's you who doesn't understand. For the most part it's the same teams that play here year after year. We have a very long waiting list."

"How long?"

"Hundreds."

"You have hundreds of teams on your waiting list?"

"Mister," he said after a long pause and a sigh, indicating his exasperation at wasting so much time with a novice, "I'm not sure why that surprises you. We're the best youth baseball tournament in the country."

CHAPTER THREE

TO WHAT END?

MY LITTLE LEAGUE career was a long and storied one. Unfortunately, hardly anyone knew about it. I manned third base and pitched for every team that I played on. I was pretty good, too. At ages ten and eleven, I played in the minors, where I was consistently one of the better players in the league. I pitched almost every game for the Orioles and was even given the honor of starting the All-Star Game. My parents only saw me play a handful of times and so my teammates and coaches were the only ones to witness my legendary accomplishments. That was true for most of the kids I played with. Only one or two die-hard dads showed up at each of our games.

My father was a good man and he loved me dearly, but he couldn't have cared less about sports. He was busy at work and pursuing his own interests. My mother similarly had precious little time to attend my games. Grades were far more important to her than were athletic accomplishments. I washed my own uniform, kept track of my own schedule, and walked or rode my bike to every practice.

It was all well and good until the year I turned twelve. That season I finally made it to the majors, where an unfortunate reality smacked me in the face. Compared to everyone else on the team, and in the league for that matter—I stunk. My new coaches were not impressed with my pitching. They kept me at third base but only as a backup. My ability to hit the ball went from above average to nonexistent. I guess I began dropping my bat too low, because I recall my assistant coach's adjusting my stance so the bat rested directly on my shoulder. It was unorthodox, uncomfortable, and unsuccessful.

The highlight of that year was the time I struck out on such a good swing that when I returned to the bench, my friend gave me a huge pat on the back.

"That was a beautiful swing," he said. "If you had connected the ball would have gone a long way."

"You think so?" I asked him, desperate for any positive feedback. I had a good-looking swing? I'd take it.

At the end of that long and painful season, the mind killer got the better of me. Instead of working hard to improve or chalking up the entire spring to a prolonged slump, I gave up on baseball completely. I guess I just wasn't as good as I thought I was, or so I said to myself. I would never be the next Sandy Koufax.

"JASON ARMON! DO you know the answer to the question?" Mrs. Abramowitz stared at him with such intensity that Jason nearly fell off his chair. She was probably only forty years of age, but looked and acted twice that. Graying hair pulled back in a tight bun and wire-rimmed glasses perched on the brim of her nose allowed her to play to perfection the part of "stern teacher." She stopped next to Jason's desk, shifting her gaze from him to the blank chalkboard in front of her as she spoke.

"I said, 'Jason, do you know the significance of Yom Kippur?'"

"No, I don't, Mrs. Abramowitz," Jason said simply, his dark eyes looking up at her. Jason was never one to be intimidated by authority, and he treated adults and kids exactly the same way. The question was an easy one, but Jason was not a rigorous academic. He had a decent head on his shoulders, but he utilized his street smarts more effectively on the playground than in the classroom. He rarely cracked a book.

Mrs. Abramowitz gave him a disapproving glare and moved on. When her back was turned, Jason held up one brown middle finger in her direction and screwed up the features of his handsome face. Those who saw him quickly shook their head in terror. It was the rare Rashi student who displayed such brazen insubordination. Jason shrugged in disappointment, not having received the response he was looking for.

"How about you, Mr. Liebshutz?" Mrs. Abramowitz whipped around, turning her attention on Rami, who was seated just behind her. She was indeed fierce but the small, cocky kid would not be intimidated.

"Yeah, I know the answer. Yom Kippur is significant because we can't eat and that makes me grouchy." He scanned the room looking for approval but found only sympathy in return.

"Is that so Mr. Liebshutz? Well, if that is how you feel—"

"I know the answer." A voice from the back of the room cut her off and Rami slumped down in his chair,

relieved that the bomb about to go off in his face had
been defused.

"Yes, Mr. Goodman. Please do tell."

Jeff Goodman did not even glance up while volunteering. He was reading a book, which he held just beneath
the desk, until the very moment that Mrs. Abramowitz
had acknowledged him. Once called upon, with a deft
and well-practiced motion, Jeff folded the corner of his
page and closed the cover, quickly moving it from his lap
to beneath his left thigh. Satisfied that he would be able
to return to it soon, he stood up and stared straight
ahead at no one in particular.

Jeff was clad in his usual attire of a light blue oxford
shirt and dark dress pants. Unfortunately, the slacks did
not quite reach his ankles and in fact, gave the appearance of capris more than pants, not that he intended it
to be that way. His black socks inside his loafers were
pushed down low and pale white skin could be seen between sock and pant leg. Jeff's sandy brown hair was
moderately disheveled, as if but one pass of a brush was
all it had seen that morning. His appearance was unique
but what his classmates thought of his style was the last
thing that ever crossed Jeff's mind. He began to speak.

"Yom Kippur is the holiest day on the Jewish calen-
dar. It occurs on the tenth day of the Hebrew month of
Tishrei. In English, 'Yom Kippur' means 'Day of Atone-
ment.' On that day we reflect on how we, as human be-
ings, can act in ways that will bring us closer to God. In
addition, we confess our sins and admit our wrongdoings.
Finally, we reenact the ancient Avodah service in the
hope that just as God forgave our ancestors when the

Temple stood, so, too, will we now be forgiven."

Jeff Goodman sat down as silence fell over the class-room. He opened his book and returned to the page with the folded corner as if the entire event had never taken place. Teacher and students looked at him in awe. Not that they hadn't seen performances like that before, but the events never ceased to amaze.

Jeff was a genius. That was clear to everyone. He had the answer to every question and his thirst for knowledge could not be quenched. The third grade cur-riculum was simply a waste of his time. Jeff spent al-most every waking moment reading. He read before class, after class, and even during class. Some teachers handled it better than others.

"Very well spoken, Jeffrey," Mrs. Abramowitz an-nounced as the bell rang to indicate the end of school. "I will see all of you tomorrow and that means you, too, Mr. Liebshutz!"

I STOOD ON the playground with my back against the metal fence, watching Gabe and his friends play football. I had been able to sneak away from the office early that day and had come to school to pick up the kids. Football at three o'clock on the playground was a ritual among the third grade boys and they would do anything not to miss it. On most days, a classmate or two would be ob-served by the group with great pity as they were dragged kicking and screaming through the parking lot to a piano lesson or other endeavor considered less wor-thy than the game. On this day, however, I had seen no one forcibly removed against his will, which meant a full complement of players and what would likely be a competitive contest.

A number of other parents milled around as the kids split into teams and took up positions on respective sides of the field. The sun was high in the sky and a cool, crisp wind rippled the leaves on the trees. The breeze caught the football in its grasp as it was kicked high in the air.

"Beautiful day, huh?" Jeremy Finkelstein approached me from the parking lot, his son running up just behind. Charlie was upset that he had missed the start of the game due to his usual delay. Unfortunately, a stop at the nurse's office for an after-school glucose check was nonnegotiable.

Jeremy, dressed in a black suit, white shirt, and gray tie, looked better suited for the playgrounds of Wall Street than for that of his son's elementary school. My typical work attire of khakis, blue button-down, and red striped tie contrasted sharply. I had pulled my tie down a couple of inches so as to release the shirt button at my neck.

"Yeah, great time of year. What's with the outfit? You look like you just came from a funeral," I responded.

"Nope, just came back from a business meeting in Brazil. Plane landed about an hour ago and I came right here to pickup the kids. I haven't seen them in a few days."

"Devoted father as always," I said.

"As are you," he responded. We looked around and saw that as usual, at least half the parents surrounding us were dads. A new era in parenting had arrived. It was something my grandfather probably would not have understood.

"Jeremy, I have to tell you about what happened in the classroom today." I proceeded to fill him in on Jason and Rami's antics, the story of which Gabe had relayed to me prior to taking the field for his football game. Jeremy chuckled. We always appreciated hearing anecdotes about this particularly eclectic group of boys.

"Hey, your nephew is sitting over there by himself, you know," Jeremy said.

I looked over at the entrance to the playground where my nephew, Ari Glasgow, sat quietly on the ground. My sister's son was about six months younger than Gabe, although he had already surpassed him in height. He was a reserved kid who rarely spoke to adults, and that included me, his uncle. I had tried many times to break down the barriers he had erected, but to no avail.

Ari wore his hair long, as was the style with many of the Rashi kids, and his bangs often fell down across his dark eyes, partially obscuring his face. He liked it that way. For reasons known only to him, Ari kept his thoughts and emotions well guarded. One thing that was clear, however, were his feelings for his cousin. The two were deeply connected despite the grade differential, and Gabe never failed to include Ari in whatever activity he and his friends happened to be engaging in at the moment. Motioning to my son, I nodded in Ari's direction. Gabe raced over and grabbed his cousin's arm, pulling him into the fray.

The football game was now well underway with Phil Perlow playing quarterback for his squad. His shorts were held fast with a belt, as he had been taking no chances since that dreadful day a few weeks earlier. Gabriel, playing wide receiver, stood a few yards to Phil's left. Gabe had decent speed to play the position, but his real strength was his hands. Over the last couple of years he had developed a reputation for catching anything within his vicinity.

Jason Armon stood a couple steps to the left of my son, itching to get into his pattern. The diminutive Rami Liebshutz waited directly across from him. Rami swiped his feet on the turf in anticipation of covering his much taller classmate. The two friends stared at each other with fire in their eyes prior to the snap.

Fresh off his impressive performance in Mrs. Abramowitz's class, Jeff Goodman was split out far to Phil's right. Jeff was used typically as a decoy. The team would pick his brain to strategize X's and O's but the ball was rarely thrown his way. Whatever satisfaction he took home with him that day would likely have to come from his exploits in the classroom.

Lined up across from Jeff was Robert Matz, the back of his blue Red Sox T-shirt proclaiming allegiance to designated hitter, David Ortiz. He was a skinny kid with long arms and dusty brown hair. The quintessential happy-go-lucky third grader, Robert's face always wore a smile, and a cross word never left his mouth. A strong desire to be liked, as well as to please, had landed him somewhere in the pack of Sam Budd's followers. However, similar to Jason, Robert struggled mightily with competing desires. A part of him wanted to run with the alpha dogs, while another desperately feared being trampled. But at that moment he was at peace. Robert considered covering Jeff Goodman to be a walk in the park.

Aaron Dines, also playing cornerback for the defense, stood casually across the line of scrimmage from Gabe. He was slightly smaller than my son, although of similar build. His full head of straw-colored hair was streaked with blond, and a faded blue baseball cap, with "Newport Yacht Club" embroidered upon it, was reversed upon his head. The rectangular outline of a thin cell phone could be made out in the back pocket of his shorts. The cap and cell phone took no one by surprise. Aaron was the son of an extremely wealthy real estate developer and there appeared to be very few limits on his ability to acquire material possessions. If he wanted it, it was his, including but not limited to a cell phone in the first grade, a working motorcycle, and regular birthday parties in his father's luxury box at Fenway.

Aaron had three homes—a Victorian near school, an oceanfront property, and a winter retreat directly on the slopes of one of the big ski resorts in Vermont. The kid had it all, but for now at least was content with an ordinary game of touch football. He adjusted his cap in preparation for the snap as Gabe sized up his coverage, looking for a weakness.

"Hike!" hollered Phil as Charlie launched the ball between his legs to the quarterback. Phil dropped behind the line, searching for an open receiver. Both Gabe and Jeff Goodman went out into their patterns, being covered by Aaron and Robert respectively. Rami desperately stuck out his foot and tripped Jason, sending him sprawling to the ground. The defensive coverage was good but not great. I watched from my vantage point along the fence as the two receivers who had been lucky enough to maintain their feet came free. Unfortunately for Phil, Sam Budd roamed the defensive line and therefore all bets were off. The bull of a third grader plowed his way through Charlie's feeble block and quickly pounced on the vulnerable quarterback. In light of what transpired next, the game of "two-hand touch" would have been more aptly named "two-hand shove." Phil fell to the ground as Sam raised his arms in a bodybuilder pose to celebrate his sack.

I took advantage of the pause in the action to continue my conversation with Jeremy.

"So I was considering trying to organize a Rashi baseball team," I mentioned nonchalantly.

"To what end?" he replied, his eyebrows pinched together in a sign of confusion.

"Gabe's cousins from Florida play in this big baseball tournament in Cooperstown over the summer and he really wants to try it. Not to mention, Sheryl's pushing me."

"Sounds interesting. Where's it at?"

"A place called Cooperstown Dreams Park," I said and proceeded to fill Jeremy in on what I knew and what I had discovered. We began to debate the merits, the flaws, and the practicality of the idea, although *debate* may have been too strong a word, as we both agreed that the merits were few, the flaws many, and the practicality limited.

"Hello, gentlemen. How was your summer?" Stan Goodman, Jeff's father sauntered over from where he had been standing near the jungle gym.

"Great, Stan, and yours?" Jeremy responded.

I watched Stan closely as he approached. He was older than Jeremy and I, perhaps in his early fifties. An interventional radiologist by trade, he had sparse curly brown hair clinging desperately to the top of his head. His appearance was not too dissimilar to that of his son, blue dress slacks, which stopped at his ankles, dark socks underneath tennis sneakers, and a wrinkled white oxford shirt. He stopped in front of us, shaking our hands in greeting.

"Josh is planning on organizing a Rashi baseball team to travel to Cooperstown and play in a national tournament," Jeremy could not resist informing the first person he came in contact with. "How does that sound to you?"

"Ambitious," Stan replied as he stared into the distance at the football game and beyond. When talking to Stan, the casual observer might have found him to be aloof. I knew differently. His quick and active mind was on par with that of his son. My guess was that for Stan a mundane conversation could be managed by a very small percent of his brain, while the rest of his gifted intellect spent the precious time working over other more pressing matters.

"Well, I like the idea, Josh," Jeremy concluded optimistically. "I'm not sure how Charlie would manage with his diabetes, though."

As if on cue, Charlie broke away from the game and ran toward us, looking a little faint.

"Dad . . . I'm low," he said.

"Okay, buddy, grab a couple of glucose tabs. They're in my briefcase." Charlie ran over to where the case was leaning against the fence and rummaged through it, pulling out a couple of pink tablets. He popped them in his mouth and slumped down on the ground next to us.

"I gotta get back in, Dad. The game is tied and this is the last drive," he said breathlessly.

As he spoke, I watched Gabe streak down the sideline directly toward us, his head swiveled around to track the football that had been thrown in his direction. At the last possible moment, he laid out for it, but the ball bounced off his hands just steps from where we stood.

"Shoot," Charlie said. "The game's over. I hate when it ends in a tie! What a bad time for me to be low!" he said, cursing his hypoglycemic reaction.

"Not a tie, Charlie," Gabe said from the ground where he lay. "We won."

Looking over, I saw Jeff Goodman kneeling on the ground, cradling the football in his arms. With the ball in the air he had shed the half-hearted coverage of Robert Matz and circled around to make the catch off the deflection.

"Not fair! We should get our last drive!" Sam Budd hollered while sitting on his knees near the line of scrimmage, pounding his fists into the ground in anger and frustration. Sam hardly ever lost and on the rare occasion when he did, had trouble figuring out how or why.

Robert Matz jogged over to him offering his hand. "Sorry, Sam," he mumbled. "My bad. I should have been there."

With the game over, Jason Armon banged his head against the soccer goal post, disgusted that the final pass had not been thrown his way. He could not have cared less about the score. "Son of a bitch!" he screamed. "Phil, throw it to me next time. Rami's half my size! Work the mismatch, for crying out loud!"

Phil Perlow looked down at his belt, thrilled that he had escaped the game with all clothes remaining on his person. "I threw to the open man. You want the ball? Get open next time." Rami, pleased with the indirect compliment, smiled at Jason in smug satisfaction.

Despite catching the winning touchdown, Jeff Goodman had no interest in celebrating. He sat down and yanked a book out of his bag, quietly opening it to a dog-eared page. Moments after making the play of the game, he sat down on the grass and resumed reading. My nephew, Ari, stared at the group with an impassive face, his thoughts unreadable, while Aaron Dines pulled his cell phone out of his pocket and began dialing his nanny's phone number for a ride.

"These are the kids that you're going to take to Cooperstown?" Jeremy said from his knees with a chuckle, while helping his son check his blood sugar.

"Are there others I'm not aware of?"

"How many coaches do you need?"

"Three besides myself," I said.

"Make it two." He looked up at me with a glint in his eye. "This is something I don't want to miss. What do you say, Stan?"

Stan Goodman silently surveyed the scene, methodically looking at each of the kids without sharing his assessments. Finally, he spoke.

"Make it one," he said quietly under his breath as he stood next to me, gazing out over the playground.

"Yeah," he said a little louder. "Make it one."

CHAPTER FOUR

INVOKING *PEYOS*

"SO, DAD, DID you think about it?" Gabe asked me quietly as I tucked him into bed. The room was dark but the soft moonlight streaming in through the window lit a sliver of his face. I looked around at the walls, which were covered in Red Sox and Patriots photos. Above his bed hung a glass frame displaying the used ticket stubs of every sporting event that he and I had attended together.

"Yes, Gabe. I thought about it. I can't make any promises, but I'll try."

He jumped up and wrapped his arms tightly around my neck. "I love you so much, Dad."

"Now, Gabe, no promises. This won't be easy. We have to recruit enough kids to get a team together, and even then, chances are we won't get a spot in the tournament."

"I know, Dad, but I have a good feeling about this."

I kissed him gently, rubbed his closely cropped hair, and walked out of the room closing the door behind me. Shani was already asleep so I went downstairs to the family room, where Sheryl sat on the couch, watching television. She was stretched out in a white terry-cloth robe, her long brown hair cascading haphazardly over her shoulders. Her eyes reflected the images of a reality show playing on the large plasma.

"You did a good thing," she said as I plopped down next to her.

"Yeah, sure, easy for you to say. You have no idea how ridiculous this is."

"Tell me," she said.

"What if it actually happens? What if I do get the team together and we get in? What then? Do you realize how badly we'd get killed? We don't belong in a tournament like this."

"Really now, how bad could it be?" She asked casually, while aiming the clicker and flipping through all sixty cable channels with practiced ease. "I mean, they take anyone, right?"

"You're right," I said. "How bad could it be?"

THE LEAVES ON the trees turned to yellow, orange and red, then fell to the ground. The temperature outside dropped and snow coated all of New England in a blanket of white. Our lives went on as usual. Sheryl shuttled the kids back and forth to and from school while I punched the clock at work. We convened at night for dinner, homework, and maybe a board game or two. It was our typical winter routine but for one small detail—I had a second job. Recruiting the boys and persuading the parents turned out to be far more challenging than I ever anticipated. Whatever limited free time I had was gone.

"Yes, Melissa, I will make sure that we get Rami ko-sher food during the week," I said into the phone, con-tinuing a conversation that had started at least thirty minutes prior. "No, I'm not sure that they have kosher food at the park." I contradicted myself, waiting for the inevitable. "Then how do I know that I can get Rami ko-sher food? I just know, okay? I have a feeling."

Most families at Rashi were not kosher, but the Liebshutzes were. Rami's family lived in a small two-story gambrel Colonial in Newton. They belonged to a local group of moderately devout Jews who had broken away from the traditional synagogue to form what they called "The Minyan"—a group of people who get together to pray. The Liebshutz family attended Minyan services routinely on Saturday mornings, and Rami was a regu-lar and vociferous participant. Their living room shelves were filled with books on Jewish culture and holidays. Rami's mother was an educator at a religious school.

"I don't know, Josh." I heard her strident voice coming through the phone line. "It's very expensive and it'll take up the first week of our summer."

"I promise it's worth the investment in time and mon-ey."

"I'm sure. But Rami has never been away from home for that long."

"From what I know of him, it won't be an issue."

"Well, really the kosher food is the thing that con-cerns me the most. I worry that he won't have anything to eat."

The Cooperstown Dreams Park cafeteria was not sanctioned by any rabbinical authority that I was aware of, but that didn't stop me from acting as if it were. "Melissa, I promise you I'll get the kid food. I'll even make the team grow *peyos* if that'll make you happy." Invoking *peyos*, the long curly sideburns hanging down to the neck that were traditionally worn by orthodox Jews, was a dangerous way to emphasize my point. It showed I was passionate about the subject but I risked offending her. I was playing with fire.

"Okay," she said finally.

"Thank you, Melissa."

"And, Josh?" she said.

"Yeah?"

"Don't worry about the *peyos*."

OTHER FAMILIES POSED different challenges and required individually tailored tactics. Although his family was also kosher, keeping to the ancient Jewish dietary laws was much farther down the list of priorities for David Perlow, Phil's father. We spoke in the hallway after school.

"Josh, I'm very concerned about the team's lack of skill and experience," he said.

"How so?"

"I looked at the Website and it seems like it's a tough place to play. They may get beaten badly. I'm worried that you might really damage the kids' psyches." I listened intently, searching his face for any trace of humor. There was none. He stood about five foot nine in loafers, jeans, and button-down shirt open at the collar. The brown chest hair escaping at the neck matched his thick beard. Large round glasses completed the picture of college professor, which indeed was what he was.

"Don't worry, David. We'll be competitive," I said disingenuously, sensing his desire to see confidence in his son's head coach. "I can't promise we'll win the tournament or anything, but we'll keep it close."

He looked me up and down as if attempting to discern whether he was being duped.

"All right," he said. "Phil can play."

"Thanks," I said, turning quickly and escaping down the corridor before he had the opportunity to question me further.

MY SISTER, JODY, and her husband, Adam, were more challenging than I would ever have anticipated. Standing in the kitchen of their large post-and-beam home while rummaging through their refrigerator, I explained the plan.

"Let me get this straight," my brother-in-law said with a look of incomprehension on his strong-featured face. "You're organizing a team of Gabe and his friends to go play baseball in a national tournament?"

"Yeah, that's right," I responded, taking a bite out of the apple I had found in my search.

"Have you lost your mind, my friend?"

Standing a little over six feet, Adam was tall and slender. His short brown hair was brushed back from his forehead and his brown eyes stared at me in consternation. I had given him a riddle and he was having trouble solving it.

"Yeah, that's right," I said. "This is something that Gabe really wants, and besides, I'm trying to make some changes in my life."

"Like what?"

"Like the fact that I never take any risks."

"That must be coming from Sheryl," he said.

I paused for a moment. Trying to lie to my sister and her husband would likely backfire.

"Yeah, it's coming from Sheryl," I admitted.

"I think it's great," Jody said. "It's good to try and improve yourself. Besides, imagine the story that'll come out of this—small Jewish day school takes on the country's best. I can see the headlines now."

She was dressed stylishly as always, sitting with her legs crossed at the kitchen table in jeans, high boots, and cropped jacket.

"Thanks, Jods. I appreciate the support," I said, taking another bite of the apple.

"But," she responded, "I am worried about Ari's being the youngest on the team. I'm not sure he can handle being away from home for so long."

"You guys will be there," I said. "Most of the families come and stay in a motel or something. Everyone'll be at the park everyday to see the games."

"That may not be enough," she said. "He gets very homesick."

"How do you know that? He never speaks."

She looked at me, lowering her eyebrows in displeasure but decided to let it pass. "Don't worry; I know what we can do. Adam will coach with you and stay in the bunkhouse with the team."

I choked on the apple, spitting up a small piece into my hand.

"I will?" Adam said in dismay, his square jaw dropping an inch.

"It's the only way," she responded.

"Jods, I'm not so sure that's such a great idea. These kids may not be the easiest to take care of for a week and it's going to be tight quarters. You know how Adam gets . . ." I said.

My brother-in-law was a rather strict authoritarian and it was well known that he had limited tolerance for disobedience. He was a surgeon by training, and despite having two sons of his own, he preferred the strict rules and order of the OR to the chaos of a room full of kids.

"Hey, I'm right here," he said. "You can talk to me."

"Honestly, Adam, I'm not sure I trust you."

"I can handle it. You know I was a camp counselor for years . . ."

"Yeah, I know," I interrupted. "That's what I'm worried about. Don't forget I was an eyewitness to your 'counseloring.'" I had known Adam since I was seven years old at overnight camp. Remarkably, he and my sister had been together off and on since the age of nine. Needless to say, he had matured over the years, but whether he had come far enough, I was not quite sure.

"Well, it's both of them or none," Jody said flatly, leaving me no choice.

"I'll take 'em," I said.

AND ON AND on it went. I began to feel like a used-car salesman, telling people what they wanted to hear and sealing each deal with a handshake. I signed up Sam Budd by conveying to his parents with abject honesty that their son's athletic skills made him key to the entire plan. It was imperative he join us. To Aaron Dines's parents I explained that I was offering their son an experience that no amount of money in the world could buy. I enticed Robert Matz by showing him the roster list that included a who's who of the Rashi third grade boys. And, of course, there was Jason Armon, who thankfully was always up for an adventure.

"Freakin' yeah, Josh!" he shouted upon hearing the plan. "Count me in!"

I confirmed with Jeremy Finkelstein and Stan Goodman that I would have their services, along with those of their sons. I visited homes, made phone calls, sent e-mails and talked up the team at parties. Gabe did his part by working the schoolyard, making our mission the talk of the grade.

As winter released her deadly grip on our small corner of the world and the snow began to melt, the team had finally come together. The coaching slots were filled and I had ten warm bodies to put on the diamond. Not surprisingly, they were all the playground regulars: Charlie Finkelstein, Phil Perlow, Sam Budd, Rami Liebshutz, Jason Armon, Jeff Goodman, Aaron Dines, Robert Matz, Ari Glasgow, and of course, Gabe.

All we needed now was an invitation to the tournament.

CHAPTER FIVE

GAME OF PICKLE

THE COOPERSTOWN DREAMS Park application sat in the middle of the dining room table, staring up at us. It was a Saturday night toward the end of March and the weather was unusually warm—so warm in fact, that I had cracked a window for the first time since autumn. Stan sat to my left, Jeremy to my right, and my brother-in-law, Adam, stared at me from directly across the table. I had called a coaches' meeting. We needed to discuss strategy on a variety of topics, the most important of which was how to get an invitation to the tournament. Against my vociferous protests, Sheryl had invited the players. The sounds of the team's horsing around in our basement were all too clear.

"I know it's me. It has to be me," Rami Liebshutz's high-pitched voice reached our ears. His words triggered a thunderous commotion and a number of challenges to his claim. The argument quickly ceased as Sam Budd roared over the tumult.

"Are you kidding me?" he shouted. "Not a chance in the world. You're about as tall as her knee!"

"Shut up! I come up at least to her waist," Rami fired back.

Word had gotten out that Tovya Kling was harboring a crush. Tovya was the most popular girl in the grade and not coincidentally the most physically mature. The boys were now engrossed in a heated debate over who might be the object of her affection. Rami, a gifted orator, had at least half the room convinced it was he.

Gabe came running into the dining room, huffing and puffing. "Dad, we have a problem and we need to know where you stand. Do you think there's any chance that Tovya Kling likes Rami?" he asked breathlessly.

"Anything's possible," I answered. "Maybe she antici-pates that he'll get a haircut and go through a growth spurt sometime soon. Now get out of here. There's a coaches meeting going on and we have work to do."

Gabe left the room dissatisfied with my noncommittal answer and we returned to our business. The question on the table was how to put our best foot forward in the application process. The paperwork was bland at best, asking for contact information, the name of our team, and a check. It had already been decided that we would include a cover letter, the contents of which had yet to be determined.

"I suggest that we enumerate the many reasons why an underdog team such as ourselves should be given the opportunity to play," Stan contributed. "We should be honest. Let's tell them that we have no experience but if given the chance, we'll grow as a team and as individu-als."

"Hmmm . . . that doesn't sound like a very sound strategy, Stan," Jeremy said while rubbing his chin and furrowing his brow in concentration. "To me, it's a simple matter of letting money do the talking. Let's offer them a little something extra on the side."

"Extra?" Adam slammed his open hand on the table. "That may be well and good for you, Jeremy, but some of us feel that we are already paying too much for this week of voluntary pain and suffering." The cost was six hundred dollars for each of the players and coaches. It was nothing to some of the families on the team, and quite a bit to others.

"Gentlemen, gentlemen," I said, "there is no need to raise our voices. I think that without actually lying, we should make it appear as if we are a talented and experienced team. I'll figure out how to word it. We should also let them know that we're from a Jewish day school and that we're hoping to become the first all-Jewish team to play at Dreams Park. Maybe that will appeal to them."

"Why would it?" Adam interjected.

"Perhaps they're looking to diversify. Had you thought of that?" I tossed out the idea, raising my eyebrows to elicit their reaction.

"Ahhh . . ." They nodded in support of the notion. We moved on to the next order of business.

"Now this one may be slightly trickier," I said. "We need to come up with a name for our team."

Stan jumped right in, "I propose we call ourselves the Rashi Beta Kappas, after 'Phi Beta Kappa.' We'll use our baseball intelligence to defeat our opponents."

The proposal engendered nothing but silence and the initiative was defeated without anyone saying a word.

"How 'bout the Rashi Raiders?" suggested Jeremy.

"Not Jewish enough." Adam shook his head from side to side. "It wouldn't fit with our cover letter plan."

"I was considering the Rashi Rams," I said.

"Why the Rams?" Jeremy asked.

"Well, the ram has plenty of Jewish and biblical associations."

"Such as?" Stan questioned. He had a vast store of knowledge on endless subjects but Jewish studies were not his strength.

"Well," I continued. "The ram played a prominent role in the biblical story of the binding of Isaac. You know, God tested Abraham by asking him to sacrifice his son, Isaac, but an angel came down and stopped him at the last moment. Abraham then found a ram caught in a nearby bush to take Isaac's place."

"Should we name our team after an animal that was dumb enough to get caught in a bush on a barren mountainside at such an inopportune moment?" Jeremy asked sincerely.

"Let's not dwell on the details, shall we?" Adam said. "Besides, you're forgetting an even bigger connection. How about the shofar? Hello, guys! We blow a ram's horn on the holiest day of the year. Did you forget?"

"That's enough for me," I said. "All in favor?"

"Aye," said Adam.

"Aye," said Jeremy.

"I still like the Beta Kappas," said Stan.

"Well, then, the motion is carried. We will be called the Rashi Rams."

WE PULLED INTO the parking lot of the Pierce School

at around ten o'clock on a Sunday morning in April.

"Okay, guys, let's go. Unload the stuff from the trunk."
It was our first practice and I had come prepared. A
bucket filled to the brim with brand-new baseballs, bases, and a few bats were unloaded from the rear of my
car.

As Gabe and Shani ran forward, lugging the equipment, I looked out onto our practice field, the only one
that had been available during any time period on
spring weekends in the entire town of Newton. Pierce, a
public elementary school, was housed in a rectangular
brick building that sat at an odd angle facing the street
in front of it. A large grass field lay adjacent to the
structure, a Little League–size diamond making up the
near corner. Behind home plate loomed a high metal
backstop, to shield the school's nearby windows from
stray foul balls. A deep left and centerfield stretched far
into the distance, ultimately flowing into some playground equipment. Right field was shorter, ceasing abruptly when it came up against a side street. Brightly
painted wooden houses lined the road in that direction,
each living room window yielding a prime view of whatever action was taking place in the park.

There was a chill in the air, and a light drizzle caused
me to pull my sweatshirt's hood up over the top of the
baseball cap resting on my head. Such is how the parents found me as the cars began to flow into the parking
lot to drop off the players.

Stan and Jeff Goodman were the first to arrive. Jeff
approached me with his baseball glove in one hand and
a book in the other. He had worn his blue dress pants to

practice, although thankfully his loafers had been replaced with beat-up sneakers. Between the end of the
pants and tops of his shoes, his trademark black socks
made an appearance.

"What're you reading, Jeff?" I asked.

"*The Outsiders*," he responded. "I'm making my way
through the Middle School reading list."

"Oh," I said. "Did you get to the part where Dally dies
yet?"

"No, Josh. Not yet, but thanks," he responded.

The rest of the team slowly trickled in. Aaron Dines
and Sam Budd would not be able to attend that day due
to scheduling conflicts. The two had been penciled in as
our starting battery. Aaron had been playing Little
League for the past two seasons and my sources told me
that he had catching experience. I knew of no other kid
on the team who could make the same claim. A reliable
catcher would be of the highest priority at Cooperstown
Dreams Park, for to my dismay I had discovered that we
would be playing with major-league rules including pass
balls and stealing.

I expected that Sam would pitch for us. He was far
and away our best athlete; countless stories detailing his
Little League prowess had made their way around the
third grade and into my home. Regardless of my plans,
these two very important cogs in the wheel would not be
present for the first practice and so we moved on short-
handed.

I gathered the team in a circle around the pitcher's
mound. They stomped their feet and rotated their arms
in circular motions, doing their best to keep warm in the

drizzle. Stan and Jeremy stood at my side, anxious to hear how I would kick things off. Adam was to be arriving shortly.

"Well, good morning, boys," I said to the crowd.

"'Morning, Josh," they muttered under their breath. I stopped for a moment considering whether to change how the team addressed me. Most of them had called me "Josh" for years.

"Before we get started I want to take a minute to explain what we're doing here and then answer any questions you may have. As you know, we have organized a baseball team. I'll be your head coach and the assistant coaches are Ari's dad, Charlie's dad, and Jeff's dad." I pointed at each of the three boys. "You can continue to call us by our first names, or 'Coach' if you like. Does anyone know why we put this team together?"

Jason Armon raised his hand.

"Yes, Jason," I called on him. He shook the straight black hair from his eyes.

"Yeah, Josh," he said. "Uh, me and the other dudes here are going to Cooperstown."

"That's right, Jason. If we get a spot in the tournament, we'll be going to a place called Cooperstown Dreams Park. It won't be until a year from now. As I said, if we get in, we'd spend a week there and play teams from all across the country."

"Yeah, and kick their butts," Jason interrupted while shoving Robert Matz in the shoulder playfully.

"I don't know about that, Jason," I said. "But I do know we would be the first all-Jewish team to play there."

They stared at each other uninspired. For the most part they had been raised among Jews, and to be the first Jew to do this or that did not seem that important or unusual to them. Rami Liebshutz broke the silence having thought of something that he deemed equally significant.

"Hey, Josh. Do they have an arcade there? Any video games?" he asked.

"I'm not sure, Rami," I said.

"How late will we get to stay up?" Phil Perlow chimed in.

"Not sure about that either, Phil," I responded.

"What do they have to eat?" added Robert Matz.

"They have some kind of cafeteria. I don't know what they serve."

"Will there be any girls there?" Jason Armon finished the round of questioning.

"Guys," I said. "Does it strike you as odd that not a single one of your questions has contained the word *baseball*?"

They looked at one another for a moment and then shrugged their shoulders.

"What are you talking about, Josh?" Charlie Finkelstein asked. "It's very important that we know the details of what's going to happen during the week. I mean, what if we find out we don't like the food? Or what if there's an arcade and we haven't brought any quarters? These are all important things . . ."

"Forget it, Charlie," I broke in. "Let's start practicing."

The wind had picked up and there was a chill in the air. The boys were beginning to shiver, and aside from

Charlie, none of them looked as if they could stand around talking for much longer. I called out their names and their positions as they scurried onto the field.

"Berkowitz to third, Perlow to short, Liebshutz to second, Matz to first!" The infield trotted out to take up their assignments and began throwing the ball around.

"Armon to left, Glasgow to center, and Goodman to right! Finkelstein, you catch for me today!" The outfielders left the huddle.

I picked up a bat and turned around. There was trouble from the very beginning. Rami Liebshutz, whom I had penciled in as the starting second baseman, was standing on second base. He was literally standing with two feet planted firmly on the bag. It was something one might expect to see from a six- or seven-year-old ballplayer but at nine years old, he should have known better.

My nephew, Ari, whom I had sent to center, was standing two steps behind our improperly placed second baseman. Ari could have reached out and put a hand on Rami's shoulder without completely extending his elbow. The shy, quiet boy was seemingly trying to hide behind his teammate, but Rami's diminutive stature made that next to impossible. Despite Ari's young age, he was a head taller than Rami. From my vantage point the two looked like some kind of odd creature with a small body and two heads, one perched right atop the other.

I called out in their direction, "Ram, do you have any idea what you're doing wrong?"

He stared at me for a moment then shrugged his shoulders. "No idea, Josh," he said.

"Move over between first and second. You're out of position."

"Sure thing," he replied, scampering over to his left.

"Ari," I called. "Move back about fifteen steps!"

I turned to tackle the next problem. Jeff Goodman, whom I had instructed to play right field, was standing on the foul line, about five steps behind the first baseman. The brim of his cap was tilted at an angle as he stood examining the stitching on his glove. He was technically in right field but in no position to do anything other than back up throws to first base. Thankfully, he had left *The Outsiders* on the bench.

"Jeff, why are you standing there?" I asked him.

"Josh, if you view the baseball diamond as a large ninety-degree right angle, then I am standing as far to the right as possible without going into negative degrees. You told me to go to the right and that is where I am." I stared at him trying to think of the best way to communicate my desires.

"Well, then," I responded. "Place yourself at about twenty degrees, please." He did as he was told.

"Josh!" I heard immediately after positioning Jeff. I turned to see Jason Armon on the pitcher's mound, looking at me and shrugging his shoulders. "Where's left field?" he asked, perplexed. He had scanned the diamond back and forth but as yet could not make up his mind. The fact that his teammates had improperly positioned themselves wasn't helping. To him it must have looked like there were two first basemen, two second basemen and no outfielders.

I pointed toward the left and he smiled in relief,

breaking into a trot. When he finally arrived at his position, we were ready to begin—or so I thought. I picked up the bat again and surveyed the group. They were in the correct locations, but now we had another problem. Most of them were standing straight up with arms dangling by their sides. They stared, glassy-eyed, back at me. The short incident with Jason had already been enough time for Jeff to find himself sitting on the ground in right field.

"Everyone bend your knees and put your gloves out in front of you! Look like you're ready to play," I hollered, reviewing the ready position with them. It didn't help, at least not for any length of time. They got into the ready position but were able to maintain it for only a few seconds at most. If no immediate action took place in their vicinity, they would resume their previous casual stance, or worse yet, end up on the ground.

"What do you want the coaches to do?" Jeremy asked as he stood next to me near home plate.

"You stay here," I said. "Stan and Shani, you two come and run the bases when I hit the ball."

Stan had been sitting on the bench staring out at the kids on the field, his face beaming. It was unclear why he was so happy, given our inauspicious start.

"Great," he said, bouncing up and jogging to my side. Shani pulled herself off the grass and came over to line up behind Stan, ready to run. My daughter had plenty of experience playing baseball with her father and brother. She could run the bases and run them well.

"All right," I yelled out to the fielders. "Nobody on, nobody out. Let's see what you can do." And thus began the chaos.

Gabe fielded a grounder cleanly at third and promptly threw it over Robert Matz's head at first, barely missing the windshield of the Suzuki that was resting in the parking lot minding its own business. Phil Perlow allowed his slow ground ball at short to go directly between his legs and into left field, where it promptly found its way past the mitt of a diving Jason Armon.

"Son of a bitch!" Jason screamed as he lay on the ground, slamming his fist against the turf while the ball continued to roll into the outfield.

"No swearing!" I hollered. "And get after that ball!"

Rami's grounder at second squirted right over his glove as he tried to field it from off to the side. Ari picked it up in center and threw it—at the school building. Fly balls to the outfield mingled with the drizzle to hit the grass and not a single one was caught.

Stan, who was running the bases, did not follow instructions and stayed on the path after each hit, making it more challenging for the fielders. He stood on second base with a wide grin plastered on his face. I had never seen him so blissfully content.

I hit one to the outfield and Stan took off for home, the curly brown hair above his ears blowing in the breeze. He crossed the plate and gave me a tap on the behind.

"This is splendid!" he hollered in joy. "I've never been involved in a team practice before!"

One hit later, Shani left my side and ran completely around the diamond, the beneficiary of a multitude of errors. She touched the plate and tugged on my sleeve, looking up at me. "Why are they so bad, Dad?" she asked confusedly.

I was quite depressed at the sight of it all and before long I felt that familiar panic begin to rise in my chest. My old friend the mind killer was back. Gabe and his friends would not be able to hold their own against a group of neighborhood kids, let alone in a national tournament. And even though it was over a year away, my first glimpse of the Rashi Rams made me think one thing and one thing only—this had all been a very big mistake.

Just when I thought I couldn't take it anymore, Adam showed up. Of the three coaches on my staff, Adam had the most legitimate team sports experience. He had been a decent athlete in his day, and of the four of us, was the only one to have played any competitive sports in college. Granted, he rode the pine for just one short season on the University of Rochester's junior varsity basketball team, but the lone hoop he scored with a baseline jumper in garbage time was a better claim to fame than anything the rest of us had ever accomplished.

Adam spent a few moments scanning the field as the practice continued. It took him no time at all to absorb what was happening and just moments after he had, he burst into uncontrollable laughter.

"This is your baseball team?" he asked me. "This is the team that is going to play in a national tournament? Josh, you have got to call this thing off right now."

"Maybe you're right, Ad," I said, hanging my head in sadness as the team reached its breaking point and dropped to the ground. The wind blew and a light rain continued to fall. I looked at my watch and saw that it was twelve noon. We had been going at it for two straight hours, and the further along we got, the worse it had looked.

Stan and Jeremy meandered over to home plate and the four coaches stood together.

"That was fun, Josh," Stan said with genuine optimism.

"Stan," I responded, "they stink."

"I disagree," he said, perplexed by my negativity.

"Stan, just trust me on this one."

"Listen, guys," Jeremy jumped in, "it's the first practice. We have plenty of time to get them ready. You can accomplish a lot in a year."

"A year? A lifetime wouldn't be enough," I said.

"Look, when I first started training, I had no idea what I was doing. Look at me now. Last year I won the Newton Jewish Community Center's annual triathlon."

"I know and now you're considered to be in the best shape of any Jew in Boston." I said sarcastically, having heard the story many times before.

"Well, it's true."

"Jeremy," I said. "We're not going to have the time or ability to train like obsessive madmen, the way you do. We've got problems here."

"What?" He sounded wounded. "I only run twenty miles three times a week," he whispered to himself.

The four of us stood looking out over the rainy field, staring at the boys who were lying on the ground hoping for practice to end soon. There was silence for quite a while as each of us became lost in his own thoughts.

Then suddenly the stillness was broken. A gentle humming sound floated on the wind and it grew in strength until I determined that it was a melody. I listened further and recognized it as a familiar one. Turning to Jeremy, I saw that it was coming from his lips. At first, he was humming just to soothe himself, but then, our eyes met, and he smiled, his voice growing stronger and louder. One by one, Adam, Stan and I joined in. The bittersweet theme song to *The Bad News Bears* filled the air.

For some strange reason, the music lifted my spirit and gave me renewed hope. Maybe, just maybe, this would work out. If that sorry team could pull it together, perhaps we could do the same.

I reached down into my bucket and took out an old yellow tennis ball that I had brought along, tossing it onto the field.

"You guys can play a game of pickle now!" I hollered.

They were off the ground in a heartbeat.

CHAPTER SIX

HOPELESSLY OVERMATCHED

DURING THE SUMMER, the team did not get together. Many of the kids were away on vacation or at camp, and, given my doubts as to whether we would get a spot in the tournament, the need to convene seemed far from urgent. As for our family's plans, that summer was to be Gabriel's first time away from home.

For some reason unbeknownst to me, somewhere along the way it became an American Jewish tradition to send children to overnight camp for a month or two during July and August. Most of the kids had an incredible experience, making lifelong friends and gaining a sense of confidence they could achieve nowhere else. Having one's children safely tucked away in some bucolic setting also ended up being a treat for the parents who typically slaved over their offspring for the remaining ten to eleven months of the year.

When the topic happened to come up with my non-Jewish friends, I invariably received one of two responses. There was the oft repeated, "How can you possibly send your eight-year-old child away from home? That is cruel and inhumane." Or the less common but equally predictable, "I wish I were Jewish."

I spent the majority of my summers as a youth at Camp Yavneh, which was located in Northwood, New Hampshire. Yavneh was a Berkowitz family tradition. My parents met there, my mother was the director for many summers, and both my brother and my sister met their respective spouses at Yavneh. Sheryl used to tease me about being a family pariah because I met her at Brandeis, of all places, a Jewish university on the out-skirts of Boston.

Summers at Yavneh defined my childhood. I lived for the end of June, and counted the hours until camp would begin. For me, there was no better part of life, and as the years went on, I slowly realized it was impossible to re-capture those sweltering hot days of living in a bunk-house with my best friends.

So, it was Gabe's turn to take a crack at being away from home as the first member of the third generation of the Berkowitz family to head to Yavneh. We drove the two hours to southern New Hampshire with Sheryl and Gabriel cuddling in the back seat. She loathed letting him go. Pulling into camp, we were quickly surrounded by counselors in Yavneh T-shirts, calling out directions.

After checking in, we took Gabriel to his cabin and helped him unpack. At Yavneh, the bunkhouses were simple wooden structures dating back to the origin of the camp in the 1950s. Not much had been done to them in all the years, aside from the replacement of an odd toilet or two. The walls were covered throughout with the names of campers who had lived there in previous dec-ades. We scanned the plywood that lined the interior of

Gabe's bunk, in search of familiar family names and dates. We took a short pilgrimage to another cabin where I knew that my friends and I had placed a plaque on the wall, listing our names and the year we called that bunk home. It was an old Yavneh tradition. Even thirty years later, those plaques remained in the same places they had been painstakingly secured with proud and loving hands. They were never removed or defaced as each successive generation of campers intuitively understood to respect those who came before.

We returned to Gabriel's bunk, where I pulled out a hammer and nails I had brought along to make his area more livable. Shelf space at Yavneh was at a premium and nails driven into the walls, to hang items from, often had to suffice. I hammered a large one just above Gabe's bed to function as a hook for his baseball glove. He looked at me with admiration.

"How did you know to bring the nails, Dad?"

"Your father knows these things," I responded.

He smiled at me. I thought how fortunate I was to have a son who was impressed by his father for simply bringing a few nails to opening day.

As we prepared to leave I could see tentative excitement on Gabe's face. Sheryl and I kissed him and walked away as he stood on the front stoop of his bunkhouse, glove and ball in hand, watching us go. He was only eight years old and it was painful to leave him. Tears welled in my eyes as I turned and walked down the path.

THE LETTERS WE received home from Gabriel that

summer told his tale, albeit succinctly. He had adjusted quite easily to being away from home and was having an extraordinary time. Much of what Gabe described in his letters revolved around playing for Yavneh's peewee softball team.

During the summer, Yavneh competed in weekly games against other Jewish camps in the surrounding areas. These opposing camps carried names such as Tevya, Tel-Noar, and Young Judea. In a league such as this, one might expect the competition to be relatively even. Nothing was further from the truth. We were considered the laughingstock of the group, not only because we were the most religious camp but also because we were just simply bad. Summer after summer, we had the worst athletes, and if we won one game during an eight-week session, we considered it a successful campaign.

It didn't help our cause that Yavneh prided itself on teaching its campers to speak Hebrew. Classes were held six days a week and public announcements were never made in English. Even the cheers the campers were taught were in the ancient language of our people.

The humiliation we suffered at the hands of our rivals was second to none as our buses pulled into the opposing camp with our voices ringing loud and clear, "*Nay-lech*, Yavneh! Yavneh, *nay-lech!*" ("Let's go, Yavneh! Yavneh, Let's go!") We were a joke. Everyone knew it, including us. In retrospect, that was probably one of the many reasons that the kids who attended Yavneh were so passionate about their experience. We were the underdogs, the losers, the Hebrew-speakers. We lived in bunks that were forty years old. We were forced to attend Judaic studies classes over the summer. Our drinking water was rusty and our showers were cold. We were in a foxhole together for two months with no one to watch our backs but one another. We loved every minute of it.

Year in and year out, the beast of our softball league was a camp named Bauercrest. It was an all-boy Jewish overnight camp that lived and breathed sports. The kids who attended Bauercrest were sports obsessed, as were their parents. In those days, people didn't readily have the opportunity to sign up their children for twelve different teams at any one time during the school year. No matter how badly they wanted it, the programming was just not available for them to turn their kid into a sleep-deprived, ultra-competitive, arrogant psychopath. But there was one remaining option. Over the summer, they could send their kids to Bauercrest.

One could never find two more opposite camps than Yavneh and Bauercrest. We were Jewish and proud of it. They were Jewish and didn't even know it. We were obsessed with our girls. Bauercrest had no females whatsoever. Our softball team struggled for one win. They were outraged by anything less than an undefeated season. They taunted us across the diamond about our Hebrew. We asked back whether they were excited about their one midsummer social with the neighboring girls' camp. It was a bitter and vicious rivalry. Unfortunately, they routinely kicked our butts.

There was one summer, however, when we got our chance. I had been attending Yavneh since the age of eight and could not recall a single game when we had even come close to beating Bauercrest. A typical defeat would be by a solid ten- to fourteen-run margin. At times it was worse.

The summer when I was twelve years old was different. I don't recall that we were much better that year than previous summers, but for some reason we were able to hang with the vaunted Bauercrest squad through six innings. We were playing at home; and entering the bottom of the sixth, the final inning in our league, we were down by only three runs. For us, that was an accomplishment in and of itself, but that summer we would not be satisfied with a three-run defeat.

I had played third base throughout the game, as I did every day of every summer that I attended camp. I had made a few solid plays in the field against our nemesis and for that reason I recall feeling confident. With two outs and a runner on first, I stepped to the plate. My heart was beating fast and my hands were slick with perspiration. After taking a couple of pitches for strikes, I stepped anxiously back into the batter's box and waited. One more and the game would end.

The sleep-deprived, ultra-competitive, arrogant, psychopathic Bauercrest pitcher went into his underhand windup. The ball looked good coming in, and I knew that if I left the bat on my shoulder it would be strike three, game over. And so I swung with all my might. It was a high pop fly, not hit solidly or with much power. But hitting with power and strength was only one factor when it came to this crazy game.

On that day, the Lord must have been with the Hebrew-speaking, girl-crazy Yavnehites because my ball had eyes. It landed in the black hole just behind second base, where no one could get to it. I ran down to first and heaved a sigh of relief, happy that I hadn't been the one to make the final out but expecting the game to end soon. With runners on first and second and still two outs, our next batter was able to draw a walk. As I stood on second base, I scanned the diamond and could not believe what I was seeing. We had the bases loaded in the final inning and were down only three runs to the almighty Bauercrestians.

By that time, the other games going on in camp had finished. The girls' volleyball teams, the peewee softball team, and other camp stragglers had made it down to watch our game. There were no stands for the fans but foul territory was littered with people sitting or standing on the grass and cheering us on—in Hebrew. I saw my older sister and younger brother, both at camp with me for the summer, jumping up and down excitedly.

Baruch Cohen stepped to the plate. Baruch was a close friend and we had grown up at camp together. He was our team's starting shortstop and our best player. He could hit the ball a mile but also struck out a fair amount. With his first two attempts, I could see that Baruch was swinging for the fences. *Not a good sign*, I thought, as he had a tendency to slip up when trying to force the issue.

With two strikes on him, what I thought was the final pitch came in. Baruch swung and missed—strike three. The entire Bauercrest team ran off the field, celebrating their victory. But as I walked slowly off of second base with my head hung low, I miraculously heard the umpire calling Bauercrest back. Baruch had remained in the batter's box knowing that it had been a foul tip and the catcher had not hung on to the ball. The game was not over. The opposition trudged back onto the field, expecting it to end shortly.

Baruch had not had a good day and the Bauercrest squad thought him to be easy prey. Just one more pitch, one more swing and a miss would end it. But they had no idea what Baruch was capable of. As the fielders settled back into their positions, the pitcher went in to his windup yet again. This time however, the results were different. Baruch connected and connected big time. His hit was a rocket that went sailing deep over the left fielder's head.

There were no fences and the outfield stretched into the distance, seemingly without end. The ball landed, rolling and rolling while the left fielder gave chase. The other base runners and I stood watching in disbelief for a long moment, our feet rooted to the ground. Then we shook off our surprise and bolted for home.

Oddly enough, the thing that I remember most about that moment was something that happened between my legs. All summer long I had worn my classic white jockeys underneath my shorts. I had owned a number of pairs for years and they were just beginning to show some wear and tear. As I rounded third, my private parts chose just that moment to slip out from one of the gaps in my underwear that was located on either side of center. Fortunately I didn't think anyone noticed my dilemma because the trouble was hidden behind my shorts. And besides, all eyes were on that softball rolling deep into left field.

I kept running, making certain to step firmly on the plate as I crossed home. The tying run came in shortly thereafter. With the final result hanging in the balance, I stayed put and hollered for Baruch to keep going. By pumping my right fist in the air, I hoped that it would keep others from noticing that I was using my left hand to stuff myself back inside.

Baruch came around with the game's winning run as the throw came in late and our team, our fans, and the entire camp danced for joy. In all my years at Yavneh, it was the only home run I ever saw hit on that field. And there will never be another as that diamond has long since been plowed over. In Hebrew, *baruch* means "blessing," and on that hot summer day at Camp Yavneh, tucked away in the backwoods of tiny Northwood, New Hampshire, my friends and I were truly blessed.

IN HIS FIRST summer at camp, Gabriel had found himself starting at third base for the Yavneh peewee softball team just like his dad. I am sure that no one placed him there because of his father's great legacy. That is just the position he was most suited for given his skill set. I thought it to be a good sign for the Rashi Rams that my son was able to make it as a starter even at the tender age of eight, although I'm sure the competition was not that stiff. Even thirty years later, things at Yavneh had not changed that much. Gabe had a wonderful first summer at camp and toward the end of his time there sent a letter home that read simply,

Dear Mom and Dad,
Thank you for sending me here.
Love,
Gabriel

WHILE GABE WAS at camp playing softball once a week against other good little Jewish boys, the competition we were to face in Cooperstown was doing no such thing. As Gabe lounged on the dock on Lucas Pond or sat in his morning class learning Hebrew, there were many serious baseball tournaments taking place all across the country. I spent a fair amount of time on the computer that summer doing research, trying to figure out just exactly what I had gotten us into.

The discoveries that I made sent cold shivers down my spine. I had some assumptions about the quality of the teams that we would be facing in Cooperstown, just as I had some thoughts on how the Rams would look once they took the field. The former were about as useful as the latter. I suspected that the competition would be good, in the same way that a good Little League team might be good. There would be some first-class players and some that were mediocre. Some of the teams would be of a high quality, others less so. Well, once again, I was wrong. I was very wrong.

Dreams Park had its own Website, which posted the scores and highlights of every game played there all summer long. They also had links to the Web pages of many of the teams that returned to CDP year after year. The fact that these teams had their own Websites was initially surprising. Surprise quickly turned to dread. I read through most of them thoroughly, my jaw dropping lower and lower with each click of the mouse.

There were the Long Island Playmakers, whose pages boasted of their "off-season conditioning program." The Rashi Rams didn't even have a "season," let alone an "off-season." I clicked on the home of the Boys of Baseball National Travel Team to read that they recruited from six different states in the South. I had recruited not from six states, not from one state, not even from one town. I had Scotch-taped and pasted a team together from just twenty kids from one grade in one small school. I read that many of the better teams required a payment just to try out—hundreds of dollars just for a chance to play for them!

I ultimately found myself on the Website of the San Diego Stars Baseball Academy, where I discovered an entire page dedicated to their players that had gone on to play professional baseball—as in, the major leagues. All-star power hitter Adrian Gonzalez was at the top of the list. The Stars' well-known head coach, Lyle Gabriel had won the Cooperstown Dreams Park ten and under tournament four out of the previous five summers.

As I read, I finally came to understand what this tournament was all about and I chastised myself for not having done my research sooner. Cooperstown Dreams Park was actually a place for baseball teams whose play was on a level above anything I had even heard of. They practiced and participated in travel tournaments year-round. Many of the coaches were paid professionals. The kids who made these teams were the best of the best. They were the elite players of the country, if not the world. We had no business being in a tournament like this. We were not even qualified to help these teams clean their equipment. It was Yavneh versus Bauercrest on steroids and multiplied a thousandfold. We were hopelessly overmatched.

After the realization of what I had done finally dawned on me, it completely ruined my summer. Many nights as I lay in bed in the dark, panic would slowly begin to rise in my chest. It grew and grew until it flooded over me like a tidal wave and I felt as if I were drowning. Despite the summer air flowing through my open window I could not breathe, and even the rare imagined visit from Sandy Koufax did nothing to calm my nerves. I would toss and turn for hours at a time as Sheryl slept peacefully beside me.

We are going to get killed, I would think to myself. And it would repeat over and over again in my mind until I would crush the pillow on either side of my head, begging God to make it stop. *We are going to get killed. We are going to get killed. I will be humiliated. I will be humiliated. Everyone will hate me. Everyone will hate me.*

I did desperately try to fight back against the rising tide of fear, however. *Fear is the mind killer—don't give in to it. Fear is the mind killer—don't give in to it.* I would repeat the mantra until I regained some sense of calm. I tried to convince myself that we were providing these kids with a once-in-a-lifetime opportunity. It would be a rare chance to step onto the field and measure themselves against the very best. Is that not worth risking utter and total humiliation?

Would I not give my right arm for a chance to throw a fastball to Adrian Gonzalez? There wouldn't be a prayer in heaven that I would get one by him. But what if on one day, just one day, the wind was blowing just right and my pitch to Gonzalez broke just so, and he swung and whiffed. For a lifetime I would be able to say that I threw a fastball by Adrian Gonzalez. How many people could say that? Just once is all it would take.

I was giving them a chance, just a chance, for that one moment, to do something special. An opportunity to round third base, totally exposed underneath their shorts, while bringing home that winning run against an unbeatable opponent. I thought of the great underdogs of all time, hoping for them to give me inspiration. I saw a vision of Buster Douglas taking a swing at Mike Tyson, soon to be replaced by Ed Pinkney of Villanova dunking over Patrick Ewing, and finally my beloved Patriots grinding the greatest show on turf to a halt in Super Bowl XXXVI.

These were the thoughts that went back and forth in my mind as the long summer came to a close. Gabriel returned home from camp and the first thing he wanted to know was when practice would begin again. My plan had been to wait until we heard from the park sometime in November before investing more time in the team. But one look at Gabe's face and I knew there would be no waiting. When school began in September, the Rashi Rams would take to the field once again.

CHAPTER SEVEN

LIKE A KETTLE ON A RANGE

THE BALL BURST through the strike zone at close to seventy miles per hour landing with a "snap" in Aaron Dines's catcher's mitt as he crouched behind home plate.

"Ouch! That hurt like hell!" he shouted, yanking off his glove and shaking out his hand. Aaron was catching Sam Budd, and even his brand-new, high-tech catcher's equipment recently acquired with his own personal credit card gave him no sense of security.

"Slow it down, Sambo!" he yelled. "You're gonna freakin' kill me!" The Rams' starting battery had joined us at practice, and brought with them a small measure of respectability.

It was early September and the players' fourth-grade year had begun. On Friday afternoons after school, we had started taking the team down to Cabot Park, a five-minute drive from Rashi. Cabot consisted of a quarter-mile rectangular swath of green grass interrupted by sporadic groupings of trees, surrounded on all sides by the back streets of Newton.

Three baseball fields were scattered along the stretch. One was a flawless Little League diamond with well-manicured grass and a forest green fence enclosing the outfield. It was always in use. The second was full size and used by the local Babe Ruth league. It was far too big for our purposes. We reluctantly settled on the third, a softball diamond with an all-dirt infield and a flat pitcher's mound. Two benches, placed behind six-foot chain-link fences, served as dugouts, and a large back-stop rose behind home plate, keeping the trees at bay.

The players were in the field at what had become their customary positions. Gabe was always at third; his consistent glove and strong arm combined to make him one of our better players. Jason Armon had nailed down left; his long legs gave him decent range in the outfield, and it was good to keep his foul mouth as far away from me as possible. Phil Perlow had found himself a home at shortstop. The proficient athlete performed well under the watchful eyes of his father, who frequently attended practice. Rami Liebshutz continued to hold down second base. He had learned where to position himself and had taken up a new habit of spitting on the ground as he stood waiting for the ball to come his way. Robert Matz frequently manned first. The cheerful youth was always in high spirits regardless of whether he was picking one out of the dirt or letting the ball go by his glove into the waiting street. My nephew, Ari, grew comfortable in center. He still uttered precious few words but showed up for practice, and given the opportunity, could usually shake the bangs from his eyes in time to catch a fly ball. Right field saw a rotation between Charlie Finkelstein and Jeff Goodman. They were a good platoon; Jeff ran out to take over for Charlie during hypoglycemic spells, and vice versa when Jeff had trouble separating himself from a good book.

Aaron Dines was our catcher and a surprisingly decent one at that. While at times it appeared that he might be daydreaming of his ski-in, ski-out winter getaway or his summer bedroom's ocean view, for the most part Aaron got the job done. He always caught Sam Budd, of course. Sam carried the reputation of the best athlete in the school for a reason. Not a practice went by where I didn't say a quick prayer of thanks for him. For a coach in desperate need of playmakers, the kid did not disappoint. Sam threw viciously hard and the majority of our team simply refused to step into the batter's box against him. At times, the players had to be encouraged to give it a go.

"Get in there, Robert," I yelled from down the third baseline. "And swing the bat!"

"But, Josh, I'm gonna get killed," he pleaded.

"Get in there. You'll be fine," I encouraged with feigned conviction.

Robert remained standing in the makeshift on-deck circle. I called him over while walking slowly down the line to meet him halfway between third and home.

"Robert," I said, placing both hands on his shoulders as he rested his bat against his right side. "Now listen to me, son. This is very important. When we are in Cooperstown, you're going to be facing pitchers that throw even harder than Sam. We're going to need you to put your fear behind you and get into that box. No matter what happens, there's no way you'll be able to get a hit if you're not in the box. Do you understand?"

"Okay, Josh," he said, nodding. "I'll do my best."

"That's all we're asking, Robert."

He left my side and walked back as Sam watched him, slowly tossing the ball in and out of his glove. Robert stepped to home plate, standing as far back as possible. His knees trembled.

"Whoosh!" came the pitch, blowing by him.

"Strike one!" Adam called from where he was serving as umpire behind the plate. Aaron tossed the ball back to Sam on the mound, who launched the next pitch in identical fashion. Robert fell backward out of the box, knocked over by the wind.

"Strike two!" Adam called, looking off to the right and pointing down the first baseline.

"Robert, come over here!" I called. He walked toward me, shoulders slumped and bat in tow. Once again, I took him gently by the shoulders.

"Now, Robert, do you understand that not only do you have to be in the box, but you also have to swing? Otherwise there's no chance you'll get a hit, okay?"

He nodded again. "I'll do my best, Josh."

"Thank you, Robert."

He turned around and walked back to the batter's box, looking over at Sam with trepidation. Forcing himself to step in yet again, Robert exhaled a deep sigh and waited. The third and final pitch came in, and as it sailed through the strike zone, he leaned forward to swing. The ball landed with another "snap" in Aaron's glove, and a good two seconds later, the bat passed over home plate.

"Strike three!" Adam called as Robert looked down at me and shrugged his shoulders.

"Don't worry, Robert." I said. "Now that you know you have to swing, you'll have three chances next time."

Rami made his way from the on-deck circle, donning a helmet that made his head look three times bigger than his body. He stepped to the plate, and Sam stared down at him.

"Josh," he called from the mound. "How am I supposed to pitch to him? The strike zone is about as big as a quarter."

"Just throw the ball," Rami called back, trying to stand up as straight as he could. The pitches came in, and Rami had no more luck than his predecessor. After three strikes, he turned to me.

"Just give me a few more chances, Josh," he pleaded. His reward for his precocious spunky nature was five more swinging strikes and seven called ones. Finally, I tried to put an end to his valiant efforts.

"Just one more and that's it," I told him.

The sixteenth fastball that Rami had seen that day sped toward home like the others and he swung yet again. This time, however, he caught the slightest piece, fouling it straight into the backstop. Remarkably, despite multiple practices, it was the first time anyone had made contact with one of Sam's pitches. A momentary silence fell upon the field as coaches and players stared in disbelief at the ball spinning slowly in the dirt. We looked to Rami who stood like a statue, eyes transfixed on the revolving sphere. Seconds passed before he awoke from his daze, ripped off his helmet, and jumped up and down as high as his small legs would propel him. Rami's screams of euphoria echoed throughout the neighborhood. The entire team followed suit, throwing their gloves in the air in celebration.

"Phil," I called. "Get in here and hit. Gabe, take over at short."

Phil Perlow hustled in from the field. He was one of the few in the group who had shown any ability to put bat on ball. Sam stood on the mound and snickered with satisfaction at the sight of him. He basked in the potential prospect of putting one of our more confident hitters in his place.

"All right, Phil, my boy, let's see what you can do!" David Perlow bellowed from behind the fence along the first baseline. I looked over to see him clapping his hands together.

"Take it easy up there, Phil. Nice level swing, now," Jeremy Finkelstein called from where he was coaching first base.

"Good luck, Phil. You can do this," Stan Goodman encouraged from his position on the bench behind me.

Phil stepped to the plate and dug in from the left side. He hit and threw left-handed, giving him a slight advantage over his teammates when facing the overpowering right-handed Budd. Sam whipped the ball toward the plate with the usual speed, and the result was predictable. Phil swung and missed.

"C'mon, Phil!" David Perlow called as he paced back and forth behind the fence. "Like we practiced! Level swing! Uncoil your body! Let's go!" Despite David's voiced concerns over the possible excursion to Cooperstown, he had been spending hours in the backyard working on Phil's swing. He was hoping his son had put the extra training to good use.

Phil stared at the ground, while burrowing his rear foot into the dirt and holding up his hand for time. He was doing everything he could to prepare himself for the next offering.

"I hate to rush an artist, Phil," Adam said from behind his umpire's mask. "But we don't have all day."

"I'm ready," Phil responded, lowering his hand and staring intently out toward the mound.

Adam pointed to the pitcher, signaling that the ball was in play. Snarling, Sam reared back as if he might ratchet his seventy-mile-per-hour fastball up to eighty, but at the last moment eased up and tossed a floater. Phil's eyes went wide and he swung hungrily, smacking a line drive into left field. Everyone stopped and stared. Even Phil was rooted to the ground. No one had ever put one in play off Sam before, let alone hit cleanly. The ball landed in front of Jason Armon in left and scooted by him.

"Son of a bitch!" Jason yelled, chasing after it.

Phil was too excited to run. He just stood, staring out at Sam, gloating.

"That was my change-up, you loser," Sam said. "You'd never be able to hit my fastball."

Phil looked out at Sam, anger and hostility boiling within him like a kettle on a range. Then before anyone could stop him, he dropped his bat and charged.

Sam immediately threw his glove down to meet the challenge, running directly at his adversary. The two made contact in between home and the pitcher's mound, falling to the ground in a tangle of arms and legs. They rolled over each other twice before Sam found himself on top, his added bulk pinning Phil to the ground.

By that point, the entire team, both coaches and players, had raced to the scene. Gabe jumped on Sam's back, struggling to pull him off, while Rami flung his small body between the two combatants. It soon became an all-out brawl with players rolling, punching, and kicking, while coaches scrambled, doing their best to reign in the chaos.

When cooler heads finally prevailed, the players lay scattered on the ground in the infield, huffing and puffing, breathless and unable to speak. David Perlow walked over and pulled his son from the ground, and they gave each other a high five in celebration of hitting the unhittable. Their time had been well spent.

As I considered my next move, unexpectedly a cell phone rang. Scanning 360 degrees to find its source, my eyes ultimately settled on Aaron Dines, standing at home plate. He was decked out from head to toe in his-top-of-the-line catcher's equipment. Fear of damaging it may have been the reason he had decided not to join the fray.

Aaron calmly took off his mask to reveal his light brown hair streaked with gold. Casually reaching into his pocket, he removed his cell phone.

"Yeah, okay, I'll see you in a few," he said and then turned to me. "Josh, I gotta go. My nanny's coming. I got an appointment to get my hair highlighted."

I stared at him in silence.

"Okay, Aaron," I said flatly.

It was odd, but for some reason, at that moment, I

was less concerned about the fight than I was disappointed to finally have my suspicions confirmed. My catcher's golden locks were not entirely natural.

"JOSH, PAY ATTENTION!" Sheryl said.

We were sitting at Café Luigi in the local town of Bedford and the discussion had turned to the possibility of adding new players to the Rams.

Luigi's was an old favorite of ours, and, in my opinion, had the best eggplant parmigiana outside the North End. It was a Saturday night and the kids were with my mother. The restaurant was crowded. Every table was occupied with patrons, many of whom called out to waitresses as they hustled by, carrying trays laden with steaming pasta and chicken. Although it was loud, I could still make out snippets of conversation from the adjacent booth. I tried to listen in so as to ignore my wife, but she would have none of it.

"Josh, I said to pay attention! This is important."

I stared at her impassively, hoping that my lack of interest would force her to change the subject. She had just finished explaining that the more our team practiced and the more the boys talked at school, the more attention we were generating. Now two additional fourth graders wanted to sign up.

"Gil Slotnick wants in. His father talked to me today," Sheryl said. "I told him that I would have to speak to you."

Gil was the son of Israelis who had immigrated to the States a few years prior. A ladies' man extraordinaire, Gil was interested in the opposite sex far earlier than were any of his friends. Word among the kids was that he currently had a girlfriend from his neighborhood. Gil had once bragged to his classmates that he would be the first to date every girl in the grade.

"Not a chance," I responded. "You have no idea what I'm dealing with here. I can't take on anyone new. I don't even know whether Gil can play baseball. Anyway, I thought all the kid cared about was girls."

"I checked with his father, and he has played Little League over the past few years. He actually told me that Gil is pretty good."

I picked at the eggplant on my plate and stared at her. She didn't understand what she was asking of me.

"His father told you he's good? Now there's a shock."

"I'm not done," Sheryl went on as if I hadn't spoken. "Carlos wants in, too."

"Carlos?" I said. "Are you kidding me? No way. Did you hear me? I said 'no way.'"

Carlos Garcia-Feinstein, born in the Dominican Republic, was the adopted son of two gay fathers, one Hispanic and one Jewish. Carlos was the pride and joy of the liberal-leaning Rashi community that embraced unconventional backgrounds. The Rashi students had been raised with an appreciation for all lifestyles and so Carlos was easily included. But, at that moment, fear and anxiety took priority over an open heart. I had never seen Carlos participate in pickup games on the playground, and I suspected that he wouldn't even know which hand to put a glove on.

Despite my protests, Sheryl pressed on. She had a unique hearing problem that happened to flare up when

I disagreed with her.

"So I spoke to Carlos's father and there is one additional concern that you should know about."

"What's that?" I said, letting out a sigh.

There was a pause. "It turns out that Carlos has a mild congenital bleeding disorder," she said under her breath. Even Sheryl hesitated when breaking that news to me.

"He *what*?"

"His blood doesn't always clot properly."

"I know what a bleeding disorder is! I'm a doctor!"

"Oh, good," she said. "Then it won't be a problem."

"Sheryl," I patiently began to explain, while gently placing my fork on the plate. "putting someone who has never played competitive baseball up against some of the top ten-year-old pitchers in the country is crazy enough. Adding a bleeding disorder to the mix is downright suicidal."

"You don't think that should be his fathers' and his doctor's decision?" she asked. "And besides, we're not going there to win, you know. We're going there for the experience and for the community."

"I'm not going to Cooperstown to win, either," I said. "But I need the team to be able to make an out, for Christ's sake!"

We sat in silence as I twirled my linguine and ripped off a few hunks of the Italian bread that lay between us. Not knowing in which direction to turn, I sat and stewed. As luck would have it, I looked over at the seat next to me and was startled to suddenly see the vision of Sandy Koufax sitting just a foot or two away. He was in full uniform with his Dodgers cap pulled low over his brow. Sheryl went back to eating her dinner, oblivious to our new guest.

"Do you believe this, Sandy?" I asked him.

He dove into his plate of pasta without even looking up. Although he had never truly helped in the past, at least Sandy hadn't been downright rude before. After curiously watching him eat for a few moments, I gave up and turned back to Sheryl.

"I refuse to take on any new players. Tell the fathers that the roster is full. It's not happening."

"Too late," she said, revealing the secret that I had known all along. "I already invited them to join."

And just like that, Gil Slotnick and Carlos Garcia-Feinstein were members of the Rashi Rams. I had two new unknowns to assess, train, and somehow work into a team that was already teetering on the brink. I sat and stared out the window, chewing on the straw in my glass. Sheryl returned to her dinner and Sandy finished his meal without so much as a word. That night, for some reason, the world's best eggplant parmigiana didn't taste quite so good.

CHAPTER EIGHT

HAPPY BIRTHDAY, DAD

"GET THAT OUTTA here!" Sam roared, rejecting Charlie's shot into the nearby lunch tables.

Sheryl and I stood against the wall, watching the team as they rotated players in and out of the pickup two-on-two basketball tournament. We were in the Rashi cafenasium, so called because it doubled as both cafeteria and gymnasium. The phys. ed. teacher had purchased a small eight-foot hoop for his corner of the undersized room, and the team managed in the cramped quarters by forgoing the preferred five-on-five.

"Gabe, come here for a second," Sheryl called.

He broke away from the game and ran over. "Yeah? What's up, Mom?"

"Dad and I are going to meet with Mr. Libenson now. Stay here, and we'll be back in a half-hour. And please keep an eye on Shani. She's in the back with her friends."

"Okay, no problem," he said, running back to the game. He stopped halfway and turned, a thought coming to mind. "Oh, and, guys?"

"Yes, Gabe?" Sheryl responded.

"Thanks for taking on Gil and Carlos. Everyone is psyched about it."

I looked over to see the two newcomers, who were waiting to get into the basketball round-robin. Gil had partnered with Jason, standing amongst Sam's crew. Carlos wandered amongst Gabe's pack, searching for someone to buddy up with.

Sheryl and I exited the cafenasium and made our way to Gabe's classroom. It was conference day, which meant the majority of the community would spend the morning within Rashi's walls. Parents roamed the hallways searching for the appropriate teachers, while the kids were left in a few reserved areas awaiting reward or punishment.

"Josh!" I turned to see a fifth grade father waving me down. He was a casual acquaintance, someone I didn't know that well. Catching up to us, he slapped me on the back. "Heard what you're doing with the Cooperstown thing. Good job, man. That's exciting."

We pushed on and were stopped once again, this time by a third grade mother. "Hey, Sher, I hear they're calling you 'Team Mom' these days," she said as she continued down the hall.

"How does she know that?" Sheryl whispered in my ear.

Finally, we arrived at Gabe's classroom and waited our turn outside the closed door. While we stood there, I saw Melissa Liebshutz heading in our direction. She pushed her midlength brown hair behind her ears as she approached. Rami's mother did not look pleased.

"Josh, is Rami pitching?" she demanded without pre-amble.

"I doubt it, Melissa," I said, waiting to hear what the

concern was.

"Well, then, can you explain to me why I just wasted fifteen minutes of my conference talking with Mrs. Metzger about pitching? She told me Rami's spending half the school day practicing his form! She can't even let him out of her sight. Every five minutes, he's jumping out of his seat to pitch some imaginary baseball. He's disrupting the class!"

"Sorry, Melissa. I'll look into it," I said, just before Gabe's teacher rescued me.

"Berkowitzes, you guys ready?" Mr. Libenson asked as he poked his head into the hallway. Sheryl and I hustled through the door, taking seats at two small desks. Mr. Libenson sat down across from us, placing a folder in front of him. He was young, perhaps in his mid-twenties, with blonde hair and a warm smile. He wore jeans and a sweater pulled down over an oxford shirt. His casual style and relaxed demeanor were impressive for one just starting out in his career. I could see why Gabe loved him so much.

"Well," he began, "you guys have done quite a remarkable thing."

Sheryl and I chuckled, slightly embarrassed. We often received positive feedback about Gabe during conferences, but this was quite a beginning.

"Well, we can't take all the credit, but yes, we're very proud of him," I said modestly.

He stared at me, confused.

"I'm not talking about Gabe," he clarified. "I'm talking about Cooperstown."

"Cooperstown?" Sheryl and I asked in unison.

"Yeah, Cooperstown," he said. "The whole school is talking about it."

"Really?" I asked.

"Yeah, it's a very cool thing you're doing. I'm a huge baseball fan. How did you find out about this tournament?"

Sheryl told him about her brother and his sons. I filled him in on our journey up to that point, discussing the difficulties of recruiting the boys and the challenges of teaching them the game. By the time our twenty minutes was up, neither Sheryl nor I had any idea how Gabe was doing in his class.

AS AUTUMN CAME to a close and the weather turned yet again, I started down a path of preoccupation that ultimately led to obsession. We had heard nothing from Dreams Park, and thoughts of whether we would be admitted consumed me. I drove my navy Volkswagen Beetle through the slush and the heavy traffic to and from work each day. The majority of my commute was spent ruminating on the batting lineup, how to work in Carlos and Gil, or other pointless plans that, in the end, would likely have no bearing on our performance. I still did not know whether we would get an invitation to Cooperstown, and while at times I wanted it desperately, there were plenty of others when I prayed to be spared the agony.

I awoke on the morning of November third expecting a fairly uneventful day. It was my thirty-sixth birthday. Birthdays weren't a big deal to me and I never made a fuss about mine, nor did most others in my life. If it allowed me control of the TV for the night or one less chore around the house, I was satisfied. This birthday however would be different.

I drove down Route 30 on my way home from work, heading west away from Boston. To my left, the cars zipped passed me on the Mass. Turnpike. The hour-long drive allowed me ample time to daydream, and I never hesitated to take advantage of it.

On that particular day I fantasized that we had won the Cooperstown Dreams Park championship by beating the San Diego Stars in extra innings. I had no problem making it happen. It's amazing what one can do with a little imagination. Sam Budd's performance on the mound wasn't even humanly possible, but that didn't stop me from continuing my reverie. Not a single batter in the tournament could touch him. He pitched every inning of every game. My nephew, Ari, was a speed demon on the bases, bunting his way on routinely and setting the table for those that followed. Charlie Finkelstein became a power hitter, knocking balls out of the park on a consistent basis, his diabetes a distant memory. And on and on it went.

There were different versions of those fantasies that played out in my head during my drive to and from work. The exact method of how our ragtag team won the tournament varied depending on the day and my mood. But, the visions all ended identically—with my standing in front of home plate, accepting a massive trophy from the park's owner and hoisting it high over my head. Those same dreams came to a halt when I pulled into the driveway.

I entered the house through the garage, which opened directly into the kitchen. The familiar white tile floor and gray cabinetry was a welcoming sight. Warm air washed over me as I hung up my coat on the rack. It was good to be home.

"Hello? Birthday boy is here!" I called out, expecting the family to be in its usual evening locations—Sheryl upstairs on the phone, Gabe watching ESPN, and Shani on the computer, e-mailing her friends. Turning around, I was surprised to see the three of them standing there waiting for me. How long they had been there, I had no idea. I reared my head back, somewhat startled.

"Hello, guys."

"Hi, Dad," Shani said.

"We have a surprise for you," Gabe reported, a large smile splitting his face in two.

"Oh, yeah? A birthday present perhaps?" It was another year, which meant handmade cards from Gabe and Shani plus with any luck an IOU from my wife promising dinner out and a movie of my choosing. I walked over and hugged the kids, giving Sheryl a peck on the cheek.

"It is a present. But not from us." She said slyly, handing me a thin white envelope that had been opened.

"What's this?" I said, before looking down to see the Cooperstown Dreams Park logo in the upper left hand corner. My hands immediately began to tremble, small beads of perspiration forming on my brow. I moved slowly over to the kitchen table and sat down still staring at the envelope.

"Open it, Dad," Gabe pressed me.

I did as instructed, and pulled out a single white

sheet of paper folded in three. The Dreams Park logo was engraved at the top and a short paragraph followed. Scanning the page quickly, it took me just a moment to comprehend its meaning.

"Congratulations Rashi Rams," it began.

I read the words again, not truly believing them. Then I looked at my family still standing in front of me, all three grinning enthusiastically. Looking down at the page for a third time, I finally grasped its significance. The decision makers at Dreams Park had invited us to play against the best ten and under teams in the country. Incredulity was my first emotion, then elation, then fear. What in God's name were they thinking? How could anyone of sound mind have invited us to play in this tournament? The questions raced through my mind.

I read through the remainder of the letter, but there was no explanation, just congratulations, an acknowledgement that we were in and a line saying that further information would follow. The letter was signed "Lou Presutti, owner Dreams Park."

Gabe came over and put his arm around me as Shani jumped onto my lap.

"Happy birthday, Dad," Gabe said, squeezing me tightly, his cheeks flushed red with excitement. I held both kids in my arms, shaking my head back and forth.

"I guess we're going to Cooperstown," I replied.

"THWACK. THWACK. THWACK. Thwack." The baseballs hit the blue gymnastic mats hanging on the walls behind the catchers. The Rams were practicing their pitching, and accuracy was an issue.

"Remember, keep your arms high over your head. I don't want to see anyone throwing side arm. Stay closed and follow through," Jeremy called out to them.

It was the dead of winter and bitter cold outside. Snow lay on the ground six inches thick, and a wild wind whipped through the air, searching for a means of entrance into the ancient Hyde Center, in Newton. We had rented the forty-year-old gym for our winter practice and so far it had served its purpose. One large, simple hall with high ceilings and paneled walls surrounded a wooden-floored basketball court with hoops at either end. The players whom I had singled out as conceivably having the ability to pitch in Cooperstown were lined up forty feet away from their counterparts playing catcher.

Soon after learning that we would actually be going to the tournament, it had dawned on me that Sam Budd could not truly pitch every game. I sent an e-mail to Sheryl's brother, Kenny, asking how many pitchers he thought we might need. He had plenty of experience seeing his sons through Dreams Park. A frightening response returned to my inbox—four or five pitchers at a minimum for the week.

"Why can't I pitch?" Rami Liebshutz stood next me, craning his head back to look me in the eye. "Do you know that I scored three goals in my indoor soccer game the other day?"

"This isn't soccer, Ram, although I hear you've been practicing your form. I'll give you a chance to show me what you can do. Hey, Stan," I called. "Catch Rami for a second, will you?"

"Sure," Stan Goodman replied, crouching down and

rubbing his fist inside an old catcher's mitt. "Let's see what you got, Rami."

Rami grabbed a baseball and took up a spot opposite his target. Staring down at Stan he waited for a sign, but with none forthcoming he shrugged his shoulders and straightened up, ready to pitch. After going through an elaborate windup that looked to be more for my benefit than anything else, Rami let the ball loose. It headed toward its target and for a moment I thought we might be on to something, but then it ran out of steam a full four feet in front of the catcher. Stan jumped up to play the carom, but the ball bounced lower than he anticipated, and the misplay cost him dearly. The hardball found its way to his groin where it landed with a thud.

"Ouch!" Stan cried, slumping to the ground in pain. Rami looked up at me.

"That's why," I said.

The two newcomers, Carlos and Gil, had shown up for winter practices and were fitting in well. They were about as incompetent as the rest, but the team and the coaches were enjoying the rookies.

"Gil," I said. "Let's see how you do on the mound." The blond-haired Israeli came up and patted me on the back.

"Good idea, Josh," he said. "The girls love pitchers."

"Try and focus on the game at hand, Gil," I said.

"Sure, Josh, get a look at this." He reared back and fired one down at Charlie Finkelstein, who was crouched opposite him. As the ball came in, Charlie's body remained frozen, catcher's mitt sticking forward giving the target, but his head swiveled upward, watching the pitch sail eight feet above him. It struck the backboard of the basketball hoop and fell directly to the ground six inches in front of his feet. Charlie reached down, picked up the ball and promptly threw it back to Gil.

"That's good, Gil. I've seen enough," I said.

Carlos approached me next. I took a deep breath that quickly turned into a sigh of relief.

"I'm really not that interested in pitching," he said.

"No problem, Carlos. We'll find a spot for you some-where. Don't worry." I was happy with Carlos, mostly because I had discovered that my fears were unfounded; at all practices, including this one, he was wearing his glove on the correct hand. He ran over to sit with Jeff Goodman, who was on the side of the gym, sitting with his back to the wall, book in hand.

I called my nephew, Ari, over to my side. "Ari, can you pitch?" I asked. Brown bangs hung low over his eyes, making it difficult to read his thoughts. He shrugged his shoulders.

"Not sure," he said.

"Well, give it a shot, buddy." I handed him a baseball and he settled in across from his father.

"All right, kid, show 'em what you got," Adam called to his son. Ari went into his windup and delivered a solid strike right over the heart of the plate. A few more at-tempts resulted in the same.

"Awesome, Ari," I said. "With a little work you may be able to pitch in Cooperstown."

"No," he said softly, shaking his head from side to side.

"What do you mean, 'no'?" I responded, unable to mask the surprise and frustration in my voice.

"No," he repeated, shrugging his shoulders.

"Why?"

By this time Adam had joined us. Ari called him over, whispering something in his ear.

"He's not pitching, Josh," Adam explained.

"I understand that. Why?"

"He's scared."

"Scared of what?" My question resulted in another father-son whispered discussion.

"The spotlight," Adam said while Ari nodded his head in agreement.

AFTER PRACTICE, I gathered the coaches together in the middle of the gym for an emergency conference.

"Okay," I said. "You saw how they looked out there. What are we going to do about our pitching?"

"They didn't look too bad to me," Stan responded.

"Have you lost your mind?" Adam barked. "Were you watching the same practice we were?"

"I just don't think they're that bad," Stan defended himself.

Adam rolled his eyes while Jeremy stood by silently.

"Listen, guys," I said. "It's not going to do any good to fight among ourselves. We're in serious trouble here. We need pitchers. Adam, do you think you can convince Ari to pitch?"

"Don't think that's likely to happen, Josh. He's pretty scared about this whole thing. Once the bullets start flying, we'll be lucky if we can get him out into centerfield."

"Great."

"Relax, Josh," Jeremy said. "Gabe and Phil didn't look that bad, and we can always use Robert or Jason in an

emergency. Let's just keep working with those four."
And that was how we left it.

THAT VERY SAME night, while sitting in my kitchen
and munching on a bag of Tostitos, I heard the phone
ring. The kids were playing in the basement, and Sheryl
was upstairs in the tub. I was the only one around to answer.

Wiping my hands on my jeans, I picked up the phone
and looked at the caller ID. It was David Perlow, Phil's
father, and while hoping for the best, I sensed trouble.
David had continued to stay for most practices, where
his frequent furtive glances in my direction made it clear
that I was under his watchful eye.

"Hello?" I said, my mouth still partially full.

"Hi, Josh. It's David Perlow."

"Hey, David, how are things?"

"Not bad. Listen, Phil came home tonight and told me
that he was going to be pitching for you guys."

There was a momentary silence as my mind raced.
Was he calling to tell me that he wanted to make sure
Phil got a lot of time on the mound? It would be a little
pushy perhaps, but I surmised that was likely the reason for the call. As it turned out Mr. Perlow was going to
a different place entirely.

"Yeah, that's right. We were hoping to pitch him. He
can really chuck the ball."

"Josh, do you mind if I ask how many pitchers you
guys have?"

"Not that many, David. But we're working on it." I
was ever aware of his previously expressed concerns

that we would be humiliated on the field.

"Well, I just need to tell you that Phil doesn't want to pitch."

Before he had finished the sentence, I stopped chewing. Placing the bag of chips on the counter, I sought to focus. David's disclosure was surprising and upsetting. I had already discussed the matter with Phil, and he had seemed very enthusiastic about being on the short list of potential pitchers. If the news I was hearing was true, it was a bona fide problem.

"I'm not really sure what you mean," I responded, not knowing what to say.

"Well, to be honest," David continued. "It's really not Phil who doesn't want to pitch. It's me."

"*You* don't want to pitch?" I asked, truly confused.

"No, not me. I don't want Phil to pitch."

"Why?"

"I'm afraid that you'll wear out his arm."

"Wear out his arm? What are you talking about?"

"Well, you don't have much of a staff and I'm worried about my son getting hurt."

I took the phone away from my ear and stared at it in utter shock. Here we were six months before the tournament with very few decent ballplayers and very few options. Now I had a father calling to tell me that his son, who happened to be one of the better players, needed not *more* playing time—but *less*. What kind of bizarre team was this?

"David, I promise you I have no intention of injuring any of the kids. Phil is a great athlete, and I would love for him to pitch, but if you don't feel comfortable with it, that's fine. We'll work around it."

For whatever reason, when David heard my response, he changed his tune. Had this been some kind of test?

"Okay, Josh, he can pitch, but try not to get him injured."

I hung up the phone completely mystified. David had been spending hours practicing and training with his son, and yet, upon hearing that he was going to play a primary role on the team, he became fearful of injury?

Picking up the bag of Tostitos, I popped one into my mouth while staring at the wall. Something told me that Lyle Gabriel, the renowned head coach of the San Diego Stars, was not dealing with similar issues.

CHAPTER NINE

MAN FOR THE JOB

THE INTERIOR OF the Boeing 747 was tight, and I felt claustrophobic. The flight was packed with Bostonians heading south for February vacation, and their physical proximity along with their body odor, cologne, and perfume made me nauseous. I leaned back and closed my eyes, praying to fall asleep prior to takeoff. Of course, I had never been able to sleep on a plane before, nor did I expect this to be the first time.

"It'll be okay, Dad," Shani said, placing her hand on top of mine. "I'm here if you need me." My seven-year-old daughter sensed how much I disliked flying, and while embarrassed to take comfort in her reassurance, I did so nonetheless. I looked over at her smiling face, jealous of her naïveté.

"Thanks, sweetheart. I'll be okay," I said, eyeballing the airsick bag in the seat pocket in front of me to ensure that it was readily accessible.

We were on our way to Tallahassee, Florida, for February vacation. Sheryl's twin nieces were celebrating their bat mitzvah that coming Saturday. I was looking forward to the time off, but the flights to and from Florida were an entirely different matter.

"You all right, Dad?" Gabe said from behind me, squirming through the crack between the seats and placing a hand on my shoulder.

"Sure, honey, piece of cake," I lied, and then changed the subject so as to avoid thinking of the impending departure. "Gabe, I spoke to Uncle Kenny on the phone, and Jordan is going to work with you on your pitching when we get down to Tallahassee."

Although the primary reason for the trip was to participate in the family celebration, secretly I had made arrangements to use the time to my advantage as it related to our upcoming pilgrimage to Cooperstown. Kenny's middle son, Jordan, was an exceptional athlete and an outstanding ballplayer. As a junior, he was starting at shortstop and was the leadoff hitter for Leon High School in Tallahassee. Jordan had graciously agreed to spend time with Gabe to teach him how to pitch.

"Great," Gabe said, flopping back down into his seat as the plane's engines revved to a start, and we began to taxi down the runway. "I was hoping to get some practice in."

SHERYL'S BROTHER LIVED in a stately brick colonial at the end of a cul-de-sac. The design of the houses that lined the street felt familiar, but the overhanging trees that pushed up against them less so. The Florida Panhandle was an odd hybrid of northern architecture and tropical vegetation. Although it wasn't home, it certainly felt more comfortable than the altogether alien environment of south Florida, where Sheryl's parents lived.

Kenny's backyard was an athlete's paradise, with a

sizable swimming pool, full basketball court, and batting cage. I wondered how anyone could drag him or herself to work in such an environment.

"You guys ready to go outside and pitch?" Gabe and I heard Jordan's voice from downstairs as we meandered around his room, marveling at the trophies. They were numerous, lining the dresser and overflowing into his closet. There were individual awards and awards for team accomplishments. Plaques and medals adorned the walls and were strewn across the floor. Most of them showed the time-honored stance of a baseball player with helmet on head and bat in hand, leaving no doubt as to Jordan's most cherished sport.

"We're coming, Jordan," I called as we descended the stairs. "Quite a collection of trophies you got there."

"Nothing too special," he said modestly. "They hand those out like water these days."

The weather was temperate, and the sun shone brightly as Jordan, Gabe, Kenny, and I went outside to pitch—two fathers and two sons looking forward to playing baseball in the Florida sun.

Jordan was a prototypical high school athlete. He stood about five foot ten, with a thin waist. Steady weightlifting had given him broader shoulders than nature intended, and his dirty blond hair was shaved close to the scalp. My brother-in-law, Kenny, was about six foot two, with dark brown hair. A handsome man, he and his son were a solid match.

The two boys began warming up by tossing the ball from one to the other. Jordan's nurturing instructions came forth with ease, and it quickly became apparent that he was indeed the man for the job.

"Catch the ball in front of your chest," he instructed. "Stay closed on your throws."

"No problem, Jordan," Gabe said, doing as advised.

"I didn't even know there was a proper way to play catch," I commented.

"It's all about consistency," Jordan explained. "Doing the same thing each and every time during practice so that when the game comes around, it's just second nature."

They worked together for about an hour, and Gabriel was taught, as if by magic, to throw a two-seam and a four-seam fastball.

"He's got it down pretty good, Uncle Josh. I'll show him how to throw a change-up now," Jordan said.

The boys continued practicing, and at the end of the marathon session, Jordan pulled me aside. "He's got a good arm," he said. "I think he'll be able to pitch in Cooperstown."

"Thank God," I replied, wiping the sweat from my brow. "We need every pitcher we can get."

"Why are you so nervous, Josh?" Kenny asked.

"I'm just a little worried about our team, that's all."

"Why, who's on it? Didn't you get together some local all-stars or something?"

"Just Gabe and his friends from school," I responded and then after a pause, "The first all-Jewish team to attend Dreams Park."

I received a skeptical look in return, and the conversation ended abruptly. Kenny and I both knew there was nothing more to be said.

THE SYNAGOGUE, ONE of only two located in Tallahassee, was smaller than most of its counterparts in the
Northeast. Of course, the size of the temple paralleled
the number of Jewish families who called that region of
Florida home. The sanctuary where services took place
also doubled as the function hall and from where I sat
during the ceremony, I could see the front door, the temple office, and the building's lone classroom. The Jewish
community in Tallahassee was so small that despite
years of effort, the congregation had been unable to recruit a rabbi. Apparently, there were few clergy seeking
to relocate to that area of the country, but from what I
observed, the congregation more than made up for the
void with enthusiasm and spirit. The bat mitzvah girls
did an exemplary job of leading the service all on their
own.

After passing out the perfunctory handshakes and
kisses, I walked to the back of the room in search of good
hors d'oeuvres. I was finding it difficult to stay focused
on the moment. Although my nieces deserved far better,
my mind constantly roamed to upstate New York. I re-
visited Jordan's lessons over and over, desperately hoping that we could turn Gabe into a solid pitcher.

As the wheels turned, I saw my father-in-law approach from across the room. Sheldon Hoffman was in
his mid-sixties, balding on top but with a moderate
amount of grayish white hair slicked back on either side
of his head. He wore a black pin-striped suit, white shirt,
and blue tie.

"Hello, Josh!" he hollered, despite the fact that he had
already come within four feet of me.

"Hey, Dad. How's it goin'?" I asked distractedly.

"Great! That was some service, huh?"

"Yeah, the girls were fabulous. You must be very proud."

"Sure, sure I am. Listen, Josh, I wonder if I could pick your brain a little."

"What's up?"

"Well, I've got a problem, and my doctor can't seem to make heads or tails of it. You see, I've got this rash that just won't go away. It's been there almost three months." And he proceeded to describe it to me in the utmost detail, which to my amazement included data points on color, location, and texture. Throughout the mini-presentation, I stood looking at him, rubbing my chin, and putting on my best "doctor is thinking over the problem" face. Yet, try as I might, I couldn't concentrate on what he was saying.

Sheldon's voice droned on and on, and as I listened, his face began to blur. The wrinkles smoothed, the nose shrank, and the hair thickened. I was staring into the eyes of my friend and confidant, Sandy Koufax. His familiar head with L.A. Dodgers cap floated above my father-in-law's midsection.

"How do I turn Gabe into a good pitcher?" I asked, not wanting to miss out on this opportunity. Sandy opened his mouth, but to my great disappointment, Sheldon's words came forth.

"The dermatologist had no idea. They gave me this cream or something. Maybe I can show it to you . . ." He dug into his pocket, searching.

I kept nodding my head up and down, listening to my

father-in-law's voice coming out of Sandy Koufax's mouth. Neither of them was any help.

"SNAP," GABE'S PITCH landed with a solid thud inside the mitt. Taking a short drive from Kenny's house, we had found an empty field in which to practice. The grass was green and long, coming to my knees as I kneeled in the catcher's position. Gabe stood across from me, his right foot in front of a dead branch we had pulled from the woods to mark a spot for the pitching rubber. I had decided to take matters into my own hands, and during the remainder of our Florida vacation, Sheryl's protests aside, we snuck off to practice whenever possible. I could already see the effort bearing fruit.

"Dad," Shani said. "I really don't want to."

"Don't worry, honey, you'll be fine," I encouraged her. "Gabe's control is much better now." She hefted her wooden bat, and stepped into the makeshift batter's box, helmet firmly on her head.

"All right, Shani. Let's see if you can handle the heater," Gabe said as he let the ball fly. It came in straight and true, blowing by his sister and landing solidly in my glove.

"Nice job, Gabe. Keep that up. Just like that," I called to him.

"No problem, Dad. I think I'm getting the hang of it." And he was. Over and over he threw, pitch after pitch, perfecting his form and technique. He sought advice whenever possible, and as the week wore on, continued to improve. If a few pitches in a row were out of the strike zone, he would become frustrated and lose his temper. But I reeled him in, encouraging him to move on to the next pitch and the next, and the next.

"Dad, why do I have to do this?" Shani asked, the brim of her oversize helmet slipping down to cover her dark eyes.

"You're helping your brother and you're helping the Rams prepare for Cooperstown. Doesn't that make you happy?"

"Not really. You're spending too much time on this thing, and it's not fair that Gabe gets all your attention."

"I'm sorry, honey," I said, feeling ashamed. "You're absolutely right. But I've made this commitment and I have to follow through. I promise your time will come."

"It better," she said as she stepped back into the batter's box, putting on her game face. "All right, bro," she called down to Gabe. "Let's see what you got."

THE INTERIOR OF the Boeing 747 felt spacious and open. There were plenty of Bostonians roaming the aisles, looking for their seats, but I hardly noticed them. It was the first time I had ever felt calm aboard an airplane. I marveled at the sensation as we sat on the tarmac at Tallahassee Regional Airport, waiting to taxi down the runway.

Sheryl turned to me and smiled. The kids were playing in the two seats behind us, and she was satisfied, having enjoyed a wonderful week of celebration with family and friends. I returned her enthusiastic grin and she assumed we were both basking in the warmth of the fun-filled family event.

I let Sheryl think what she wanted. Unbeknownst to

her, there was a far more compelling reason for my tranquility, a secret reason that only I knew. All the hard work and effort had paid off. By the time we flew home from Florida at the end of the week, the Rashi Rams had their number two starter.

I put my head back and closed my eyes, falling asleep just before takeoff.

CHAPTER TEN

AN EXTRAORDINARY GIFT

AS SOON AS I saw him, I knew. I knew it beyond any shadow of a doubt. It was over, and he didn't have a chance. I was twenty-seven years old, and yet still very close to my parents whom I visited frequently. They lived in a large, beautiful home built in 1903 that spoke of the quality craftsmanship of the day. Located in an affluent neighborhood of Newton, my parents had been fortunate enough to buy it at below market value in the mid-1980s.

Alone, I walked up the small hill upon which the white Colonial was set, looking down on the street below it. Sheryl was at home, tending to Gabe who had been born just six months prior, while I had taken a detour after work to say a quick hello to my folks who had recently returned from a short vacation.

After receiving a slight push, the heavy oak door swung open, unlocked. The spacious entry hall that greeted me was lined with dark wood trim, and the antique chandelier hanging from the ceiling glowed warmly.

Dad was puttering around the living room off to my left, and I watched his back for a moment as he rearranged a few odds and ends on a coffee table.

"Hi, Dad," I interrupted him. He turned, recognition crossing his face accompanied by a familiar, gentle smile.

"Josh, I didn't know you were stopping by. We just got back from our weekend in New York. It's so good to see you," he said warmly, approaching me with open arms.

I moved to greet him, but my light mood rapidly darkened with concern. It was indeed my father who approached me, and yet it was not. His thinning curly brown hair and bushy eyebrows were the same. His thick, soft hands and casual gait were also familiar. But he appeared gaunt, much thinner than I remembered from the last time I had seen him just a few weeks before. And even more worrisome, his skin was tinged a faint yellow.

"Dad," I said immediately, not thinking to restrain myself. "What's wrong?" I gave him a quick hug as he approached.

"Nothing," he responded. "What are you talking about?"

"Come into the kitchen where the light is better. You look a little jaundiced."

"Jaundiced?" he questioned. "I feel fine."

I drew him into the brighter lights of the kitchen, and examined his eyes. After that, there was little doubt; they were imbued a pale yellow.

"Your eyes are jaundiced, Dad. We've got to get you checked out."

"What do you think it is?" he asked.

"I'm sure it's okay," I backtracked, not wanting to scare him. "Don't worry. We'll go tomorrow to see your doctor. I'll come with you."

I continued to reassure him as best I could, but it was disingenuous. Maybe it was my medical training, my understanding of the limited differential diagnosis of painless jaundice, or perhaps it was just the keen intuition of a son who loved his father more than life itself, but I knew in my heart right then that it was all over. My father's story had been written, and all that could be done now was for him to play out the final act.

A week later, the diagnosis of a rare bile duct tumor was made. The location and the extent of the spread ruled out surgery. Dad did his best to handle the chemotherapy, and we supported him through it, but it had no effect, and perhaps even hastened his demise.

Not three months later, he passed away in his bed, just steps from where I had greeted him in the front hall on that fateful evening. I sat with him and held his hand until there was no life left in his body. I told him I loved him so many times that the words lost their meaning. But it did nothing to ease the pain.

"BUZZ. BUZZ. BUZZ." I looked down at the black Sprint cell phone attached to the belt at my waist, and considered not answering it. Exhausted after a long day at work, I needed to concentrate on driving. The VW Bug sped down Route 128 south. The light snow made for poor visibility and slippery roads. The trees on either side of the highway were dusted white as were the multitude of other vehicles trying to make their way home in the growing darkness.

I glanced at the incoming number and recognized

Sheryl's cell.

"Hey, honey. What's up?"

"Bad news," she said. "Where are you?" I could hear a faint tremor in her voice, as if she had been crying.

"On my way home. What's wrong?"

"I just hung up the phone with Marci."

"Stan's wife?"

"Yeah."

"And?"

"He's been diagnosed with a brain tumor," she said flatly.

"What are you talking about?"

"A brain tumor," she repeated.

"How is that possible?"

"They went skiing for the weekend, and Stan started becoming slightly confused. You know, he was forgetting things, unable to remember certain words. Marci thought that it might have been the result of an injury he had a couple weeks ago when he hit his head, so she took him right to the emergency room. They did an MRI, and found a tumor."

"That can't be true."

"It is."

"What are they going to do?"

"He is scheduled for surgery this week. They're going to try to remove it."

And that was it. One day our friend and fellow coach, Stan, was living a normal life, enjoying work and his family. The next day, he had been diagnosed with a brain tumor. Not knowing the details, I feared the worst.

IN TIME, THE warmth of spring returned to New England. The trees sprouted new shoots and the lawns in front of the homes turned green. The sun embraced us with its rays, allowing the Rashi Rams to return to practice outdoors. Whether it was at the Pierce School on Sunday mornings or Cabot on Friday afternoons, the results were much the same—a mixed bag of enjoyable times, funny sights, and depressing moments.

The diamonds that we practiced on did not have the same dimensions as those at Dreams Park, and that alone kept me up more than a few nights, wondering how it would affect us. The distance from the pitching mound to home plate was a good one to two feet shorter than what we would see in Cooperstown; and outside of Sam Budd, the pitchers were struggling even at that distance. Of course, we used the term *pitching mound* euphemistically, as neither field had a raised platform. The rubbers of both diamonds were more or less on the same level plane as home plate. If anything, the softball field at Cabot had our pitchers throwing uphill rather than down.

"I like the new shirts, Josh," Charlie Finkelstein said, adjusting the insulin pump at his waist. We sat on the bench along the first baseline at Cabot.

"Yeah, what do you think of the logo?" I asked, and then regretted it instantly.

"Very cool, but I probably could have made it better. The Ram looks good, but I'm not so sure about the bat. Also, the colors don't seem quite right . . ." He went on as I nodded my head up and down, listening as any good coach would.

With the help of Gabe and an online graphic design company, we had created T-shirts for the team. The logo consisted of an angry ram with curling horns, staring straight ahead while biting a baseball bat in two. The colors were those of the Rashi School, teal and white. Rami's father had printed out the logos and ironed them on to white T-shirts for all the players and coaches. It wasn't exactly a uniform, but at least it gave us the illusion of being organized.

"We had a banner made with the same design. All the teams march in the opening parade with a banner. We also ordered team pins," I told Charlie. "You know in Cooperstown, you'll trade pins with the other teams. It's a lot of fun."

"Great," he said. "Hey, Josh, can I start practice on the bench? I think my blood sugar is dropping. I feel low."

"Sure, Charlie. Go find a snack in your bag."

I turned to the rest of the team, "Okay, everyone, before we take the field, we're going to have some special hitting instruction today."

David Perlow had asked me if he could help out by teaching his hitting techniques to the team. As I had spent an inordinate amount of time on fielding, and because David's son was one of our better hitters, I thought it a gamble worth taking. Besides, I was in no position to turn down offers of assistance.

Wearing old jeans and a T-shirt, the college professor stepped in front of the bench to address the team. He carried a bat in his right hand.

"Okay, guys, what most young players don't understand is that hitting power comes from your legs, not from your arms. What you want to do is coil your body and when the pitch comes, rotate your hips and turn on it."

He swung the bat violently, causing the disturbed air to make a whistling noise. The team looked on in awe.

"Phil," David said. "Come up here and show everyone."

Phil bounced off the bench and took the bat from his father.

"Okay, keep an eye on his form, guys," David said. He soft -tossed a ball in front of Phil, who drove it out into the field away from the bench. A few more tosses resulted in similar sharp line drives that traveled a fair distance.

"See how that works, boys?" David asked.

The team nodded in comprehension as Phil looked up at his father with pride. I watched confused. David seemed to be an excellent teacher, but given our previous conversations, I didn't know whether he wanted to completely dismantle the team or pick us up on his back and carry us to the Dreams Park championship.

"Thanks, David," I said. "Okay, everyone, Phil's dad will do some individual work with you on your swings after we do some fielding. Let's have a crisp practice today. Take your positions."

The team ran onto the field while I grabbed a bat and strolled up to home plate. "Here we go, Gabe. Make the play at first."

"Gotcha, Dad," he said as he scooped up the grounder and whipped it cleanly across the diamond. His arm had strengthened considerably over the past year. Robert extended his glove and picked the ball cleanly out of the air, throwing it down to Aaron, who was standing next to me at catcher.

"Nice play, guys!" I yelled, proud to see my son holding down my old hot corner position with such authority. "Not quite as good as I used to do it, Gabe, but we'll take it, buddy!"

"Not funny, Dad," he responded with a smile and a laugh as Aaron flipped me the ball.

I continued to scatter them around the field. Rami snatched his slow grounder, and tossed it over to first. Phil did the same at short.

"Nice job, boys. Keep it up!"

My nephew stood quietly in center. "Ari, here you go," I yelled, and hit one high and deep to him.

"Get back, Ari! Get back!" Gabe screamed at his cousin. Silently, Ari spun on his heels and ran—fast. As the ball approached, he turned at the last minute, shaded his eyes and caught it.

"Nice job, Ari. Lookin' good out there," I yelled.

"Thanks," his quiet voice floated over the air to me from center.

"You're next, Slotnick!" I yelled to Gil who was also out in centerfield, standing next to Ari. He reached into his pocket and pulled out a pair of dark sunglasses, sliding them over his eyes just underneath the bill of his cap.

"Ready, boss," Gil said with just the slightest hint of an Israeli accent. He had been raised in Israel for the first part of his life, but after six years in the States it was hard to detect anything but America in him. I hit it high and deep, and then watched as Gil slowly faded back on the ball. After a few moments, he casually reached up over his head and made the catch.

"*Oogah!*" he called out loudly.

"What did you say?" I yelled.

"I said '*oogah.*' It's Hebrew for 'cake.'" And he threw the ball in on a line to home plate.

"Carlos, your turn!" I called out to left field where he waited anxiously, fidgeting with his glove and stamping his feet up and down.

"Go get it, kid," I yelled as the ball sailed off my bat. Carlos stepped back slowly and then faster as he saw that it was hit harder than he thought. He ran backward at a good clip, never taking his eyes off the sky, and finally settled down in what he felt was the best location. As I watched the ball crashing down toward earth, the thought of Carlos's bleeding tendency briefly crossed my mind, but it was too late to do anything about it. Seconds felt like minutes as the entire team waited on edge to see if he would make the catch.

Finally, the ball came within Carlos's reach, but he had miscalculated. It passed over the top of his outstretched glove. Just then, from out of nowhere, Gil flew in from centerfield. He dove a foot or so behind where Carlos was standing, and picked the ball just inches before it hit the ground. Carlos looked over the back of his shoulder in amazement. Gil lay on the ground behind him, sunglasses slightly askew, raising his glove and the ball contained therein.

"Son of a bitch!" Jason Armon screamed from where he was standing on the pitcher's mound. He threw his mitt on the ground. "Never seen anything like that before."

"Catch the ball, Carlos!" Sam Budd roared as he stood next to Jason. "You can't count on people backing you up like that every time!"

"Hey, stop swearing, Jason!" I yelled. "And let's try to support our teammates please, Sam. Nice catch, Gil. That's the way to back each other up. Everybody should be doing that. Carlos, don't you worry. You made a good play on the ball. Next time will be different."

I felt a tug on the back of my shirt.

"Josh, my sugar is dropping." Charlie stood next to me, a glassy look in his eyes.

"What do you mean your sugar is dropping? I told you to have a snack!"

"I know but I can't find the bag with my diabetes supplies. I think I left it in my mother's car when she dropped me off."

Charlie's father, Jeremy, was not coaching that day because he had to be in New York for a meeting. Stan had not joined the team since his diagnosis, and Adam had been unable to get out of work. David Perlow and I were the lone adults on the field. Phil's father looked at me helplessly. The professor had come to teach hitting, not deal with a medical crisis.

"You left your bag with the diabetes supplies in your mother's car?" I repeated to Charlie in disbelief. "What's your glucose reading?"

He looked down at the meter on his waist. "Sixty-four and dropping," he said.

"Sixty-four? Go have a seat on the bench."

I turned to the team. "We've got a situation here. Practice is on hold for a minor emergency. Everybody get

in here, and find something for Charlie to eat or drink."
They started slowly moving to the bench without any
appreciation for the urgency of the moment.

"Hurry!" I screamed.

"Fifty-eight, Josh," Charlie called from where he sat
as the players started rummaging through their bags.

"Does anyone have anything?" I hollered, looking
around for a store but knowing that there was nothing
within walking distance.

"Fifty-two, Josh."

"I have water!" Robert Matz called with excitement.

"Thanks, Robert, but that's not going to help."

"Forty-seven, Josh."

"Does anybody have anything to eat? A candy bar? A
cracker? A multivitamin? Anything?" They shrugged
their shoulders rifling through their bags with increasing alarm as they sensed my own.

"Try this." I heard a familiar voice from behind me.

Turning, I saw Stan Goodman standing there. He
wore gray sweatpants and matching sweatshirt. One
arm was draped over his son's shoulder while the other
was raised in front of him. In his left hand, he held his
old beat-up baseball glove; in his right, a small bottle of
orange juice.

I had spoken to Stan once or twice after his surgery,
but had yet to see him in person. He was keeping a low
profile, and had not made any appearances at school or
the spring practices. Half of his head was shaved, and a
six-inch scar extended the length of the left side of his
scalp, visible for all to see. I was overjoyed at the sight of
him.

"Welcome back, Stan. We missed you," I said, giving him a warm hug. "How are you feeling?"

"I'm doing okay. Getting through the surgery was difficult, but I'm improving. I'm ready to get back to my coaching duties," he said.

"Great, we're happy to have you back. And how are things with you, Jeff?"

"I'm doing well, Josh," he responded.

"Forty-two," Charlie called groggily from the bench. I grabbed the orange juice out of Stan's hand, and rushed over to pour it down Charlie's throat myself.

"SO HOW HAS the team looked in my absence?" Stan Goodman looked at me, but appeared distracted.

"Not bad, at least by your standards, Stan," Adam responded lightheartedly on my behalf.

We stood in front of the sink in our kitchen on a Saturday night in early May. It was dark outside the window, but the light of the moon was visible through the glass. Sheryl and I had invited the coaches and their families over for dinner. The meal finished and bellies full, the fathers gathered in the kitchen talking while I placed the dishes in the dishwasher.

"I must say, Stan, the team is really making strides. It's slow but there's noticeable improvement and what's more, I'm really enjoying coaching them," I said.

"Really?" Adam asked.

"I mean it. Of course, it's challenging at times, but I discovered something about myself. Give me a bat and a ball and my son down at third base with a glove, and I could be content forever."

The coaches nodded in agreement.

"How are things going with you, Stan?" Jeremy asked.

"Not bad," he responded. "I have eight more radiation treatments left, and then I'll have another scan. As it happens, the follow-up MRI is going to be done the Saturday after we return from Cooperstown."

"Stan, you know that you don't have to come to the tournament, right? We would miss you, but we can make do without if necessary," I said.

"I understand, Josh. But I want to come. Jeff is extremely excited about the week, and he is counting on me. It's important that I be there for him."

"Okay, as long as you know that you're free to opt out whenever."

"Thank you."

"Dessert is ready!" Sheryl called from the dining room, prompting Adam and Jeremy to excuse themselves from the kitchen.

Stan and I stood there alone. His face was drawn and his hair had yet to grow back after being shaved for the surgery.

"Josh, there is another reason why I have to go to Cooperstown with you guys," he said wearily.

"Why is that, Stan?"

"The type of tumor I have . . . it's a glioblastoma . . . you know what that means, right?"

Unfortunately, I did. Glioblastoma was one of the deadliest of cancers, spreading by sending squidlike tentacles out among the cells of the brain so that by the time it was diagnosed, there was no way to remove it all. There was no known cure and prognosis was marked in months, not years.

"I know what it means, Stan."

There was silence for a moment as he stared at the floor and continued, "What I'm really worried about is Marci and the kids. You never expect this to happen to you, of course." There was more silence while he stood and thought.

I looked at him with sympathy, reaching out and grabbing his hand in mine. "No one ever expects something like this to happen. All you can do is take it one day at time and keep fighting."

He nodded.

"You're giving an extraordinary gift to your son, Stan. To keep on coaching like this, and to go to Cooperstown with everything you're dealing with. What you're doing is incredible."

We held hands and he looked at me, smiling. It was not the smile of peace, contentment, or happiness, but the simple smile that came with the knowledge that he had a friend.

CHAPTER ELEVEN

DON'T GET COCKY

I SAT IN my family room on a Sunday afternoon late in May and stared at the desktop Apple computer. Outside the window, directly before me, Gabe and Shani played with the neighbors' kids on the front lawn. I could hear their muted screams of laughter as they chased each other in a game of tag. Sheryl was busy cleaning the kitchen. She was out of sight, but the clinking of dishes mixed with the gentle sounds of Norah Jones coming from the radio was proof that she was there.

Sorting my e-mails, I scrolled through the usual spam, something from my younger brother, Jonathan, about getting together to play basketball, and a note from my secretary with a question about my schedule. I was just about to shut down the computer when a curious new message appeared in the in-box. Fellow Rashi father Milton Schwartz had sent it with the subject line "base-ball." I knew who Milt was, having heard several stories over the years about his rabid passion for youth sports, but was surprised that he was aware of my existence. I double-clicked on the message.

Josh. Saw a picture of the Rams in the

*paper. Would like to get together a team of
Rashi third and fifth graders to play you.
Might help you get ready for Cooperstown.
Let me know. Milt Schwartz.*

I stared at the words for a minute, taking in both
their apparent and latent meanings. Milt was an omni-
present figure at Rashi. He had been responsible for creating the only organized school athletic program, prior to
the founding of our baseball team. He and his third
grade son had started a basketball squad that competed
in the local YMCA league. Milt was widely known to be
passionate about his son's sports—too passionate, some
said. He was ultracompetitive when it came to coaching,
and many parents felt he placed far too much emphasis
on the proverbial "W." I had even heard talk that he was
videotaping his third graders on the court so that he
could break down game film.

Apparently, Milt had seen us in the paper. Sheryl,
having taken on the role of Rams' promotional director,
had arranged for us to have a picture and small article
in Boston's *Jewish Advocate*. The two-paragraph piece
hailed us as the first all-Jewish baseball team to travel
to Cooperstown Dreams Park.

The team photo had been taken after school in front
of the playground. The boys had stood or kneeled in
three rows with those in front proudly displaying the
Rams' banner. The players' ridiculously cocky smiles exhibited far more confidence than they deserved. Those
blissfully smug fourth-grade faces must have piqued
Milt's competitive spirit.

While some spoke of Milt's style disparagingly, I actually admired it. He had the guts and the fortitude to teach kids how to win, and that was a rare thing in the politically correct world from which we came. And win Milt did. So much so that every other YMCA basketball team had refused to participate in a play-off, so as not to be humiliated at the hands of Milton Schwartz's Rashi team.

A seasoned lawyer at a Boston law firm as well as a business owner, Milt was a wealthy man. So wealthy, in fact, that he had recently retired even though he couldn't have been much more than ten years my senior. Due to his hard work and good fortune, Milt now had plenty of time to spend with his family and to pursue his hobbies, first and foremost of which was coaching his son. He had the ability to drop off and pick up his kids at school on a daily basis, and whenever I saw him, I felt envious, shameful as it was. Milt Schwartz had a life that I could only dream of, a Mr. Mom with endless time to watch television, read a book, or play ball with his son. I can only imagine his biggest concern was finding time to manage his financial portfolio. Milt's schedule also allowed ample time for him to lay down the gauntlet before me. I knew his e-mail was not as altruistic as it appeared. He was challenging me at my own game.

The mind killer began to take hold once more. It was one thing to practice alone with just a few parents or random passersby watching us, but playing against real competition in an organized game was a far different matter. The fact that we were only weeks away from playing eight highly organized games against the very

best teams in the country still seemed remote and unre-
al. In any case, at least in upstate New York we would
not be known. This would be a local and potentially very
public display of our ineptitude.

"WHAT SHOULD I do?"

"You know what you need to do," Sheryl answered me.
It was late at night and we lay in our bed in the dark
under the covers, her disembodied voice once again
prodding me in the direction of healthy decision making.

"But it's Milton Schwartz. He's probably going to
make it his top priority to humiliate me."

"Josh, it's a baseball game for kids. Do you understand what I'm saying?" she asked.

"For you maybe it's a baseball game for kids. For people like Milton Schwartz, it's much more than that."

"Well, you're not Milt Schwartz."

"Yeah, right," I said mulling it over. "How can you be
so sure about that, anyway? Why am I doing this whole
thing? Is it for Gabe or am I doing it for myself? How do
you know I'm not trying to live vicariously through my
son? I hate parents who do that. Maybe I've become one
of them." There was silence for a few minutes as we lay
next to each other. I wasn't even sure whether my wife
had heard me.

"You're not Milt Schwartz," Sheryl repeated quietly
before rolling over to go to sleep. "Set up the game."

I turned her words over and over in my mind, but it
didn't help and it wasn't long before I realized there was
no way I was going to fall asleep. I stared at the clock as
the minutes passed by, and continued staring as those

minutes turned into hours.

At three in the morning, I got up, walked down the hallway and quietly opened the door to Gabe's room. Cautiously, I slipped inside to stand by the head of his bed. Gabe's chest rose and fell with ease, and he seemed at peace. Whenever I watched him sleep, I could easily see the face of the newborn that I had brought home nine years earlier. There was not a trace of fear upon him, asleep or awake, and I felt his strength, while at the same time feeling ashamed of my own weakness.

Going downstairs, I sat in front of the computer, listening to the machine purr while waiting for the screen to come to life. Steeling my nerves, I opened Milt's e-mail again and hit reply. It was time for the Rashi Rams to face some competition.

"AARON, GET OFF your phone and get into your gear!" I called to our starting catcher, who was loafing on the bench.

It was Sunday morning, just around ten o'clock, and Schwartz's team was to be there momentarily. We had arrived at Pierce field early so that we could warm up. Mother Nature had cooperated: The sun shone down on the diamond unobstructed by a single cloud. The school was keeping the field in decent shape. The dirt was well raked, and although the infield grass had seen a fair amount of foot traffic, it was green enough to satisfy even Milt Schwartz and his team.

Warm weather had brought the neighborhood outdoors. The homeowners that lived just beyond right field could be seen cleaning garages and tending to yards. Focused on their to-do lists for the day, they paid us little attention.

The team had taken the field, and Adam was hitting practice balls to the boys. His trim six-foot frame knocked out each one sharply as they were sprayed from left to right. Stan, Jeremy, and I stood nearby, discussing strategy.

"We should pitch Sam first," Adam said definitively as he hit a grounder down to Gabe at third. "It'll give the team some confidence."

"No way," Jeremy rebutted, standing next to me in his sneakers, shorts, and Rashi Rams T-shirt. There were sweat stains under his arms from the six-mile run he had put in that morning. "We know what he can do. We need to take this opportunity to check out the rest of the pitching staff."

"That incessant running you do has diverted the blood supply to your brain, man," Adam said. "Sam's got to start, and he's got to go for as long as possible."

"I think we should just let the boys have fun," Stan interjected, absentmindedly running a hand over the healing scar on his scalp.

"Of course, you pitch Sam first. The team needs to get some confidence." We all looked down to see Jeff Goodman standing with his arms crossed in the middle of our group. He wore his Rams T-shirt tucked into his far-too-short sweatpants, his black socks pushed down just above his sneakers.

"You coaching now, Jeff?" I asked.

"Just saying," he answered. "Pitch Sam first."

I looked at him and nodded. He seemed to know what

he was talking about.

"Okay. We'll go with Sam for the first inning, and then we'll move on to the bullpen," I said.

The decision just made, a red Honda minivan drove into the parking lot. We watched uneasily as it pulled to a stop in one of the spaces.

"Here come the Marauders," Adam announced.

"Who?" I asked.

"The Marauders," he repeated as if I should have known. "You know . . . Milton's Maurauders."

And so the enemy was identified and named.

Milt came out of the car first, carrying a black duffle bag overflowing with equipment. He was probably just shy of fifty years old, with thin black hair combed straight back. His nose was sharp and came down to a point just above his upper lip, resulting in an eaglelike appearance. He wore a Newton Little League championship sweatshirt, which reminded me that he had served as head coach of his son's "World Series" winning team the year before.

Behind Milt, a couple of small Rashi third graders popped out of the van, and I heaved a sigh of relief. I recognized the kids, your garden-variety eight-year-olds, not the baseball titans conjured up in my imagination. I chuckled at my own insanity.

"Hey, that's Bill March!" Robert Matz screamed, pointing his long arm from where he stood at first base. "What the heck is he doing here?"

"And that's Tony Gusto!" Rami yelled from second, not a moment later.

I grabbed Aaron's arm from behind the plate as he

finished buckling his chest protector. He tossed his gold-
en bangs out of his eyes, and looked up at me.

"Who are those kids?" I asked.

"Only the two best pitchers in all of Newton Little
League," he responded casually. And it continued. More
and more kids piled out of the minivan as if it were a
clown car that Milt had stacked with players from floor
to ceiling. The more who exited, the bigger they got. Finally, when the last two climbed out, I saw that one of
them stood taller than his coach, and the other was
sporting facial hair.

Milt approached me.

"Milt, what's going on here? I thought we had agreed
that your team would have third and fifth graders only.
Those kids look like they're fifteen," I said.

"Sorry, Josh. I just couldn't get enough of the younger
ones together on such short notice. Don't worry though,
we'll take it easy on you. You don't mind, do ya?"

"HERE WE GO, Sam!" Gabe called from the hot corner.

Sam Budd kicked the dirt from his cleats and wiped
his right hand on his gray baseball pants. He looked
calm and confident as if he had done this before, and indeed he had. Compared to playing in the Newton Little
League Majors at age ten, this was nothing.

Despite the fact that he had promised to take it easy
on us, Milt sent his fifteen-year-olds to the plate first.
But Sam Budd was not easily intimidated. With little
wasted motion, he went into his windup and released
the ball overhead. It flew toward home plate with a
vengeance and landed crisply in Aaron's glove as the

leadoff hitter with facial hair swung and missed.

"Strike one!" called the umpire, a friend of Milt's who had been brought along to officiate the game.

The batter glared down at Sam as the ball was tossed back to the mound. The next pitch was a carbon copy of the first. Again and again, Sam just reared back and hurled it by the best of the Marauders' hitters. He struck out the side, making quick work of them. He and Aaron were the only ones to touch the ball for the entire top of the first. Adam, Jeremy, Stan, and I all nodded back and forth to one another. It was as we'd expected.

The team hustled off the field with a hop in their step, giving each other high fives all around, even though the vast majority of them hadn't done a single thing.

"Don't get cocky, boys!" I hollered. "Budd can't pitch every inning for us!"

The Marauders took the field and began to toss the ball around. Milt had enough restraint not to send to the mound his player who had shaved that morning. Unfortunately, some of the others who had yet to go through puberty were nearly as intimidating.

Bill March took the hill, and began warming up. He was a slender kid with a deceptively gentle look to him. As we watched, he coiled his lean body tightly before each pitch, ultimately releasing an incredible amount of stored energy, flinging the ball toward home with surprising speed and accuracy.

"That's not fair," said Charlie. "I thought we were playing other Rashi kids."

"Yeah," Phil chimed in. "I've seen this kid pitch in Little League. He's unhittable."

"Just focus on getting some good swings, gentlemen," I said. "We'll face tougher than this in Cooperstown."

I sent Gabe up to bat, and for the first time since we had organized the team I saw a trace of anxiety on his face.

"I don't know if I can hit this kid, Dad," he whispered.

"Just do your best, Gabe. That's all I ask."

He walked up to the batter's box, and dug his rear foot into the dirt, grinding it back and forth while watching Bill March's body contract into a sphere. The pitch came in and Gabe wasted no time, swinging with all his might. His aluminum bat just barely nicked the ball, and it rolled six inches in front of home plate.

"Run, Gabe!" I screamed, jumping up off the bench and motioning him toward first. But before he could get out of the box, the catcher grabbed the ball and applied the tag.

"Out!" hollered the umpire, and my son came back to the bench, shaking his head in disgust. His contact would prove to be the offensive highlight of the inning, as the next two batters struck out on three pitches each. After one inning, there was no score.

"Can I pitch, Josh?" Rami Liebshutz asked as the team was about to take the field.

"Not now, Rami. We've got to get some work for the players that will be pitching at Dreams Park."

"But I can shut these guys down!" he said earnestly.

"I have no doubt, Rami. Now, get going to second base." He shook his head in disappointment and ran onto the field. "Phil," I said. "You're pitching this inning. Sam you take over at shortstop."

Phil Perlow nodded, and walked out to the mound, anxiously picking up the game ball from where Bill March had dropped it in front of the rubber. He squeezed it tightly in his hand, looking over at his father.

David Perlow, after agreeing that his son could pitch, had taken it as his personal responsibility to get Phil ready to take the hill in Cooperstown. Although batting practice always took priority in the Perlow household, the father and son duo made certain not to neglect Phil's pitching mechanics. It was showtime.

"Don't open up, Phil!" David called, while pacing back and forth down the right field sideline. "Remember to follow through!"

Nodding to his father, Phil turned toward Aaron Dines behind the plate, while straightening the bill of his cap. The southpaw twirled the ball in his left hand, feeling for the seams.

"Here we go, Phil! You got him, now!" Gabe called from third. Working into an elaborate windup, Phil released the ball, but the angle of his throwing arm was too low. It went straight from his hand to the dirt, bouncing a good foot in front of home plate.

"Ball one!" called the umpire.

"Over the top! Come down over the top, Phil!" David instructed from behind me.

Phil paced back and forth for a moment, considering how to correct his mistake. Going back to the rubber, he tried again but overcompensated, and the next pitch went a foot too high. His problems continued, and by the time he was able to throw a strike, the lefty had walked in two runs.

"Don't worry about it, Phil. You did a good job," I said as he trudged off the mound halfway through the second inning, shoulders slumped.

"Not good enough," he replied. Instead of taking a seat on the bench, Phil walked over to his father and the two huddled together to discuss where their plans had gone awry.

The game continued but things only got worse. We had agreed to allow stealing after the ball crossed the plate, and the result was a variety of mortifying errors on our part. Our pitchers were wild, our infield a sieve, and our outfielders scampered around seemingly without a clue. Each inning brought additional frustration and embarrassment. After the third, we were down ten to nothing, and I decided to make some changes.

"Carlos, get up to bat," I called.

Carlos Garcia-Feinstein had yet to play, up until now watching the game from his seat on the bench. When he heard his name called, he looked up at me with surprise, eyes wide. Seconds passed.

"Carlos?" I said slowly, raising my eyebrows. "Please grab a helmet and get up to bat."

He picked a helmet up off the ground, and approached me nervously. "Josh, I have a question," he said.

"Yes, Carlos?"

"Should I swing when I'm up at the plate?"

"What do you mean?"

"My Little League coach doesn't allow me to swing," he answered. Because Carlos had never played organized baseball, I had encouraged his fathers to sign him up for Little League, and they had mercifully complied. Carlos had noticed a difference in style between his two coaches.

"You mean that you have to take a strike first before swinging, right?"

"No, my coach says that I'm not allowed to swing."

"Ever?" I asked.

"Yeah, ever."

Because of time constraints and practice priorities, I hadn't seen Carlos hit much, and I wondered what his Little League coach was thinking.

"Of course, you can swing," I said to him. He went to the plate, dragging the bat limply behind him, and was back seconds later after having swung and missed at two balls in the dirt and one that was a foot over his head. He had not come remotely close to making contact.

"Carlos," I said. "You're not allowed to swing anymore."

Sam Budd was up next, and he was in a foul mood. Sam was not accustomed to losing in such a fashion, and as the game wore on, his rage was mounting. He angrily pulled his helmet onto his head, grabbed the biggest bat he could find, and stepped to the plate. The first pitch was close enough. Sam released his pent-up aggression and swung fiercely, driving the ball deep into left field. The Rams jumped off the bench in excitement, desperately looking for the team's first hit of the morning. For a moment it appeared that we would certainly have it, but the Marauders' left fielder came flying in to make the grab.

Sam stopped halfway down the first baseline, and realizing that the ball had been caught, turned back toward the team. Then, ripping off his helmet, he threw it with all his might against the fence that stood between the bench and the diamond. Tears welled up in his eyes as he stormed off the field and sat down next to his teammates where he promptly slammed his fist into the fence that now stood in front of him.

"Sam, that will get you kicked out of the game in Cooperstown. Do you understand me?" I reprimanded him despite wishing that I could behave in a similar manner.

He nodded in response, but did not raise his head. Jason, Aaron, Robert, and Gil gathered around and patted him on the shoulder, mumbling words of encouragement. Then they slid down the bench as far away as possible. Gabe, Charlie, Ari, and Phil gave him a wide berth, not saying a word. Everyone recognized when to give Sam Budd his space.

Only Jeff Goodman remained sitting next to Sam. It seemed that Jeff had paid little attention to the drama unfolding before him. But then allowing himself a momentary break from the book he had brought to the game, Jeff looked up at his teammate and spoke.

"Nice hit, Sam," he said. "Left fielder made a good play. I wouldn't cry about it, though."

He then returned to reading as Sam looked down at him, too shocked to say a word.

ALL IN ALL, our first and only spring training game against Milton's Maurauders was an unmitigated disaster. We scored no runs, had no hits, and gave up a total of sixteen. After it was over, I walked off the field, head hung low. Sheryl approached me.

"Sorry," she said.

"Yeah—me, too." We stared at each other for a moment. "How am I going to take this team to Cooperstown?"

"Don't worry. It's going to be fine."

"Sheryl, this isn't some movie where I can actually bring a truly terrible team to one of the most-sought after and praised national youth baseball tournaments. There won't be any theater-going audience who will be happy to sit there, eat popcorn, and delight in our ineptitude. This is real life!"

She looked at me and started to speak, but whatever words she had been attempting to string together died in her mouth. Sheryl had no idea what to say. For the first time in my life, my wife, who had an answer to every question and a solution to every problem, was stumped.

"GOOD GAME YESTERDAY, Josh."

It was the day following our humiliating defeat at the hands of the Marauders, and I had run into Milton Schwartz in the hallway at school after dropping off the kids. Seeing him a few steps ahead, I slowed my pace so that he wouldn't notice me. Milt would have none of it.

"Uh . . . yeah . . . well, thanks for getting us some practice," I said, while looking at the floor, trying to hide my shame. He waited for me and I had no choice but to walk with him out to the parking lot.

"Do you mind if I give you a little advice?" he asked.

Normally, I would have. But on that day, I was too

desperate to care. I was battered, beaten, and without pride. If Milt had invited me to sit with him on the bench in front of school and cry into his lap while he stroked my hair, I would have agreed in a heartbeat.

"If you have any ideas that could help us, I would love to hear them."

"Have the team look at the pitcher's shoulder and not at his face. That way they won't be as intimidated."

"Okay," I said.

"Also have them stand back in the batter's box to give them an extra half-second to see the ball."

"That sounds good."

"If you need help, I'm available."

We walked side by side for a few more steps while his words sank in. There was too little time to take Milt up on his offer, but his advice felt like water in the desert. With those four sentences he had somehow given me hope. His message was simple and straightforward, but inspiring. Perhaps I was reading too much into it, but what I heard from Milt was something far more mean-ingful than words of wisdom on how to hit a baseball. What I heard was that I was not alone. The Rashi com-munity was backing us. Tons of sports-obsessed Jewish fathers were praying for us. We were the ultimate un-derdogs with no chance of success, but we were loved and supported.

Milt had no idea what he had done. I had been in a dark, dark tunnel, and he had shown me a light. Mil-ton Schwartz—sportsman and devoted father, attor-ney, businessman, and early retiree—barely escaped the parking lot without a kiss.

CHAPTER TWELVE

NO TURNING BACK

"VIHAERETZ HAYITAH TOHOO vivohoo vichoshech al pinai tihome."

Gabe straightened his pastel-colored, tie-dyed T-shirt, and sat down on the stage after proudly performing his one Hebrew line of the play. His eyes glowed brilliantly with excitement. I sat in the auditorium between Sheryl and Shani, and gave my son a thumbs-up as he squinted into the bright lights searching for our reaction. Looking down at the printed program resting on my lap, I found the translation of his words, "The earth was uniform and desolate, and darkness covered the surface of the abyss."

We had two weeks before the end of school, which also meant we had two weeks before leaving for Cooperstown. On this Thursday evening, the fourth grade families had come to watch the end of year performance, an artsy production of the book of Genesis that was titled *"Breishet,"* meaning "In the beginning."

The auditorium was probably the most impressive part of a not so impressive Rashi building. The spacious hall took up at least a quarter of the overall square footage of the school, and the forty or so fourth grade families fit easily into the first ten rows of chairs. The students were dressed in matching tie-dyed shirts as they moved about the stage, striking unusual poses and rattling off biblical Hebrew verses. The final lines and class bow brought the crowd to their feet for a standing ovation.

As I made my way down the aisle, avoiding the crush to get to the after show refreshments, I could see Jeremy Finkelstein also fighting through the mob to get to me. I didn't like the look on his face.

"Did you hear about Aaron?" he asked in a low conspiratorial whisper.

"Aaron who?" I asked absentmindedly.

"Aaron Dines," he said furtively. "You know, our starting catcher?"

"No, I haven't heard a thing. What's going on?"

"His Little League team is in the play-offs," Jeremy said, his eyes quickly darting from side to side as if someone might steal our team secrets. "If they make it to the championship, he's going to be late to Cooperstown."

"What are you talking about? How late?" I raised my voice, doing everything I could to stifle the scream rising in my throat.

"Hush," Jeremy said, looking around again. "He'll miss at least the first game."

Our starting catcher missing the first game and maybe more, the mind killer immediately gripped me, and held on tight. The precarious house of cards that we had spent so much time and effort building was about to collapse.

"This can't be," I said to Jeremy. "It's not possible."

"Go check for yourself," he said, nodding behind me. "Joyce is right over there."

I turned around to see Joyce Dines standing twelve feet behind me. Thin and muscular from her daily workouts, Joyce had worn a summer dress and high heels to her son's performance. Blond hair cascaded past her shoulders.

"Joyce," I said, grabbing her gently by the elbow and pulling her to the back of the room, "we need to talk."

"Yes, of course, Josh. I was actually hoping to speak to you at some point."

"Please tell me the rumors aren't true."

"Unfortunately, I can't. Aaron's team made the playoffs, and Matt has made it clear that Little League takes priority over the Rashi team."

"But does he understand what he's doing? This trip to Dreams Park is a once-in-a-lifetime opportunity. Aaron will never have a chance at something like this again," I pleaded.

"Matt understands, but he feels that Aaron has made a commitment to his Little League team."

"But what about his commitment to our team?"

"I'm sorry, Josh. There's not much I can do. It's out of my hands."

"So that's it, then?" I said to Joyce.

"Sorry," she repeated. "But don't worry. If he has to play in the Little League championship game, then I'll put him on our private jet immediately afterward and fly him up to Cooperstown. Hopefully he'll only miss one game."

"Hopefully," I said, the private jet being little consolation. Without a catcher, one game would feel like a hundred. I thought back to Gabe's line in the play—the earth was uniform and desolate, and darkness covered the surface of the abyss—much the same could be said about my mood.

I PLACED THE final bat inside the duffle bag with the rest of the equipment and threw it on top of the luggage in the trunk of our SUV. Looking around, I made sure that I hadn't forgotten anything. My garage was not as clean as it normally would be at that time of year. The frenetic pace of the previous two months had resulted in neglect of my usual springtime chores. The winter shovels were strewn upon the ground, the garden hose lay uncoiled, and an old paint can had tipped over and fallen off the shelf.

"Sheryl, are you ready? Let's get going!" I called through the open door into the house.

It was Friday, the last day of school, after which the team was set to leave for Cooperstown. The bags under my eyes were prominent given that I had been awake much of the previous night, tossing and turning over what was to be. But the time had finally come, and the only thing left to do was finish packing and head out.

Sheryl had arranged a small pep rally to take place during the final Rashi Shabbat at school. Every Friday afternoon, Rashi celebrated the coming of the Jewish Sabbath, or Shabbat, with a ceremony of stories and song. Parents, siblings, and friends were always invited, and on the last day of the year there was certain to be a good turnout.

"Sheryl! Let's go!" I called again, coming back into the house.

"Here I am, all set," she said, descending the stairs in jean shorts and a Rams T-shirt.

"Looks good," I said. "Now let's go."

As we exited the house, I looked at the *mezuzah*, which hung at a slight angle on the doorpost. That *mezuzah*, a small ornamental object containing a parchment with the most sacred Jewish prayer inscribed upon it, had likely gone untouched by human hands since it had been affixed a few years prior. Jewish tradition commanded that one hang from every door of the home so that you could touch it and kiss your fingers when entering or leaving a room.

"Better late than never," I whispered to myself. Grazing the silver object, I put my fingers to my lips, and walked out the door.

THE FINAL SHABBAT ceremony took place in the Rashi cafenasium. The room was too small for its current purpose, and the lunch tables had been put away to allow space for the event. All three hundred students sat on the floor as visiting parents pulled up chairs behind them. As expected, it was a good turnout for the final day of the year, and there was a buzz in the air in anticipation of summer.

I saw the team, all wearing a Rams T-shirt, sitting together in the front row. Gabe spotted me, jumped up, and ran over.

"Hey, Dad!" he called, leaping into my arms. "Are you

ready?"

"Ready for anything," I said, squeezing him tightly. "How's the team doing?"

"Look for yourself," he responded, motioning toward the group.

I surveyed the players. I noticed Charlie Finkelstein first, his thick brown hair reaching toward the ceiling. His head was tilted toward Phil Perlow, who looked on numbly as Charlie yapped ceaselessly in his ear. The topic of discussion was unknown, but Phil was clearly on automatic pilot, barely listening.

Beside Phil, Jeff Goodman sat cross-legged. I was surprised to see him clutching a small handheld video game device. There was not a book in sight. By the look on his face, I suspected that Jeff had found a new love.

Rami Liebshutz was next in line. With an empty hand and a slow exaggerated motion, Rami was taking advantage of the momentary lull before the ceremony to practice his pitching form.

Behind Rami sat my nephew, Ari. His long brown bangs covered both eyes, and I was disappointed to see that it had not been cut despite repeated appeals to my sister. I was hoping to eliminate any possible obstruction that might interfere with our centerfielder's ability to see the ball, but apparently Ari had been unwilling to part with his precious mane. He sat silently with head in hands awaiting the start of Shabbat.

Next to Ari, stood Carlos, pulling on the bottom of his Rams T-shirt, which was a little too small for him. He saw me and waved.

Just apart from that group, Sam Budd held court, sitting in the center of a circle surrounded by his minions. His curly brown hair had been clipped tight to his scalp, and his elongated torso allowed him plenty of clearance to monitor his gang, making sure all was in order. Robert Matz was one of those being monitored. He lay prone on the floor, listening to Sam and barking out laughter at the slightest hint of a joke.

Next to Robert was Jason Armon. He stood tall and proud in his Rams shirt and khaki shorts. His eyes darted back and forth, one moment on Sam Budd and the next on Charlie and Phil's tedious conversation that he so longed to be a part of.

Gil Slotnick sat within the same circle. A dark-haired fourth-grade girl lay next to him, rubbing the top of his blond head, and Gil was relishing every minute of it.

Finally, set apart a few feet and in a chair by himself sat Aaron Dines. The Shabbat ceremony had not yet begun, yet he had already found himself in a time-out for some nameless indiscretion I dared not think about.

I surveyed the entire group with Gabe standing by my side, watching me.

"They're ready," I said.

"AND NOW . . . LAST but not least . . . the first-ever all-Jewish team to play in a national baseball tournament at Cooperstown Dreams Park . . . let me present the Rashi Rams!" Rabbi Joe, Rashi's head of school, made the announcement. The boys jumped up and ran to the front of the crowd, proudly displaying their eight-foot-long team banner that contained our angry Ram logo surrounded by the last names of all the players.

I stood in the back of the room and watched as the entire audience rose to its feet and cheered. It seemed as if parents, grandparents, brothers, sisters, teachers, and students all had been waiting for this moment to voice their passionate support. The players smiled back and waved to the crowd enthusiastically.

"Wow, that's heartening," Jeremy said as he stood next to me watching the team.

"I'm not sure we deserve it."

"Well, we'll find out soon enough. Are we ready to hit the road after this?"

"As far as I know," I answered. "I think all of the parents are here, except for the Dines, of course."

"Yeah, that's going to be a problem."

We had been informed earlier in the week that Aaron's team had indeed made the Little League championship game, which was to take place on Sunday morning. "At least it will only be one game," Jeremy finished his thought.

"Yeah, one game without a catcher against one of the best ten-year-old baseball teams in the country. I'm sure we'll be fine."

"We'll find out soon enough," he repeated.

"Where is Stan? Have you seen him?"

"Yeah, he's waiting outside. He told me he wanted to get a little sun."

"Let's go see him," I said. We walked out just as the final bell of the school year rang, and the Shabbat ceremony ended. Stan stood silently by the side of the building, staring up at the cloudless blue sky. He also wore his white Rams shirt, khaki shorts, and the trademark

Goodman black socks with sneakers. He appeared to be deep in thought.

"How're you feeling, Stan?" I asked.

He took a moment to rouse himself before answering me. "Good, Josh. I'm feeling really good."

"Do you still feel like you're up for this?" I was well aware that he had just recently completed his radiation treatments.

"Without a doubt. Jeff came into my bed last night and told me how proud he was that I was coaching. I know it's going to take a toll on me, but I couldn't be happier with my decision."

"That's good," I said. "Because we're going to need you."

A loud honking sound coming from the parking lot interrupted our conversation. I looked over to see Adam. He was pulling up in his green Ford Explorer, his head hanging out the window. The back of his truck was overflowing with suitcases.

"Ready, boys?" he screamed. "Let's get the show on the road!"

As if on cue, a mad rush of screaming kids flooded out of the building. The momentary chaos soon faded, however, as most of them were quickly whisked away by parents looking to get a head start on the summer. The Rashi Rams had seven cars leaving that afternoon, and it took us a little while to get the team and luggage organized. By the time we were ready to go, the parking lot had mostly cleared out, aside from a handful of our most loyal fans that stayed to see us off.

We drove out in single file, heads sticking out of the

windows and horns blowing wildly. At that very moment, ninety-five other teams from across the country were also making their way toward Cooperstown. One thousand or more of the top nine- and ten-year-old baseball players in the United States were converging in one small valley, for one short week, to face off against one another. By some strange twist of fate, twelve very ordinary Jewish boys from one very small Jewish school were to be included among the elite.

We hopped on the Massachusetts Turnpike, heading west toward upstate New York with Boston in our rearview mirror. The safety and security of the Rashi School was left in our wake. There was no turning back.

PART TWO

AWAY

CHAPTER THIRTEEN

SWITCH 'EM AROUND

"WHAT DO YOU guys know about Sandy Koufax?"

We had been driving for close to four hours, Gabe in the front seat, Phil and Ari in back. Somewhere along the way, we had separated from the remainder of the caravan. The drive through western Massachusetts and into the Berkshires was a long stretch, our only company being one another and John Fogerty's *Centerfield*, which I played repeatedly on CD.

"He was the best Jewish baseball player ever," Gabe responded with confidence, having heard much about the great Mr. Koufax over the years.

"That's right," I said. "The best ever and one of the greatest left-handed pitchers of all time, Jewish or not."

"Just like me—a left-handed Jewish pitcher," Phil said. "Do you think Koufax was better than me when he was ten?"

"Most likely, Phil. Although I will say that he didn't have an easy road to the majors. When he was young, he was actually a better basketball player than baseball player, and he struggled with his control for a while. But hard work and persistence paid off."

"Boys, did you know that Al Campanis, who was a

Dodgers scout at the time, once said that there were only two times in his life when the hair on the back of his neck stood up? The first time was when he saw the ceiling of the Sistine Chapel. Do you guys know when the second time was?"

"When he saw Sandy Koufax throw a fastball!" Gabe yelled.

"That's right. When he saw Sandy Koufax throw a fastball. Imagine that—having your fastball mentioned in the same breath with the Sistine Chapel—not too shabby."

"What's the Sistine Chapel?" Phil asked for clarification.

"It's a famous church where the pope lives in Rome. It was painted by some very well-known artists, like Michelangelo."

"Michael who?" Phil persisted.

"Don't worry about it. It was a great compliment to Koufax, trust me."

It was quiet in the car for a few minutes as the boys thought about becoming the next Sandy Koufax. John Fogerty crooned on. The road led us along, each stretch of highway looking similar to the one before, green hills interrupted on occasion by a house, farm, or roadside diner.

For one of the first times in his nine short years, Ari broke the silence.

"I'm scared," he muttered as he looked forlornly out the window, watching upstate New York pass by. The other two boys looked at him and nodded in agreement.

"I'm scared, too, Ari," I said.

"You are?"

"Sure, I am. But if you let fear hold you back, you're going to miss out on a lot of great things in life. I'm living proof of that."

"What do you mean?"

"Well, there were a lot of things that I should have done when I was your age, things that I didn't do because I was scared. Now I regret missing out on some great experiences."

"Like what?"

"Well, I never liked to be away from home. So I avoided trips with my friends, overnights and things like that. One summer, all my camp friends went to Israel and I didn't go because I was nervous."

"What were you nervous about?"

"I'm not sure really . . . being away from home, not knowing what would happen . . . the unknown, I guess."

"That's sad," Ari said.

"Yeah, and believe me, I regret it now. My father, your grandfather, also made some poor choices when he was young, and by the time he figured it out it was too late."

"What do you mean?" Gabe chimed in. "What poor choices did Abba make?"

The use of the affectionate moniker brought back old heartache. *Abba*, the Hebrew word for "father," was the name we used when telling the children stories of their grandfather.

"Well, he didn't have the same problems as me— being afraid and all. But when he was young, he didn't spend as much time with his kids as he would have liked.

He was very focused on work. When he started having grandchildren, however, it seemed that he was determined to make changes. He began focusing on his family and spending quality time with everyone. But he was only able to reap the benefits of those changes for a few years before dying young. And when that happened it was extra tough on the family, because we could all see that he was just coming into his own. He had finally figured out what he really wanted out of life."

"So what are you saying, Uncle Josh?"

"I guess I'm saying that life is short—too short to waste time on being afraid, too short not to try new things, and too short not to spend as much time as you can with family and friends.

"But I'm rambling. The bottom line, Ari, is that you worked hard and prepared for this, and now it's time to face your fears. You'll be a better person for it, and you won't regret it. I promise you that."

"I hope you're right," he said, never turning his eyes from the window.

No one said anything further and we drove on in silence, the tension gradually rising as we came closer and closer to our destination.

Pressing a button on the CD player, I did my best to lighten the mood. "C'mon, boys. Let's sing along. Do you guys know the words to 'Centerfield'?"

"We do now," Gabe said sarcastically. "You've played it twenty times already."

"What can I say? It's a great song."

We sang together about beat-up gloves, homemade bats, and brand-new pairs of shoes. The mounting pressure eased slightly, and the boys began to relax, jostling playfully with one another.

But as we came over a small rise in the road and looked into the distance, John Fogerty was left to sing by himself. For there, perhaps a half mile away, cradled in the loving arms of the mountains and lit up in the summer twilight, lay a valley that left us speechless. It was unlike any we had ever seen before, and although I shall likely return many times, I doubt I will ever see it quite the same way again.

The sun set over the tops of the hills, illuminating a seemingly endless number of perfectly manicured, entirely symmetrical, glorious baseball fields. Although at the time they seemed too numerous to count, there were, in fact, twenty-two of them, clustered in groups of three and four around various buildings and tents. An array of lights surrounded each diamond, all brightly lit, revealing the brilliance of the green grass and the crisp brown base paths lying beneath.

Even from where we gazed, nearly half a mile away, I could make out the individual white bases on every field. The foul lines were clearly delineated with white powder, stretching at right angles from home plate to the outfield fences in both left and right.

A long line of cars snaked through the park and back onto the road in front of us, waiting anxiously to get inside. The picture spread out before me was exactly as I had envisioned it in every one of my numerous dreams and my even more frequent nightmares.

The four of us sat transfixed in the car. I stepped gently on the brakes to maintain control. John Fogerty sang on, oblivious that we had reached our destination. I turned off the CD player without taking my eyes from the scene. Indeed, I had not blinked since we crested the rise. "Cooperstown Dreams Park," I whispered.

We had arrived.

"FLORIDA!" GABE SCREAMED, pointing at the license plate of the car in front of us.

"Maryland!" Phil called out, pointing at another.

"Georgia," Ari sighed under his breath.

As we sat in the queue about to enter the park, the boys sized up the competition. The cars surrounding us were decorated with names, uniform numbers, and inspirational messages. From inside the backseats, nine- and ten-year-olds peered back at us. There were big kids and small, tall and short, chubby and scrawny—young baseball players in all shapes and sizes.

"He doesn't look that good!" Phil yelled out, pointing at a round kid with a small head.

"That's a younger brother. Look next to him," Gabe said, pointing at a thickly set, muscular boy with a crew cut.

"Oh," Phil responded dejectedly. "Too bad."

"They're just kids like you guys," I said halfheartedly. "No need to panic."

We made our way through the entrance and passed under a large gold sign that read COOPERSTOWN DREAMS PARK. Employees, decked out in CDP shirts and caps, walked to and fro, directing cars and answering questions.

I rolled down my window and motioned to one of them.

"Where to?" I asked.

"Players or visitors?" he questioned.

"Coach and players."

"Which team?"

"The Rashi Rams." He checked the clipboard that he was carrying, flipping through a couple of pages.

"Bunkhouse number eighteen," he said. "Keep going straight until you hit the Baseball Village. You can drive your car down to the bunkhouse to unload. Bring it back to the parking lot when you're finished."

"Eighteen, did you say?" I asked, giving him a look of surprise.

He double-checked. "That's right. Why?"

"Could be a good sign for us, that's all."

I drove on. Eighteen was a special number in the Jewish tradition. It was the numeric value of the Hebrew word *chai*, which meant "life." The concept of *chai* was integral to Jewish culture. A Jewish toast said at a wedding or bar-mitzvah often ended in the word *l'chaim*, or "to life." Traditionally gifts of money or charity were given in multiples of eighteen for good fortune.

"That's definitely a sign," Gabe said, understanding the significance.

"You see, boys, things are looking up already."

THE BASEBALL VILLAGE at Cooperstown Dreams Park was designed to house 1,000 kids, 400 coaches, and 100 umpires. A grand total of 1,500 bodies lived for a week at a time in an area that was less than a quarter of a square mile in size. The tightly packed plain wooden cabins stretched row after row, lining the sides of three paved roads. Painted a crisp white and labeled with large red numbers, the exterior of each bunkhouse also displayed a picture of one or two well-known ballplayers. Each of the cabins housed two teams separated by a thin, paneled wall.

A large, white circus tent marked the entrance to the compound and functioned as both mess hall and central meeting place. Beneath the large tarp, numerous picnic tables were placed in neatly ordered rows.

Adjacent to the tent, sat a rectangular wooden building with the word *arcade* written in bold letters above the entrance. All the necessary distractions were available for the players to blow off steam, in between heated contests on the field. The blinking lights and loud noises of video game machines, pinball, and air hockey tables could be heard as one passed by.

Next was a snack bar with an open serving window shaded by a yellow awning. Inside could be found the usual suspects—hot dogs, nachos, pizza and ice cream—all of which beckoned young ballplayers.

We inched our car down the road toward Bunkhouse 18 as hundreds of players and coaches wandered across our path. They hauled around suitcases and inspected bats and helmets. The pin trading had begun in earnest. Everywhere we looked, a deal or swap had either just been completed or was in the process of being negotiated. Players were already showing off large collections, some numbering in the fifties or sixties.

"Let us out," Gabe begged as we finally pulled up in front of our cabin. The boys had their bags of Rashi Rams pins ready to go as they sprang out of the car and into the fray. I put the Suzuki in park, and went around the back to unload.

"Welcome to your home away from home, Coach. Let me give you a hand." Jeremy Finkelstein came out of the bunkhouse and grabbed a bucket of baseballs from the back of the car.

"How do things look?" I asked.

"Well, the accommodations are . . . interesting."

"Not as nice as your Manhattan apartment, huh?"

"Not quite," he said, opening the door to the cabin and ushering me inside. My head swiveled from left to right, taking in what was to be our living quarters for the next seven days.

It was a stark square space, with two small windows set high in the walls on either side. The floor was made of cold, gray cement and cried out for carpeting. Each side of the room was lined with black metal bunk beds at the foot of which lay two black plastic trunks to hold clothing. All of the Rams had arrived, and those who were not outside trading pins were making their way through the bleak landscape, arguing over bed assignments.

"Sorry, Jeremy, I was hoping for better," I said, dropping my bags and raising my eyebrows. "Where did all the parents go?"

"They announced that all family had to be out of the Baseball Village by seven. Everyone left and headed to their motels. Sheryl said to call her when you get a chance." Sheryl had driven up with Jeremy's wife. The two of them and Jason Armon's mother had rented a nearby house for themselves and the younger siblings.

"And how about our fellow coaches?"

"Adam went to park his car, and Stan is checking out the park."

A loud voice from the back of the bunk interrupted my train of thought.

"No way! You can't sleep here. This bed is reserved."

I turned to see Sam Budd shouting at Phil Perlow, who had brought in his bag from the car and thrown it on the top bunk, above Sam. Phil arched his back ready to defend himself.

"Let him sleep were he wants," Gabe said, pushing his way into the bunk behind me.

"Like I would want to sleep near you anyway, Sam," Phil chimed in, gaining strength from his friend's presence. "I didn't even see that you were there," he continued, picking up his bag and moving toward the front of the room.

"Settle down! We're supposed to be a team and I want to see you guys acting like one!" I announced loudly.

Adam entered the cabin behind me, letting the screen door slam shut. "I don't want to hear anymore fighting!" he hollered. "Everyone find a bed and start unloading your stuff, before I really get pissed!"

The boys responded quickly to his stern voice, and petty arguments were rapidly placed on hold. I turned and looked at him. He had just returned from parking his car.

"Thanks for backing me up. It's good to have you on board. I think we're going to need someone to instill some discipline around here."

"Among other things," he said.

The team dispersed to the four corners of the bunk-house, and finally settled on sleeping arrangements. I was disheartened to see that, after all these months, they were keeping to their dual camps. Sam and Gil chose beds in the back, along with Robert, Jason, and Rami. The group made sure to save a bed for the tardy Aaron Dines. Meanwhile, Gabe led his troops to the front, near the door. He chose a top bunk and Ari threw his bag down underneath him. Surrounding them on either side were Phil, Charlie, and Jeff.

The counselors also chose beds near the entrance. As I unloaded my bags into the plastic black trunk, Carlos approached me, looking bewildered.

"Josh, where do I sleep?"

"Aren't there any beds left?" I asked.

"A few," he said.

"Okay, then pick one."

"How about the one above you?" he asked, his sad puppy eyes wide and pleading.

"That's fine, Carlos," I said, and he hopped up on the bunk above me with a grin.

I surveyed the group, unhappy with the division that was persisting within the team. Something would have to be done, but at the moment I had bigger problems to deal with.

THE HEAD COACHES' meeting was called for eight p.m. in the large pavilion at the entrance to the Baseball Village. Stan had returned from his inspection of the park, and I left him, Adam, and Jeremy in charge of the team while I walked down to the tent. We were to be addressed by Dreams Park owner Lou Presutti.

Darkness had fallen over the village as I made my way down the path between the cabins. The deep shadows of the mountains could be seen surrounding us, above which the stars shone brightly. Many of the other head coaches were leaving their bunks at the same time, heading to the meeting.

As I entered the tent to grab a seat, I looked around, sizing up my own competition. To my eyes, every one of my fellow head coaches looked to be a hard-core veteran of the ten and under baseball circuit. Their grizzled faces, firm stances, and tournament caps struck fear in my heart. Many of them greeted each other with familiar handshakes and pats on the back. These guys knew one another from previous contests.

The picnic tables under the tent had been removed for the meeting and multiple rows of foldable chairs had taken their place. They were rapidly filling up. I picked a spot in the back, listening anxiously to the chatter going on around me. There was talk of practices, schedules, and game strategies. I heard discussion of tournaments past and those yet to come, war stories that were as alien to me as this place that I had found myself in.

Of the ninety-five coaches present, not a single one spoke to me or acknowledged my presence, and I wondered what it was that gave me away as a rookie. I slumped down in my white plastic chair, feeling small and alone.

After a few minutes, a buzz rippled through the crowd as Lou Presutti made his way to the front of the tent. A middle-aged man of medium height and build, he walked

down the center aisle, greeting this coach or that with a
nod, a handshake, or a smile. He wore a Cooperstown
Dreams Park shirt with a matching baseball cap that
was perched gently atop his balding crown. The scant
hair that escaped from either side was dyed brown and
clipped close to the scalp. His facial features were nota-
bly sharp and angular. After arriving at the front of the
tent, he wheeled on his heel, surveying the group before
him. For a moment, I felt his sweeping gaze pause on me,
then pass on.

"Good evening, gentlemen," he began. "Welcome to
Cooperstown Dreams Park, home of the best youth
baseball tournament in the country. To those of you who
have been here before—welcome back, and to those of
you who are new to us this year—I hope that your team
is prepared."

Lou spoke for some time, reviewing with the group
how the week would be organized. He began with the
mundane details about mealtimes, the dress code, and
the laundry service. I listened and took in the information. But when he started in on the history of CDP,
my heart began to beat faster. He discussed the elite
level of competition that we would be facing, and it triggered pounding in my ears. He spoke of the supreme talent level of the invited teams and mentioned casually
that we would be participating in the highest level of
baseball competition for this age group in the nation, if
not the world. The sweat began to pour from my forehead, and I wondered, neither for the first time nor the
last, what in God's name we were doing there. Lou went
on and on. The more he spoke, the more physically ill I

became.

I had a roommate in college who was a passionate New York Giants fan. Whenever Todd Kanterman would watch a game, he would sit on the edge of the bed, staring at the television, while leaning forward with his right knee bouncing up and down uncontrollably. He would maintain that position for the duration of the game, more than three hours if necessary.

As I sat there listening to Lou speak, looking at the casual, calm poses of the coaches surrounding me, I was the spit and image of my old friend, Todd, watching his beloved Giants. It took every single fiber of strength I had to keep from standing up, walking to the car, and driving straight home, leaving the team and my fellow coaches to deal with whatever might be coming.

"Finally, I would like to say one last thing," Lou wound down his speech, the crowd paying close attention. "There are a few 'park and rec' teams present here for the week." The crowd groaned. *Park and rec* stood for "park and recreation," local town teams with lesser talent. Lou raised his hand to quiet the disgruntled masses who were not thrilled at the news. "Now, boys, we have to allow some of them to participate here as well. I would respectfully request that if things get out of hand, you switch 'em around."

He was talking about us. That I knew immediately. It was also clear that the majority of coaches present were not happy to have us there. I had no idea what Lou meant when he advised that they "switch 'em around," but for some reason I felt it very important that I find out.

A heavyset thirty-something-year-old guy with a face covered in razor stubble rocked back on his chair next to me. If his cap was accurate, his team hailed from California. Summoning as much courage as I could, I leaned over in his direction, and spoke for the first time since entering the tent.

"What does he mean, 'switch 'em around'?" I asked.

He looked over at me and stared, apparently finding it incomprehensible that I didn't know.

"He means if you come up against one of those park teams and you're kicking the snot out of 'em, you should have your boys bat from the wrong side of the plate. You know, if they're righties, then bat 'em lefty." And as if to emphasize his point about the snot, he rubbed one large meaty paw under his nose and snorted.

"Oh, yeah . . . sure . . . switch 'em around . . . got it," I said. Turning back toward the front, where Lou was continuing to speak, I pressed both hands firmly down on my right knee to keep it from running out of the tent and leaving the rest of me behind.

"HOW DID IT go?" Jeremy asked as I walked into Bunk 18, letting the door close gently behind me.

"It was . . . educational. How are things going here?"

"Probably about as well as it went for you," he responded. It was approaching ten p.m., which according to park rules was time for lights out. I was expecting to see the kids ready for bed, with their teeth brushed, but that was far from the case.

Jason Armon, wearing only pin-striped boxers, was hanging from one of the rafters by his knees. His long brown arms were held in the tight grips of Sam Budd and Robert Matz as they swung him to and fro.

Rami Liebshutz was standing on his upper bunk bed, practicing his pitching form. His empty right hand, delivering a make-believe fastball, accidentally slammed against the ceiling and he screamed in pain.

Gabe and Charlie sat on a bed, engrossed in a game of backgammon. Ari lay propped up on his elbows behind Gabe and Phil stood behind Charlie as they cheered on their respective teammates in what was apparently a round-robin tournament. I waved my hand across the board to get their attention. The players barely noticed.

Stan and Jeff Goodman lay next to each other on Stan's cot. Jeff was engrossed in his new handheld video game and Stan was reading.

"Stan, don't you think it's time to put the kids to bed?" I said. He looked up distractedly.

"Yeah, bed . . . right . . . just give me a minute," he said as he dove back into his book.

I moved over to Jeff.

"Jeff, ready for bed?" I asked. There was no response, and I realized that if I was not on his game screen, there was no way he would recognize my presence.

I turned to see who else I might be able to corral, when Carlos walked by me. He was shirtless, with a towel wrapped around his waist and flip-flops on his feet.

"Where are *you* going, Carlos?" I asked.

"To the shower house to take a shower," he responded casually. The bathrooms, which included the sinks, showers, and toilets, were located in a separate building, a short distance from our cabin.

"Carlos, its ten o'clock at night. Get into your pajamas and get into bed," I said sternly.

"Why haven't you done anything?" I asked Jeremy.

"It was just too much. I didn't even know where to start."

"Where's Adam?" I asked.

"Out looking for Gil."

"What are you talking about?"

"Gil left the bunkhouse, so Adam went looking for him."

"Do you know where he went?" I asked.

"No idea."

I opened the door to look, myself, and right at that moment, Adam came walking toward me, dragging Gil Slotnick by the neck of his Rams T-shirt.

"Where the heck did you go, Gil?" I asked as they approached.

"I went looking for the girl's cabin," he responded unapologetically. His short blond hair had been spiked up with gel in preparation for his outing.

"What are you talking about?"

"I found out that some of the teams here have girls, so I went looking for their bunkhouse."

"Don't ever leave without telling someone again," I said as Adam threw him inside with the rest of the team. He followed on Gil's heels, taking in the chaotic scene.

"GET INTO BED, YOU ANIMALS!" Adam shouted at the top of his lungs. They looked up with shock and scrambled for their sleeping bags.

AS THE LIGHTS were turned out, I noticed Stan walk

over to his son's bed to say good night. Jeff lay calmly under his covers, resting comfortably in matching *Batman* wing-patterned pajamas. They whispered quietly to each other, and then Stan kissed his son gently on the forehead and walked away. I approached him in the dark.

"You doing okay, Stan? I know this has got to be tough on you."

"I'm fine, Josh. I'm just tired. I think I'll turn in."

"We're going to sit outside and talk for a little while if you want to join us," I offered.

"No, thanks; I'm beat. I'll see you in the morning."

"Good night, Stan," I said, watching him climb into his bed and roll over.

I went outside to find Adam and Jeremy sitting on plastic chairs in front of the bunkhouse. There was a slight chill in the air at that late hour. All around the Baseball Village, coaches were congregating outside their cabins. Most of the bunks had at least two or three men sitting in front of them, shooting the breeze.

We sat in silence for a moment, caught up in our own thoughts. At times other coaches would pass by, and we would exchange brief pleasantries, mostly in the form of stern nods, but if someone happened to be in a generous mood we heard a muffled, "Good luck this week."

In my mind, a war raged back and forth between the fear of competing in this tournament and shame at my petty anxieties, especially given what Stan was dealing with. I could not imagine the true fear he must be experiencing and I was in awe of his courage. He had undergone major brain surgery and until recently was receiving daily radiation treatments. He was scheduled for that ominous MRI the day after we returned home, an MRI that would reveal whether there was tumor remaining. And yet, on some level, he also clearly understood that the results of that MRI were not all that significant. His tumor was incurable and his disease had only one end. Yet he persevered, coming with us for the week, out of love for his son and commitment to the team. I had no idea whether I would have been able to muster similar strength.

"Amazing," Adam said, reading my thoughts.

"What is?" Jeremy responded.

"That Stan is here, doing this. You know, given everything that he's going through, you'd think living and sleeping in a hot, cramped bunk for seven nights with twelve boys wouldn't be his first choice of how to spend the week."

"Maybe it's the best way for him to spend his time," I thought out loud. The three of us sat in silence, lost in our own thoughts and wondering what we would do under similar circumstances.

"I'm scared, guys," I said, trying to change the subject. "You should have been at the meeting tonight. This is no ordinary baseball tournament. All these teams are good, really good. I'm not sure that we'll even be able to get an out. What happens if we can't get off the field?"

"Relax, Josh," Jeremy said. "Remember what this is all about. If not for you, these kids would never have a chance to experience a place like this. You're giving them a once-in-a-lifetime opportunity."

"Yeah, an opportunity to make fools of themselves."

"An opportunity to see how they measure up. It may serve them well to be humbled."

"Oh, they'll be humbled all right," Adam piped up. We sat in silence again until my cell phone buzzed.

"Hi, honey," I answered.

"You were supposed to call me," Sheryl's voice sounded crisp, as if she were sitting right around the corner.

"Sorry, hon. You have no idea what's going on here. It's taking all my energy to stop myself from having a nervous breakdown, not to mention keeping the boys in line. Their behavior has been less than stellar."

I filled her in on the head coaches' meeting and the events of the night, while Adam and Jeremy sat and listened.

"Okay, just hang in there. I'll see you tomorrow," Sheryl said. "And Josh . . ."

"Yes?"

"You're doing a good thing here."

"Thanks, honey. Love ya," I said and hung up the phone.

We sat and chatted for another hour, during which time Adam and Jeremy also fielded calls from their spouses. As midnight approached, Jeremy stood up.

"I have to check Charlie's blood sugar," he said.

"At midnight?" I asked.

"Yeah, too much junk food around here. I think it's going to be a nightly affair this week."

Jeremy's words were yet another reminder of my absurd and foolish fears. My fellow coaches were dealing with issues of far greater significance than how our team would perform in the tournament.

We said good night as Jeremy quietly roused his son. I climbed into my sleeping bag on the bottom bunk and listened to the deep breathing of Carlos, sleeping soundly above me. Then, closing my eyes, I drifted off while wondering what the following day would bring.

CHAPTER FOURTEEN

ERRANDS TO RUN

THE SUN ROSE early above the mountains, shining its rays past the trees, over the baseball diamonds, into the village, through the windows of Bunk 18, finally coming to rest upon my closed lids. I refused to open my eyes, dreaming that it was Saturday morning and I was home in bed, able to sleep late and spend the day as I pleased.

I slowly climbed out of my sleeping bag and stepped on the cool floor, looking around the bunk. Blankets had fallen off of bodies, sheets were no longer tucked in, and clothes were already hanging from the rafters. Random arms and legs protruded from the sides of beds and deep snores could be heard from one or two corners of the room. I was the first awake, and from the looks of it, it would remain that way for a while.

Changing out of my sweats, I threw a towel around my waist and grabbed my toiletries, heading for the shower. The coaches had facilities separate from those of the players, although the outhouses were practically identical square, cinder-block structures with tin roofs. One side of each building was lined with toilets, the other with sinks. Communal showers were in the back.

Two other coaches moved quietly about the bathroom,

and we nodded to one another in greeting during our shower and shave. I returned to the bunkhouse to find everyone still asleep, and decided to use the free time to explore. Pulling on sneakers, khaki shorts, and my CDP coaches' blue polo shirt provided by the park, I set out to see the lay of the land.

The practice facilities were located behind our cabin at the foot of a small slope. I wandered down the path and noted between twenty and thirty metal batting cages off to my left. Each contained bat racks, a plate, and an adjustable screen to protect the vulnerable pitcher. To my right lay a large, open expanse that the teams used for fielding practice. The morning dew still covered the grass, and at this early hour, a distant groundskeeper was the only soul in sight. For just a moment, I was able to take in the physical beauty of the quiet park.

Pushing on, the path guided me to the baseball fields. I marveled at their exquisite perfection, one followed by another. This area contained only half of the park's diamonds. I counted four in sight of where I stood, each surrounded by a dark green eight-foot fence. Doorways along the outside were labeled *home* or *visitor* with white painted letters.

I approached one of the fields, pushed open the "home" door, which was upon the third baseline, and stepped inside. I had entered the third base dugout, looking out upon the diamond. The grass was cut neatly and rested about a half-inch above the ground. The infield dirt had been raked clean and straight lines of white powder stretched along the foul lines.

In right and left field, the visitors' areas beckoned to

family and friends. The stands made me long to be a guest and not a participant. I counseled myself that the pressure of performing should not keep me from enjoying the magic of this place. The size of the diamond far surpassed the typical Little League fields that we had practiced on, and I looked from third to first, judging whether Gabe could make the throw.

Not surprisingly, the serenity of the park could not protect me from my anxiety, which grew as I stood looking out upon the field. There was no place here for a team to hide. You could not avoid the spotlight. The humiliation would be everlasting. The mind killer grew in strength, and my breathing quickened. I fought back, forcing myself to leave the dugout before it could take full control. In my wake, the "home" door swung silently back and forth on its well-maintained hinges.

RETURNING TO THE bunkhouse, I found that everyone was still asleep, except for Jeremy. He had woken for a jog before dawn, although I hadn't realized it earlier. He stood in the middle of the cabin, huffing and puffing after the long run. Sweat stains covered the front of his gray T-shirt and ringed the armpits. His dark hair was damp and swept to the side.

"Six miles," he said. "Good run."

"What time did you get up?"

"Five a.m."

"You know that's not normal, right?"

He simply shrugged his shoulders, as if those of us who attempted to sleep as late as possible were the ones who were truly crazy.

"We all have our ways of dealing with stress, Josh. Some are better than others."

"Right," I smiled. "Listen, I have some errands to run this morning. Do you think you guys can handle the boys?"

"No worries. After a run like that I can handle anything."

I looked at him and grinned. "Jeremy, where would the world be without people like you?"

Leaving the bunk, I walked down to the entrance of the Baseball Village for a prearranged meeting. By now the early risers were up and about, making their way to the shower house. A few stood with their food trays in the breakfast line under the tent. Approaching the low gate across which parents and visitors were not allowed to pass, I saw Jonathan and Diego Garcia-Feinstein, Carlos's fathers, waiting for me.

Jonathan was the Feinstein of the Garcia-Feinstein partnership. He was about five foot six with dark hair, pale skin, and large, square glasses that partially covered his handsome face. He wore jeans and a gray sweatshirt that fell loosely over his thin frame.

In contrast, Diego was broader, two inches taller, and of darker complexion. He wore a yellow T-shirt that showed off his defined musculature. Physically, they were a mismatched couple, but word had it that they had a strong marriage and provided a loving home for their three adopted children.

In his wide arms, Diego held a large Styrofoam container with a fitted lid secured to the top. The contents of this box was the subject of our early morning meeting.

"How are things going, Josh?" Jonathan asked as soon as I came within earshot.

"Not bad. We're getting adjusted, but the boys seem to be having a good time."

"Great. How is Carlos doing?"

"So far, so good. He's sleeping in the bunk over me, so I'll be able to keep a close eye on him."

"Wonderful . . .so, anyway, here it is." He motioned to Diego, who passed the Styrofoam cooler over the gate and into my arms. It was surprisingly heavy.

"Now, tell me again, what am I supposed to do with this if it's ever needed?"

"Just bring it to the emergency room with you. They'll know," Diego answered my question.

"Remember, guys, I'm just a primary care doctor. If you want me to prescribe some high blood pressure pills I'm your man, but I don't do trauma."

"We trust you, Josh," they said in unison.

I said good-bye and turned back toward the village with cooler in hand, immediately seeking out the park's medical offices. A passing employee directed me to the administrative building behind the large pavilion.

I knocked on the door.

"Come in," called a female voice.

I entered to see Dreams Park's lone nurse sitting behind a counter. She was middle-aged with thick brown hair pulled high over her head in a bun. A white lab coat covered her shoulders.

"Hi, are you Terry?" I asked.

"I am," she smiled.

"I'm Josh Berkowitz. We spoke on the phone about

my player with the bleeding disorder."

"Right, I remember. So is this the plasma?"

"So I've been told," I said, handing over the cooler.

"Okay," she said taking the box and placing it in a freezer that stood behind her. "Hopefully we won't be needing this."

"Agreed," I responded.

WITH THE RISK to Carlos's life now significantly diminished, I moved on to the next item on my checklist. Lou Presutti had instructed all head coaches to pick up their team uniforms that morning at the pavilion. Dreams Park provided each player with two sets of uniforms, red jerseys for home games and blue for away. Included in the package were matching socks and a CDP cap. My next responsibility was to get the Rams their gear.

Despite the early hour, a line of coaches had already formed in front of the uniform table and I got at the back of the queue to wait my turn. Against my better judgment and for lack of anything else to do, I eavesdropped on the two men talking to each other in front of me. The topic of conversation piqued my interest, as it turned out our teams had something critical in common.

"This isn't going to be pretty," one said to the other. The speaker was tall, gangly, and something about him screamed "father" not "coach." I could smell the fear on him. A Boston Red Sox cap rested awkwardly on his head.

"Yeah, they should have warned us. This is ridiculous. I'm ready to head back to Concord," his shorter counterpart responded. His pudgy broad face was covered by a scant amount of stubble, and a New England Patriots T-shirt barely contained his protuberant belly.

"Are you guys from Massachusetts?" I interrupted them, sensing that I might have found some compatriots.

"Yeah, we're with the Concord-Carlisle Minutemen," the tall one answered. "How 'bout you?"

"I'm with the Rashi Rams. We're from Newton. Sorry, I couldn't help overhearing. It's good to learn that someone else is nervous about this tournament."

"Yeah, we send a team every year, but it's always a new group of coaches. Now I know why. No one told us it was going to be like this," the pudgy one declared.

His words were a welcome relief from all the other chatter I had heard at the park to that point. "Yeah, it's a little overwhelming. How did you guys get your team together?" I asked.

"Basically, we tried to recruit the best players we could find from Concord and Carlisle—two towns' worth of Little Leaguers. We both have sons on the team. How 'bout you guys?"

"We're from a small Jewish private school. It's pretty much just my son and his friends."

"Oh," the tall one said with a hint of surprise in his voice. "Are you any good?"

"Good? I wouldn't exactly say 'good.' Coming here might have been a bit of a reach."

"Us, too," he said forlornly as they arrived at the front of the line and turned to pick up their uniforms. "Well, I guess it's our turn. Good luck to you. I think we're all going to need it. Maybe we'll meet up at some point."

"Maybe," I said. "Good luck to you, too."

I was not sure whether the encounter put my mind at ease or not. The Concord coaches felt considerably over-matched, but they, at least, had been able to recruit the premier players from two towns' worth of Little Leaguers. We had attempted to cull players from a sig-nificantly smaller talent pool. If the Boys of Baseball National Travel Team had the entire ocean to fish in, the Concord-Carlisle Minutemen had gone fishing in a small pond. The Rashi Rams, on the other hand, had tried to fish in a driveway puddle after a brief rain.

I finally had my worst fears confirmed. There was no one else at Cooperstown Dreams Park like us. Even among the so-called park and rec teams, we were truly unique. And in our uniqueness, one thing was eminently clear—in no way, shape, or form did we belong.

CHAPTER FIFTEEN

FRONTING UP OUR THROWS

"LET'S GO, GUYS! It's time for practice!" Adam's booming voice reverberated throughout the bunk. "Move it!"

The Rams filed out of the cabin and we made our way to the designated practice area I had visited that morning. The majority of teams were using the free time to get some work in on this early Saturday afternoon.

We walked down the path dressed in a haphazard array of T-shirts over sweatpants or shorts, immediately standing out like fifteen sore thumbs. Most of the competition practiced in matching baseball pants and Under Armour tight-fitting shirts. Many of their practice uniforms displayed printed slogans plastered on chest or back. The messages were appropriate for the players that wore them. PAIN IS WEAKNESS LEAVING YOUR BODY and HARD WORK BEATS TALENT WHEN TALENT DOESN'T WORK HARD were a couple that caught my eye. Surveying our own sweatshirts, I read my son's chest which proudly proclaimed SPECIAL PEOPLE MAKE CAMP YAVNEH A SPECIAL PLACE, and that was probably the best of what we had to offer.

The opposition walked in single file behind their

coaches, carrying their bats, helmets, and gloves in matching wheeled equipment bags. Our kids ran ahead, pushing and shoving while Adam, Stan, Jeremy and I trailed behind, hauling our gear in old duffle bags that we had dredged up from the basement.

We stopped outside of the batting cages. They were all occupied. If we had any hope of using them, now was not going to be the time. As we stood and watched, my jaw went slack. Gone were the realities of Stan's tumor and Charlie's diabetes, which had given me some perspective just the night before. The mind killer returned, and quickly.

"Why are their coaches hitting?"

I looked down to see Rami Liebshutz standing next to me. The long brown hair sprouting from under his cap covered his ears. His expression was one of puzzlement and confusion. I looked at the logo above the bill of his hat which read JEWISH COMMUNITY CENTER— NEWTON.

"Those aren't their coaches, Rami," I said.

Inside the cages, the players were crushing each and every pitch thrown their way. Coaches had dragged the movable screens up close to their batters, perhaps only fifteen feet away. And even from that short distance, they pitched fast, extremely fast. Ringing line drive after ringing line drive left those bats with a sound that made me think I had shown up early at Fenway Park for batting practice. It made no difference which batter stepped to the plate. Regardless of the player or the team, each looked better than the next. I couldn't find one who was worse than Sam Budd, the best hitter on our team.

It quickly became obvious that our equipment was also lacking. As each kid stepped to the plate, he carried with him an extremely thick aluminum bat. Despite my best efforts to get us the appropriate gear, I had failed. These teams were using bats that I had never seen before—heavy-barreled things with thin grips that the players whipped around their bodies in an incredible blur of motion. I started to feel nauseous.

"Now I know why I always liked soccer more than baseball," Rami said as he stood at my side. "Maybe I won't pitch after all, Josh."

"Perhaps that's a good idea, Rami," I said.

"OKAY, IS EVERYONE in their uniform?" I called out to the team.

Two hours had gone by. Two hours after we had seen the other teams at Dreams Park practicing for the first time, and two hours after each and every one of us had come pretty darn close to wetting our pants.

The opening ceremony that kicked off the weeklong tournament was set to begin. The teams were scheduled to march from the Baseball Village to Field No. 3, which was the largest of the stadiums and had the biggest seating capacity for fans. We had our choice of uniform and the Rams selected blue for the occasion.

"Take a look at this, Dad," Gabe said as he and Ari came over to my bed. We were in the bunk, rushing to get dressed with only five minutes remaining before the scheduled meeting time. Gabe was dressed in his blue CDP jersey with a blue T-shirt underneath. His legs were adorned with white baseball pants pulled up to the knees and blue socks that stretched south until they found his black cleats. His blue cap with a red bill and the Dreams Park logo on the front completed the picture.

"You look like a ballplayer. That's for sure," I said.

"That's not what I'm talking about. Look at me and Ari," Gabe insisted as they both turned for me to inspect them. On the left I saw a large white 1 emblazoned on the back of Ari's jersey. To his right, Gabe wore the number 8.

"Eighteen, Dad! When we're together, it's the number eighteen!"

"If my father could see his two grandsons now, he would be so proud. Another *chai* is a good omen, Gabe."

"You really think so?"

"Well, it's no burning bush, but beggars can't be choosers."

MAKING OUR WAY through the village, we were one of the last teams to arrive at the large, white open-aired tent. Inside, the seating had been rearranged from the previous night and the tent was now filled with row up-on row of picnic tables. The setup would remain in place for the rest of the week. Each table was packed with nine- and ten-year-olds, every one dressed in the Dreams Park colors, either red or blue. The edges of the pavilion were lined with portable tiered bleachers, and our team commandeered one of the empty ones. The excitement was evident by the noise level, which reached a peak as we arrived.

Lou Presutti, wearing the same uniform that he had donned the night before, once again stepped to the front of the tent, motioning with his hands for quiet.

"Hello, young ballplayers!" he called, to which he received a rousing cheer.

"Welcome, my friends, to Cooperstown Dreams Park!" This engendered another prolonged roar from the crowd.

"I know that many of you have been waiting for a long time to come here, and I hope that this week meets your expectations. Rest assured that if you are sitting in this tent tonight, you are one of the best ten and under baseball players in the country!"

I looked over at our team to see Phil Perlow nodding at Charlie. Apparently, Phil was not surprised to hear the news.

Lou continued, "Now, young men, please be aware that participating in this tournament is a privilege! There are thousands of kids your age across this great nation that would give their right arm to trade places with you. I cannot tell you how many teams we had to turn away this summer and how many ballplayers we disappointed. So do your best to live up to the great tradition of this park, and show us that you have earned the right to be here."

"He's taking this pretty seriously," Jeremy whispered in my ear.

"You ain't seen nothin' yet," I responded.

"And one more thing!" Lou called out loudly. "I want to take a moment to congratulate ourselves. You should all know that this past year, Cooperstown Dreams Park experienced a first. This was the first year that *ten*, let me repeat, *ten* of this year's major-league baseball's first-round draft picks played here when they were your age. Our previous record was eight!"

I looked over at Adam and raised my eyebrows in surprise. He raised his at me in return. Then we both looked at Jeremy, who responded in kind. All three of us looked over at Stan, who shrugged.

"That's impressive," he said casually, nodding his head.

"RASHI RAMS, YOUR turn!" We had waited in the tent as each team was called, one by one, to line up for the opening parade. Finally, our time had come, and after a brief debate we allowed the coaches' kids to carry our banner in front of the team. Gabe, Ari, Charlie, and Jeff took the lead, proudly clutching the long sign. Robert, Sam, Jason, Rami, Phil, Gil, and Carlos followed. The coaches brought up the rear. Aaron Dines had yet to arrive. He was not due until the following day.

The parade route was short but the wait time long, and the line of ninety-six teams began to bulge outward as discipline gave way to boredom. We clustered together while the remaining teams formed up behind us, and I took the opportunity to call Sheryl on her cell.

"We're almost ready to start marching," I said. "How are things going there?"

"Great. Shani is trading pins. All the families are in the stands waiting for you guys. We're in right field."

"Okay, we'll be coming soon. I love you."

"Love you, too," she said and hung up.

Never in my life had I felt the need to reach out to those who loved me, more than at that moment. Finding the strength to lead the Rashi Rams in a parade alongside the country's best ten and under baseball teams was easier with some emotional support.

The front of the line began to move and space soon opened up before us.

"Let's go, boys," I called. "This is it."

We moved out slowly, leaving the village and the tent behind us. The parade made its way to the front of the park, toward Field No. 3. As we approached, we saw the rear of the packed stadium. Thousands of screaming, cheering friends and family awaited our arrival, many of them hanging over the outer walls of the field, waving at us from the top row of the stands.

The head of our great snake was halted just outside the entrance, however, as we heard the buzz of a small plane flying overhead. At first, I thought it was a coincidence or perhaps a local trying to get a look at the festivities. However, it wasn't long before we saw three skydivers launch themselves into the air and hurtle toward the stadium. After a few seconds, they pulled their ripcords and floated down in great circles, trailing red, white, and blue smoke. They landed gently in the infield to raucous approval from the crowd.

"This is getting even more serious," Jeremy said to me as the divers gathered up their parachutes and made their way out of the stadium. The teams began marching in, one by one, as Lou Presutti announced their names on the loudspeaker. We waited for a few minutes, while they entered the field in alphabetical order.

"From North Carolina . . . the Outer Banks Baseball Academy!"

"From Miami, Florida . . . the Pinecrest Pumas!"

And finally our turn arrived. "From Newton, Massachusetts . . . the . . . Rushi . . . Rams!" I noticed the mispronunciation, but was not surprised. I had a feeling that our first formal introduction to the CDP community might involve some sort of hiccup. We entered the stadium, crossed over home plate, and proceeded to walk down the first baseline, following the teams that preceded us.

Among the thousands of boisterous fans, the first person I recognized was my mother. She had brought my grandfather to watch us play. Papa was still a spry man, even at the ripe age of eighty-eight. After all these years, his curly light brown hair still remained the envy of his peers, at least the one or two who had made it as far as he had. He wore blue shorts and a white T-shirt that hung loosely over his stick-thin torso.

Papa pumped his fists in the air, and cheered for his beloved grandson and great-grandsons. I had never seen him so excited. He had lived through the Great Depression and had served in World War II. He could bear witness to Watergate, Vietnam, and the crumbling of the Berlin Wall. He had seen quite a lot in his time, but in all his long years, he had never seen anything quite like this. Papa had desperately wanted a professional ballplayer in the family, and this was as close as he was going to get.

My mother sat next to him. She was in her early sixties but looked far younger. Her long hair, dyed brown, fell close to the middle of her back, and, at times, could still be seen pulled back in a ponytail. Her skin remained smooth, with only the faintest of lines. But the vision of this young and open-minded product of the 1960s was overshadowed by the narrow-mindedness that had consumed her with age.

"You're craaaaaaazy! You're craaaaaaazy!" she yelled down at me from just a few rows up in the stands.

Mom had always done things her way, and if I did something that didn't fit into her entrenched view of the world, well, then, I was crazy. At that moment in time, she wasn't able to fit what we were doing into her schema of familiar choices or experiences, and so it qualified me as certifiable. Maybe she was right. I smiled and gave her a tip of my cap.

Making our way along the right field foul line toward the bleachers, we came upon the majority of our fan base. The Rashi families cheered long and loudly for their representatives in the tournament, and we responded with smiles and waves. Sheryl blew me a kiss, and Shani held up her hand, crossing two fingers in our long-shared tradition that indicated how close we were to one another. I reciprocated the gestures to the two most important women in my life.

The teams were then directed to line up in the outfield facing home plate, and we each took off our cap while silence fell among the crowd. Lou's voice sounded over the loudspeaker. "And now please welcome team mom Nancy Merlino, who will sing the national anthem!"

Nancy stepped up to the microphone that awaited her on the pitcher's mound. She remained quiet for a moment to let the crowd settle down. Then her voice floated across the field and into the stands.

"Oh, say can you see, by the dawn's early light . . ."

One thousand ballplayers mouthed the words along with their coaches, families, and friends. One and all watched Nancy with admiration before shifting their gaze to the large American flag whipping in the breeze above the stadium. I caught Gabe's eye and he smiled excitedly.

The other three coaches and I stood side by side. My right hand clenched the bill of my cap, which I held over my chest as we swayed to and fro. I took in the moment as Nancy finished her rendition of Francis Scott Key's original poem.

"O'er the land of the free . . . and the . . . home . . . of the . . . brave!" Stan stood next to me, singing loudly. Our eyes met and he smiled just before the crowd erupted in furious cheers.

SATURDAY NIGHTS AT CDP were reserved for the skills competitions—group or individual contests that pitted teams against one another in various baseballs drills. It was considered a "low-key" way to kick off the week, prior to the start of the actual games.

We sat in foul territory on Field No. 3, waiting for our turn at "Around the Horn," an event where each team threw the ball in a set pattern to all nine positions. The team clocking the fastest time would win.

Gabe, Phil, and Sam had already represented us in the individual contests. The coaches selected Gabe for the "Golden Arm" competition, as his was one of the best on our team. His throws from center consistently fell ten feet short of the target, however, and he finished in the bottom third. Phil, being the fastest of our group, served as our representative in the "Road Runner." Unfortunately, fast in Newton was not the same as fast in Cooperstown, and he suffered a fate similar to his friend's. There was never a doubt that Sam would be our nominee for the home run challenge, "King of Swat." If he didn't hit one out, at least he would maintain our dignity by making contact with the balls lobbed in by the JUGS machine. And indeed he did make contact, but not enough to fare better than his teammates.

With the individual events now behind us, I stood with my fellow coaches and watched other teams perform the final drill. It was immediately apparent that we were ill prepared. "Around the Horn" was not simply "Around the Horn." Many of the teams had concocted elaborate schemes for their players to back one another up. Each player who had completed a throw would run to stand behind a teammate who would receive the ball two or three tosses later. During practice, we had worked hard on teaching the boys where to make the throw, but it had not even occurred to us to teach them how to back up one another. The oversight was sure to mark us as novices. I felt a tug at my sleeve.

"Josh, why didn't you teach us that?" Rami asked.

"Because they're as poorly prepared as we are," Jeff Goodman explained before I had a chance to formulate a response.

Jeremy watched the other teams with disgust. He could handle the fact that we were physically inferior to everyone else in the park, but he took personal pride in being mentally prepared.

"Ugh!" he said. "That was so obvious."

"Don't worry everyone," I responded. "Just focus on making the catches, and we won't need some complicated plan to back each other up."

The stands were still overflowing, the crowds cheering for each and every throw. I looked up to see people of all ages, men and women, critiquing each team. The sun was near setting and the stadium lights had been turned on as the contest continued.

"Rashi Rams! You're up!" one of the CDP staffers called out.

"All right, guys, go take your positions. Take it slow out there. Do your best," I told them. Gabe and Phil stood by my side as the rest of the team ran out onto the field and took up their spots. There could be only nine players in this drill, and I reluctantly left two of my best on the bench so that everyone would have a chance to participate in the opening-night festivities.

Carlos was on the mound. It was a short throw from there to the plate and I thought it might be his best chance for success. Sam Budd served as catcher, an important position, as he had two throws to make in the routine. Gil Slotnick manned third; Jeff Goodman, short; Rami was at second; and Robert Matz, first. The outfield consisted of Charlie in right, Ari in center, and Jason Armon holding down his usual position in left.

The kids were given the green light, and Carlos started off well by throwing the ball gently down to Sam behind the plate. Our very first team-oriented baseball activity done in public had been a success, and I heaved a great sigh of relief. Sam threw down to Gil at third, and it looked as if things were going pretty smoothly.

But then, just as I was starting to relax, I noticed something fascinating unfold. Inexplicably, as the ball started working its way around the infield, Carlos began chasing after it. The ball was thrown from catcher to third, and Carlos ran at breakneck speed from his spot on the mound to the base, putting the brakes on just a few feet in front of Gil. Then as the ball was thrown over to second he did the same, not backing up the play but for some unknown reason just chasing after it. It was a credit to the rest of the team that they were able to stay focused during the bizarre distraction.

I looked up into the stands to see many fans pointing and questioning. They were confused. Had this team come up with some new and impressive strategy to back up its throws? I grabbed Jeremy by the neck in total panic, looking for an explanation.

"What the heck is he doing?"

"Don't worry," Jeremy said, doing his best to think it through. In seconds, he had an answer. "We're just the first team in the history of Cooperstown Dreams Park to be 'fronting up' our throws. See how he positions himself in front of the player that's receiving the ball? If it bounces off that person's chest, he's set up perfectly to make the play."

Ultimately, the ball made it out of the infield, off to Charlie in right and then to Ari in center, both of whom performed well. But on the final throw, which had to go from left field back to home plate, Jason Armon threw it into the third base dugout. Gil graciously retrieved it and tossed it over to Sam. For better or for worse, the Rams' first challenge was complete.

"Son of a bitch!" Jason swore as he jogged off the field.

GIVEN THE CIRCUMSTANCES and despite everything that was stacked against us, the "Rushi" Rams performed reasonably well in "Around the Horn." We finished with a barely respectable mid-forty-second performance, whereas the top teams completed the drill in the mid-twenties. If we were only half as bad as the best, I could live with that.

The Rams clapped one another on the back, and the smacks of high fives were heard all around. They had completed the first team activity without any nightmarish disasters, and that was enough for them. We bought the boys pizza, which they gulped down hungrily while sitting in the stands and watching the teams that followed us.

"Not bad, hey, Josh?" Robert Matz, ever the optimist, asked me as we each sat with slice in hand.

"Yeah, you guys did pretty well out there," I responded.

"Do you think that means we're going to win some games in this thing?" Phil questioned.

"Not a chance in the world," Sam Budd said as he took a ravenous bite out of his piece of pizza. "My Little League team that won our division last year couldn't win a game in this tournament—let alone us."

Phil Perlow's face dropped at the disappointing news.

"Don't listen to him, Phil," Gabe jumped into the debate. "We'll win at least one game. I'm sure of it."

"Wanna bet?" Sam said, sticking out his hand to seal the deal.

Gabe looked up at him. They wore identical blue Cooperstown uniforms, their outfits matching to a T; however, Gabe's head came just short of Sam's shoulders. The rest of the team inched closer to hear the terms of the arrangement.

Robert, Jason, and Gil stood behind Sam, offering their support. "You know he's right, Gabe. There's no way we're going to win." Robert said, looking up at Sam for approval.

"Yeah, there's no way," Gil seconded.

Gabe looked over at his troops in an effort to shore up his confidence.

"I don't know," Charlie said. "I hate to admit it, Gabe, but Sam may be right." He ran a hand through his tall, thick brown hair, and it was momentarily lost from sight.

Gabe eyed Ari, but his younger cousin just shrugged his shoulders. He agreed with Charlie.

"Okay, what's the deal?" Gabe said to Sam.

"If I win, when we go back to school in the fall and the teacher asks how the summer went, you stand up in front of the whole class and tell them how we were the worst team here and how badly we stunk!" Sam negotiated, glowing with pride at his creativity.

"And if I win," Gabe responded. "You apologize to Phil for picking on him . . ."

"Deal," Sam interjected.

"I'm not finished. Also, you promise never to pick on him again."

Sam thought it over as his posse whispered back and forth, debating what he would do. Phil stood silently next to Gabe, hoping that the deal would go through.

There really wasn't much downside for him.

Finally, with the pros and cons having been weighed and the enticing vision of Gabe's publicly admitting our failures in front of the Rashi fifth grade dancing before his eyes, Sam came to a conclusion.

"Deal," he said.

"Deal," Gabe responded, shaking Sam's large hand, which enveloped his own.

And the bet was on.

CHAPTER SIXTEEN

THE ISRAELITES TREMBLED

"ALL RIGHT, GUYS, I need everyone's opinion. What should we do?"

It was Sunday morning, just hours before our first game was scheduled to start. We had two games that day. The first was to be against the Tustin Extreme from California. We knew little about them, but I expected the worst. Warm-weather states typically produced the best talent, and a team that had made the commitment to travel 2,500 miles to play in the tournament was likely to pose a challenge for us.

We woke early, and after dressing in our home red uniforms, made our way down to the tent for breakfast. The mess hall was overflowing with players and coaches. Everyone was in uniform, waiting for morning or early afternoon games. The Rams sat at one of the picnic tables, jockeying for position, tossing cereal at one another and heatedly debating the merits of the previous night's bet between Sam and Gabe.

Adam, Jeremy, Stan, and I sat at the table next to them, continuing our own debate that had been ongoing for a couple of weeks. Our starting catcher, Aaron Dines, was not scheduled to arrive in Cooperstown until that evening. In fact, at that very moment back in Newton, he was suiting up to play in the championship game for his Little League team. The problem was clear—Sam Budd was our backup catcher, but of course, also our best pitcher.

"We've got to start Sam on the mound," Adam argued as he had done multiple times before we arrived in Cooperstown. "We have no other choice."

"Gabe can pitch," I said. "I'm confident he can do it. Besides, if we don't start Sam at catcher, then I've got to put Gabe behind the plate. I'm not sure he can handle that." Gabe was our emergency third-string catcher, but I desperately hoped never to be forced to use him.

"Doesn't matter," Adam persisted between mouthfuls of Froot Loops. "We have to start our ace in game one. We have no choice. Start Gabe on the hill and you might as well change our team name from the Rashi Rams to the Sacrificial Lambs."

"Clever," I said. "But there *is* a choice to be made. What does it matter if Sam throws strikes, when every pitch goes to the backstop? You do remember that we're playing with major-league rules here, don't you? You know, steals, pass balls, and such?"

"You asked for my opinion. I'm giving it," Adam said and went back to eating his cereal.

"What do you think, Jeremy?"

"I think Adam's right. We've got to go with Sam."

"Stan?" I asked for a third opinion.

"I trust you, Josh. You decide," he said casually.

I thought about it for a few more minutes, while the coaches quietly ate breakfast. Looking over to the other table where my son was talking to his friends, I observed the lines of his face and his body language. He was calm and composed.

"Sorry, guys, but we're going with Gabe," I said. "It just makes the most sense to me."

Adam shook his head in dismay, Jeremy shrugged his shoulders, and Stan nodded his approval. The decision made, my attention was quickly diverted elsewhere.

"Josh, where do I get my kosher food?"

I turned to see Rami Liebshutz standing next to me, his chin just reaching the height of our table. A shock of brown hair took up the majority of what could be seen of him. I was thunderstruck, having completely forgotten about the promise I had made to his mother. With all the stress and anxiety I had been dealing with since arriving at Dreams Park, I had neglected to follow through on one of my most important assignments.

"What have you been eating since we've been here, Rami?"

"Well, I'm allowed to have this cereal," he said, holding up a small box of Rice Krispies. "And I can eat fruit, and they have prepackaged peanut butter and jelly sandwiches at lunch. That's about it. But everyone else in this place is having bacon and eggs for breakfast. That's just not fair," he said.

"Hang on. I'll see what I can do."

I walked up to the front of the tent near the food line and spoke to one of the servers. It was last minute and I didn't have high hopes, but maybe they were prepared for unique food requests.

"Hi, can I please speak to the head of the mess hall?"

"Sure, hang on," he said, calling into the back of the tent where a small, closed-off area functioned as the kitchen. "Al, coach here wants to speak to you!"

A few moments later, a bald-headed man with a potbelly emerged from the back. He wore an apron stained dark with black and brown grease. The original color of the thing could no longer be ascertained.

"What can I do for ya, Coach?" he asked, his baritone voice deep and rumbling.

"Well, I was wondering if there was any chance you could assist us. We're a Jewish team that's here from Massachusetts and one of our players is kosher. There's not much here that he can eat. Have you ever had any players here who were kosher?"

"Kosh—what?" he looked at me, confused.

"You know, kosher . . . the traditional laws that some Jewish people follow regarding what food they can and cannot eat."

"Oh, yeah, right—kosher—well, I don't think we've ever had any kosher kids here before. Not that I can recall."

"So you can't make any special accommodations?"

"Wish I could help you out, Coach."

"All right, we'll make do. Thanks anyway."

"Anytime, Coach," he said and walked away.

I returned to the table and motioned Rami to my side. "For now you're gonna have to make do with the peanut butter and jelly, fruit, and cereal, buddy," I said.

He nodded as if he expected as much. "Okay, Josh, and don't worry, I won't tell my mother. This'll remain between the two of us."

"I don't want you lying to your mother, Rami," I said guiltily.

"Okay, Josh, but trust me on this one. Lying is probably the way to go."

BY THE TIME we finished breakfast, the early games were well under way, and we took the team down to the fields to see some of the action. There were four scheduled times when games were played: seven or eleven in the morning and three in the afternoon or seven in the evening. Each team played two games per day, one during an early slot and then again during a late one.

The sun was shining brightly as we exited the Baseball Village and walked toward the entrance of the park, where many of the fields were located. Picking a game at random, we filed through the guest entrance and found ourselves in the right-field bleachers, looking out across the diamond.

The game was a contest between the Blue Devils, hailing from Fresno, California, and the Lakeshore Graysox, out of Maryland. We watched with intense curiosity, it being the first time we had seen any of our competition ply their true craft.

The play was as good as advertised. Balls were thrown crisply and cleanly, pitching was fast and accurate, and the base running was smart and sharp. These kids were not just equivalent to very good Little League players; they were something entirely different. It was baseball being played in a manner that previously I would have felt impossible for ten-year olds. It had the appearance of a professional game, only with smaller players.

Gabe stood by my side, watching in silence. I could feel his tension mounting.

"Gabe, you know that Aaron is not coming until tonight, right?" I asked him.

"Sure, Dad, I know."

"So we have to start Sam at catcher," I explained.

"Makes sense," he responded.

"Do you understand what that means?"

"Yeah, I'm the starting pitcher," he said flatly.

"That's right," I said, putting my arm around his shoulder. We stood watching as one of the Blue Devils knocked a screaming line drive into the gap in left center. Moments later, he slid head first into second with a double. "Are you okay with that?" I asked.

It was a loaded question and he knew it. Could he take the pressure? Could he pitch our first game in full uniform, in front of family, friends, and strangers, with all our dignity on the line?

He looked up at me with his beautiful oval face and stared for a moment. After thinking over the question, he gave a simple but honest answer.

"I'll do my best, Dad," he said.

"RAMS, I WOULD like to read you a story from the Bible. I'm sure that you've heard it before, but I feel that it's particularly relevant today."

It was approaching game time, and we had returned to the cabin for final preparations. The boys were jittery as they sat on their bunk beds and black trunks, listening in silence to the pregame speech. They were in full uniform. Cleats had been tied and retied so as to get the laces just right. Shirts were tucked in and then pulled out just so. The sun shone outside, but with few windows the cabin was cast in shadows.

I pulled a folded paper from my pocket and opened it, reading aloud: "A long time ago, the people of Israel were at war with their old enemies, the Philistines. During one very important battle, the armies of the Israelites and Philistines faced each other from opposite sides of a hill. Each day, the Philistines sent their champion, Goliath, who was fully armed and gigantic in size to shout across the valley.

"'Choose a man to fight with me, and if he is able to kill me, then we will be your servants. If I kill him, then you shall serve us.'

"The Israelites trembled as they heard the voice of Goliath. Nobody was brave or strong enough to fight with the giant Philistine. But one day, a small shepherd boy named David came to the Israelite camp. He heard the words of Goliath and was amazed at the fear of the people of Israel.

"'I will go and fight with this Philistine,' David said.

"When the king heard of David's intention, he tried to stop him. 'David, you are just a boy and the Philistine is a giant warrior.'

"But David replied, 'The Lord will deliver me.'

"The king relented, and allowed David to challenge Goliath. With only his shepherd's sling and a few stones, David went to confront the giant.

"Goliath was angry when he saw that the Israelites had sent a shepherd boy to meet him.

"'Am I a dog that you come to me with sticks and stones?' Goliath shouted.

"'You are a man like any other,' David responded. 'The Lord shall deliver you into my hands.'

"David ran fearlessly toward the Philistine giant, slipping one of the stones into his sling. He skillfully slung it, hitting Goliath in the forehead, and he fell to the ground. When the Philistine army saw that their champion was dead, they fled the battle. David was the hero of the people of Israel," I said, ending the story.

Looking up, I quietly surveyed the team. There was complete and utter silence. I had their attention as never before.

"Rashi Rams, you are David. The teams you'll face today and the rest of this week are the Philistine giant, Goliath. You must confront them head on and without fear." I stopped momentarily, and they stared at me enthralled. "Boys," I said, finishing my pregame speech. "Let's go out there today and sling some stones."

A great cheer erupted from Bunk 18, which to this day may still be reverberating among the rolling hills of upstate New York.

TOGETHER, WE HOISTED our duffle bags full of equipment onto our backs, and made our way across the Baseball Village to our destination. Remarkably, it was Field No. 18 upon which our Cooperstown baseball career was to be christened, or perhaps circumcised, as the case may be. It was the third number eighteen that we had come across in the short time that we had been there, and I was beginning to actually think that there might be some meaning behind it.

Field No. 18 was on the far side of the park, an area we had yet to visit. We found it easily, however, as many teams were heading in that direction, while others were returning from battles already fought there.

Jeremy walked by my side, and we talked as we went.

"I did some research on the Tustin Extreme," he said.

"Let's hear it."

"They're from Tustin, California, and this is their second or third year at Dreams Park. Last year they only won three out of eight games. This may not be a bad team for us to start out with."

"How did you find all that out?" I asked.

"Listen, this is what I do for a living. I research. Usually its companies and multimillion-dollar businesses, but I can apply my skills to a youth baseball team when necessary."

"What else did you discover?"

"One of their starting outfielders is a girl, the head coach's daughter."

"Interesting," I said. "If you come up with anything else, let me know."

We walked on, passing by other games. A few were still ongoing, while many had just finished. Players and coaches milled about, discussing outcomes, strategy, and schedules. Fans rushed to and fro, desperate not to miss a single pitch. There were parents and siblings, friends and family, many who had traveled thousands of miles to root for their loved ones.

We were the first to arrive at our field and entered through the home door, dropping our equipment in the dugout along the third baseline. Every one of our hearts was hammering away furiously as we looked out over the diamond. As with every field at the park, it was perfectly groomed. The grass had been fastidiously trimmed and the infield dirt was without rock, stone, or blemish. The team was silent and edgy.

"Guys, do you know the movie *Hoosiers?*" I said. Most of them nodded.

"Do you remember when Gene Hackman's team arrives at the state finals in that huge gym and everyone is panicked looking at how big it is?"

"Yeah, I remember," said Robert.

"Well, what does the coach do to settle them down?"

"He has them measure the height of the hoop!" Robert gushed. "So they can see that it's the same as back home!"

"That's right, Robert," I said. "And this is a baseball diamond like any other. And we will play on it the way we have played and practiced on our fields at Pierce and Cabot back home."

"There's a problem," Jeff Goodman piped up.

"What's that, Jeff?" I asked.

"These base paths are sixty feet long. That's ten feet longer than what we practiced on at home. And the distance from the mound to home is forty-eight feet here, two feet longer than what our pitchers are used to."

"Jeffrey," Stan said with admiration in his voice. "Good for you for analyzing the diamond's dimensions. That's very good planning. I'm proud of you."

"Thanks, Dad," Jeff responded giving him a hug around the waist.

"Well, no matter," I said to the rest of the team. "It's still baseball."

"Yeah, but them ain't Milton's Marauders," Adam said, pointing across the diamond as the Tustin Extreme entered the visitor's dugout.

The opposing team came in, dropped their bags, and without delay ran into right field to warm up. We stood there watching as they assembled into a large circle and began stretching, each player doing the same exercise for the same precise length of time. While we stared transfixed, they formed into two even lines, each pair of players fifteen feet across from his or her partner. Baseballs materialized from their gloves and the duos began tossing them back and forth.

"Go out to left field and do what they're doing!" I yelled to the team.

The Rams scurried into the outfield and paired off in a predictable manner—Sam and his cronies in one section, Gabe with his friends in another. They began throwing balls back and forth.

Meanwhile, the left-field stands adjacent to our dugout started to fill with our fans. Most of the players had family who had come for the week, and the clicking of cameras soon could be heard along with shouts of encouragement. I noticed David Perlow pacing back and forth, wringing his hands while watching his son warm up. Melissa Liebshutz tracked Rami's every movement with a video camera. My mother and grandfather took seats in the front row.

"HEAD COACHES! COME to home plate!" The umpire

called to both dugouts.

I looked over at Adam. "Get the boys in," I said. "I'm going to the managers' conference."

"Good luck," he responded.

I had never attended the traditional pregame meeting between coaches and umpires, and so had no idea what to expect. Jeremy shoved our lineup card into my hand just before I left the dugout.

"I think you'll need this," he said.

Walking slowly to home plate, I did my best to appear confident, as if I had done this many times over. The umpire was tall, perhaps in his early thirties, and carried a large chest protector held at one side. His mask was pulled up to the top of his head.

"Nice to meet you, Coach," he said, shaking my hand.

"Pleasure," I returned the greeting, waiting for my counterpart from the Extreme to arrive. He appeared to be about my age and we were dressed similarly, in light brown shorts and navy blue CDP coach's polo shirt. It had taken me only a day to discover it was the standard attire.

"How ya doin', Coach?" he said casually as he approached. We shook hands as I prayed silently that he wouldn't notice the moistness of my palm.

"I assume you guys know Dreams Park rules. It's basically the same as the majors. If a ball goes under the fence, play will be stopped; otherwise, you know the drill. Any questions?" the umpire asked.

We had none.

"Then, Rams, you guys take the field."

I turned, relieved that I had escaped unscathed from

my first umpire's meeting, and began walking back toward the dugout. But before getting far, I was stopped dead in my tracks.

"Coach," the umpire called after me. He had one final question. "Forgot to ask . . . is your team properly equipped?"

I froze and panicked. For the life of me, I had no idea what he was talking about. Did we have our gloves? Were we in our uniforms? I stammered momentarily, thinking of a way to buy time, and then thankfully it hit me. He was asking if our catcher was wearing his protective cup. I breathed a sigh of relief, nodded in ascent and walked back to the dugout, feeling that I had performed rather well in my first managers' conference.

The umpire signaled once again for us to take the field, and I gathered the team in a circle in front of the dugout for a few final words.

"This is it, guys," I said, looking into their faces. "Are we ready?" I asked.

"Ready," they responded.

"Gil," I said, looking at him, "what is the Hebrew word for 'defense'?"

"*Haganah*," the son of Israelis responded.

"*Haganah* it is," I said. "Hands in, on three." Fifteen hands met in the middle of our huddle.

"One, two, three . . . *HAGANAH!*" The word came forth mightily. Hearing our cheer, the Tustin Extreme looked at us from their dugout in bewilderment. The Rams disbanded. The time had finally come.

"Well, this is it," I repeated to Adam who was standing next to me. "Can a group of Jewish boys from a small day school in Newton, Massachusetts, keep pace with an all-star team from California?"

"Your question is about to be answered," Adam replied.

The Rashi Rams took the field.

CHAPTER SEVENTEEN

THE SANDLOTS OF EVERETT

GABE DUG HIS black cleat into the dirt in front of the rubber, scooping out a small hole in which to plant his right foot. He looked small on the mound, but confident. His torso had yet to catch up to the growth of his long arms, but for now, that worked to his advantage. Wiping his right hand on his red jersey, he felt for the ball in his glove and adjusting it slightly, placed two fingers across the seams. A four-seam fastball would be his first pitch of the tournament.

The umpire called, "Play ball!," and Gabe risked a quick glance over to the dugout, where our eyes met for an instant. I wiped all doubt from my face and gave him a half smile and a firm nod.

"Go get 'em, kid!"

He smiled back and turned to face the batter.

Pitching from the stretch, as his cousin Jordan had taught him during our trip to Florida so long ago, Gabe went into his windup and his body reached toward home. Released high over head, the ball sailed straight and true.

"If there was ever a moment when a young Jewish pitcher needed your blessing, this is it," I muttered to

Sandy Koufax, while standing in the dugout with fingers of both hands crossed behind my back. I felt Sandy's presence as Tustin's muscular leadoff hitter let it go by, and the ball landed with a thud in Sam's catcher's mitt.

"Strike one!" yelled the umpire.

"That-a-boy, Gaaaaaabriel!" I hollered out to him through the dugout screen.

"Nice pitch, Gabe!" Sam called from behind the plate. "Just like that!"

Gabe nodded, and after retrieving the ball, went back to his spot on the mound to begin again. The next pitch was a little outside.

"Ball!" called the ump.

"That's okay, Gabe. Stay focused now!" I yelled.

The batter worked the count full as I paced back and forth in the heat of the dugout. Small droplets of sweat, brought about from anxiety as much as from the temperature, formed on my forehead.

Just before the payoff pitch was thrown, I surveyed the team in the field and noticed a problem. Gil Slotnick, whom I had placed at third base, looked as if he were posing for a modeling shoot. He was the only player on the team to wear sunglasses, and they rested on the bridge of his nose just below the bill of his cap. He stood nonchalantly, glove hand tucked under his armpit and right hand on hip, as if he didn't have a care in the world.

Gil had probably seen the Tustin coach's ten-year-old daughter during warm-ups; he looked nothing short of a peacock with feathers on display. Her long blond ponytail was a serious distraction, and while she may or may not have been watching him from the dugout, he wasn't taking any chances.

"Gil, ready position!" I shouted just in time. Right at that moment, Gabe delivered his three-two pitch, and the leadoff batter promptly popped it up in the direction of third base. Gil, jarred back to reality by the sound of my voice, saw the ball coming toward him and casually raised his glove skyward. He never appeared to be working too hard. The ball went about twenty feet in the air and then slowly returned toward earth, where it landed gently in his outstretched glove.

"*Oogah*," he said as he tossed the ball to Rami at second, where it subsequently made its way around the infield. I looked at Adam and Jeremy, who were standing next to me. They were staring out at the Rams as if they had seen a miracle.

"We just made an out," Adam said. "I don't believe it."

"Yeah, only a hundred and forty-three more and we'll make it out of the tournament. Did you see that, Stan?" Jeremy asked.

We turned around to where Stan was sitting on the bench next to his son, who had not started the game. "I told you guys we weren't that bad," he smiled.

The contest proceeded. Gabe gave up a single to right, and on the next two pitches the runner easily stole around to third. The batter struck out, however, and with two outs and a man in scoring position, the cleanup hitter stepped to the plate. The fans on both sides of the field were yelling loudly now, but I heard one familiar voice rising above the rest.

"They can't hit you, Gabe! They know they can't touch you!"

I looked down the left field line to see my eighty-eight-year-old grandfather hanging over the low fence, screaming at the top of his lungs. He had worked himself into such a lather as the inning wore on that his face had turned beet red. His cheeks were hotter than the Cooperstown summer sun, and as he hollered, spittle flew over the fence to land in the foul territory at his feet. He soon became so boisterous that everyone on both sides of the stands and in the field began to curiously observe this new oddity. Unfortunately, even the umpires turned to see what was happening.

I stared at him incredulously, not believing this was actually occurring. And as I did so, the situation went from bad to worse.

"They're no good, Gabe! They can't hit you, Gabe!" Then ultimately, with the last bit of air remaining in his ancient lungs, Papa took it to an unimaginable level. "*THEY STINK, GABE!*" he bellowed. And with his opinion thus irrevocably declared, Papa finally doubled over the fence, gasping breathlessly, his emotional tirade complete.

My beloved grandfather had no idea that he had done anything out of the ordinary. Indeed, heckling like that was not only acceptable but the rule, when playing on the sandlots of Everett or Chelsea, Massachusetts, where he had been raised during the 1920s. He was completely unaware that in the present day, one simply did not show up for a youth baseball game and holler across the diamond that the other team stinks.

Despite my grandfather's blissful ignorance, not a single person on the field was amused, and his actions propelled me into an unusual out-of-body experience. My mind, so desperately wanting to escape, began to drift. I floated above the field and saw the scene from on high— the back of my grandfather's head as he hung over the fence gasping for air, the top of Gabe's cap pulled low over his face to hide his shame, and the front of the umpire's mask as he pushed it up, looking to our team for an explanation.

I was quickly dragged back to earth, however, when I saw the Extreme's third base coach approaching my mindless body, which was standing at the edge of the dugout. He was an older gentleman, sporting a gray beard and the typical coach's attire.

"You have some passionate fans over there," he said to my lifeless shell, kindly implying that I needed to take some action.

I returned to my body just in time to offer a feeble response. "Sorry . . . it's my grandfather . . . I'll see what I can do," I mumbled under my breath while staring at the ground and walking down the third base foul line toward the stands. The first person I saw there was Sheryl.

"Someone needs to shut down Papa," I said.

"I'll take care of it," she responded, and mercifully she did.

PAPA WAS BROUGHT to the back of the stands, where soothing words were whispered into his ear and a cold compress was placed upon his forehead. Gabe turned back to face Tustin's cleanup hitter and the game resumed. The batter adjusted his helmet, stepping into the box. He was a tall, lean kid who carried one of those thick bats that I had noticed earlier in the cages.

His intimidating presence, combined with Papa's distraction, caused Gabe to lose focus. Afraid to throw one down the heart of the plate, he tried to get the batter to chase. But his strategy backfired. The ball sailed wide, getting by Sam and rolling to the backstop. The runner on third raced home, and just like that, we were down one.

"Don't worry about it, Gabe!" I yelled to him. "Clean slate now. Just go after the batter!"

Gabe went back to work, and the next pitch was grounded up the middle. Phil Perlow charged the ball, backhanded it, and threw over to Robert Matz at first for the final out of the inning. As the team came off the field, I ran out of the dugout to greet them.

"Way to go, Rams. Good work!" I congratulated them, giving each a high five as he passed by. We emerged from our very first inning at Cooperstown Dreams Park, having allowed only one run.

I grabbed Phil in the dugout, as he was our leadoff hitter. "Remember, Phil, wait for your pitch and swing early. These guys throw harder than what we're used to."

"Josh, no worries. I can hit this guy," he said with his usual misplaced confidence. He pulled a pair of thick-rimmed dark sports glasses from his equipment bag, pushing them onto his nose and sliding the head strap over his ears.

"What the heck are those?" I asked, never having seen them before.

"My new special sports goggles. My dad got them for

me right before we left. They were really expensive. He thought I wasn't seeing the ball that well. I don't need them in the field, only when I'm hitting or pitching."

"All right, Clark Kent, whatever works for you. Just get on."

I wandered out to the third base coach's box and watched the Extreme's pitcher warming up. It was the tall, lanky kid who had just grounded out in the bottom of the inning. His delivery was all arms and legs, and the speed of the ball seemed to be at least twice that of what Gabe had been throwing.

Phil dug in from the left side, and stared down the third baseline. At first I was pleased to see that he was checking for a sign, but I soon realized that he was looking right past me, into the stands where his father was standing.

"Level swing now, Phil! Just like at home!" David called out to him. Phil dug in his left foot and curled his body tightly, waiting for the pitch to come. But when it did, it took him by surprise. The ball was in the catcher's mitt by the time he had started his swing.

"Strike one!" yelled the umpire.

"A little earlier, Phil!" I called. "You can do this!" But two pitches and two swings later, the umpire was back at it.

"You're out!" he called. Phil pulled off his dark glasses and looked down at them as if searching for an answer, then walked slowly back to the dugout, shaking his head. He found Sam Budd waiting there to greet him.

"Those glasses ain't gonna help much," Sam said. You're better off just closing your eyes."

"Don't worry, Phil." Gabe patted him on the back. "That guy's throwing heat."

Our next two batters did not improve on Phil's performance. Gil struck out on four pitches; and Sam Budd, our great hope, could only muster a ground out to the pitcher. Gabe and Phil chuckled as he returned to the dugout, slamming his bat into the rack.

"At least I made contact," he growled in frustration.

Before we knew it, we were hustling back out onto the field.

"C'mon, guys, let's hold 'em," Rami Liebshutz shared words of encouragement as he ran out to second base and started taking his warm-up grounders.

"Yeah, let's hold these sons of bitches!" Jason seconded Rami's idea while trotting out to left.

Gabe picked up the ball, which was sitting on the rubber and threw a few warm up pitches down to Sam.

"You're lookin' good, Gabe," Sam said. "You ready?"

"Ready," Gabe replied and the second inning began. The coach's daughter was the first batter Tustin sent to the plate. She was tall and lean with a blond ponytail that escaped from the back of her helmet to fall halfway down her back. It whipped back and forth furiously as she swung two bats in the on-deck circle. Dropping one of them, she stepped to the plate.

Gabe took off his cap and wiped a small amount of sweat from his brow. Then, digging his right foot into the small hole in front of the rubber, he let fly a fastball. The coach's daughter wasted no time. It looked good to her and she swung away, making solid contact. With a piercing ring, the ball flew off her bat and sailed high into centerfield.

Ari had been standing there, silently praying that no balls would come his way. But now he had no say in the matter. With heart in throat, he turned and ran backward toward the fence. His fast legs carried him quickly to the warning track, and with time to spare he settled underneath the towering fly ball. Shading his eyes from the sun, he raised his small black and brown Wilson A-450 glove, catching the ball just above his head. Ari looked at it quickly to make sure that what he thought had happened had indeed taken place. Then with a calm that I had never witnessed in him before, he threw the ball back into the infield.

Adam, Jeremy, and I began jumping up and down and screaming as we pumped our fists into the air.

"That's my son!" Adam called.

"Great catch, Ari!" I yelled.

"I didn't think that boy had ever played in an actual game before!" Jeremy screamed.

"He hadn't! Just the one against Milt's Marauders! That was it!" Adam screamed back as we hopped around in a circle chest-thumping each other.

"Why are we so excited?" Stan yelled from the bench.

"Because Ari made a catch!" we all screamed.

IT WENT DOWNHILL after that. A single, a stolen base, a walk, an error at shortstop, three more walks, and another single resulted in five runs. Finally, Gabe's second strikeout and another fly ball to Ari in center got us out of the inning but trailing six to nothing.

Our offense showed no signs of life. We were only able

to get three runners on base the entire game, all of them from walks. When Tustin scored their ninth run in the fifth inning, I finally pulled Gabe and gave the nod to Robert Matz for mop-up duty. Six hits, eight walks, and eleven runs later, the final out was made. The Rashi Rams trudged off the field, having lost twenty to nothing.

We lined up behind home plate and congratulated the Extreme on their definitive victory. As they passed by, hands were slapped and the proverbial "good game" was muttered back and forth from one line to the other. The Rams then turned on their heels and walked dejectedly back to the dugout.

"You pitched well, Gabe," Sam Budd said, coming up from behind him and throwing an arm over his shoulder.

"Thanks, Sam," Gabe replied, surprised by the compliment. He stretched his neck to look up at him. "You caught a good game—only one pass ball."

"That wasn't a pass ball. That was a wild pitch, man."

"Not so sure about that," Gabe said.

"Well, anyway, we lost. So that's one down. Pretty soon you're going to be blabbing your guts to the whole grade about how bad we were."

"Not so sure about that, either," Gabe said, and the two left the stadium side by side.

CHAPTER EIGHTEEN

PROPERLY EQUIPPED

"THAT WAS A tough one," Charlie said as he plopped down on his bed back at the bunkhouse. "I don't think any of us even made contact."

"I fouled one off," said Phil.

"Yeah, barely," Rami interjected, throwing his CDP cap onto the floor in disgust.

"Listen, guys, it's not like we lost to Schecter or something," Gabe said, referring to Rashi's archrival, another Jewish day school back home. "These guys are good. I think we held our own pretty well."

"I agree," I said to the boys as they sat on their beds kicking off their cleats. "Listen, we were only down nine to nothing after five innings. That's better than I expected."

"That is, until Robert took the mound," Sam Budd announced.

"Sorry, Sam. I did the best I could," Robert pleaded his case.

"That you did, Robert, and I'm sure things will work out better next time," I said. "Now listen, guys, you'd better get some rest. We have our second game right after dinner.

"Who are we playing, Coach?" Rami asked. I reared my head back in surprise.

"What did you call me?" I asked.

"Well you're our coach, aren't you?" Rami challenged.

"Yes, I am, Rami. I am your coach."

"Well then, Coach, who are we playing?"

"We're playing the Westfield Rocks, our bunkmates," I replied.

The Rocks, who hailed from Indiana, were living on the other side of our cabin. At that moment, only a thin wall separated us. "Maybe this one will be a little more competitive."

"Coach, what will we do if Aaron doesn't show up?" Jeff Goodman asked as he picked up one of his books and began to leaf through it.

In all the stress that I had experienced over our game against the Tustin Extreme, I had completely forgotten about Aaron Dines. He was scheduled to arrive sometime that afternoon, but as of yet, I had heard nothing from his mother.

"Don't worry about it, Jeff," I said. "I'm sure that he'll be here in time."

"And if he isn't?" Jeff persisted.

"Then I'll put you behind the plate, Jeff," I said flatly. He looked up from his book.

"Seriously?"

"No, Jeff. Not seriously."

AT 6:40 P.M., the mind killer came for me with a vengeance. After dinner, the Rams had gone back to the bunk and changed into their visiting blue uniforms. Then making an about-face, we headed out of the Baseball Village and toward the front of the park for our evening tilt. The game against the Rocks was to take place at Field No. 4, one of the larger stadiums located near CDP's entrance. It was likely that we would have an even bigger crowd than was on hand for the afternoon debacle.

As we walked toward the field, we passed players, coaches, and fans coming and going from other games. The park lights came to life as the sun sat low on the horizon. Game time was at seven that evening, and twenty minutes beforehand I still had heard nothing from Aaron Dines or his mother.

Hoping against hope, I had one of the boys bring Aaron's uniform down to the field, but as the minutes ticked away and there was no sign of him, I realized that I would have to start Gabe behind the plate. There was no other option.

I opened the visiting team's door to Field No. 4 and stepped inside, the Rams trailing behind me.

"Aaron!"

Twisting quickly and sticking my head back outside, I saw Charlie Finkelstein standing and pointing. My eyes traced the path of his outstretched hand, and there, cresting a small hill near the park's entrance, came Aaron Dines, starting catcher for the Rashi Rams.

He was still in the Little League uniform he had worn that morning, knees stained brown from the dirt that had collected on them while performing his duties as catcher during their championship game. He walked casually with his left hand in his pocket, while the right held a cell phone to his ear. His mother marched behind, hauling his duffle bag as if she were expecting a big tip for her efforts.

"Who is he talking to, his stockbroker?" Adam asked as we all stood and stared.

"Beats me," I said. "But, man, I've never been happier to see anyone in my life."

I looked down at my watch—6:50 p.m., ten minutes until game time. "Thank you, Lord," I said, looking to the heavens. "Thank you."

"I CAN'T TELL you how glad I am that you guys have a private jet, Joyce," I said, grabbing Aaron's duffle bag and ushering her toward the visitor's gate of Field No. 4. "Aaron, come with me."

We hustled over to the public restroom that was connected to the refreshment stand directly adjacent to the stadium. I shoved Aaron into the nearest stall and threw his Dreams Park blue uniform in with him.

"Get dressed quickly. The game starts in five minutes."

Leaning against the outside of the stall, I heard Aaron's voice resonate from underneath the green metal barrier.

"I'm not wearing a jock strap and this cup won't stay in place." I had included a protective cup in the bag with his uniform.

"Just stick it in your underwear, and hurry," I responded urgently.

"It won't stay in place and it's uncomfortable. I'm not wearing it."

"You don't have a choice, Aaron," I said. As the words

left my mouth, the cup came flying over the top of the stall to land in one of the sinks standing in a row behind me.

"Either I play without it or I don't play," he said abruptly.

There was no time to argue. "Fine," I said. "Let's just get going."

We ran from the bathroom and into the visitor's dugout of Field No. 4 with forty-five seconds to spare.

"COACH, IS YOUR team properly equipped?" the heavyset umpire asked, staring right through me. It was my second manager's meeting of the day, and I stood at home plate uncomfortably shifting my feet as the game's two umpires and the head coach of the Westfield Rocks awaited my response.

The Rams and Rocks had already warmed up in their respective outfields. As visitors, our dugout was along the first baseline and our fans gathered a short distance away in the right-field stands. The Rams had practiced with their usual partners, the team's fault line easy to recognize. The Rocks appeared a more united front.

Physically, the opposition's players painted a sharp contrast to our own. Each of them had blond hair clipped tight to the head. If more than a quarter inch remained it must have been considered long by Indiana standards. Their coach was the same, clean-cut, trim, with blond hair buzzed to the scalp. It was hard not to wince under the pressure of his firm handshake.

"Coach," the home plate umpire repeated. "I asked if your team was properly equipped."

I hesitated. Risking a potentially embarrassing scene by arguing with Aaron about sticking the cup in his underwear was not something I was willing to do. Besides, who knew how helpful it would be to have the thing floating around in there, anyway? On the other hand, I couldn't very well admit to the ump that our starting catcher was without protection. I resorted to my only option.

"Uh . . . yeah, Ump . . . we're properly equipped," I lied.

"LET'S GO, PHIL. Start us off now!" I called from the third base coach's box. As the visiting team, we were to hit first and Phil was leading off. Dozens of family and friends on both sides of the bleachers were shouting words of encouragement, and I again saw David Perlow pacing in the stands. My mother had Papa sitting in the rear for this game. I saw her rubbing the back of his neck gently in an attempt to keep him calm and also to afford easy access to his shirt collar should she feel the need to restrain him.

Once again putting on his black framed sports goggles, Phil stepped into the left-hand batter's box and dug in. The Rocks right-handed pitcher appeared to be throwing slower than had Tustin's starter, and I realized that because this was their second game of the day as well, we were likely not seeing their ace.

The ball flew through the air between mound and home plate, to land at Phil's feet.

"Ball one!" called the ump. Phil stepped out of the box and looked around.

"Good eye, Phil! Good eye!" his father called from the stands. Phil stepped back in, waiting for the next one. It sailed high.

"Ball two!" called the umpire.

"Wait for yours, Phil," I instructed. "Wait for yours!" Two more balls followed, and we had a leadoff walk on four pitches.

"Nice job, Philster!" I called. "You're glasses worked that time, buddy!"

Phil jogged down to first base and stood there staring at me. I was confused, thinking that he might be upset about the sarcastic glasses comment. But as he kept staring, I suddenly realized that he was waiting for a sign. We had so few runners during the first game that I hadn't even had the chance to give one.

After touching the brim of my cap, I rubbed both hands together then reached down and tapped my right foot. If Phil read it correctly, he would be off on the next pitch.

Aaron Dines stepped out of the on-deck circle and up to the plate. He took a few practice swings before entering the batter's box.

"Let's go, Aaron! Let's make some contact!" I called.

The pitcher started his abbreviated windup and released the ball. Phil watched closely, and with the first move toward the plate, he bolted for second, beating the throw with ease. He took another cautious lead while Aaron worked the count to two and two, before striking out swinging.

Sam Budd was up next. Stepping in, he eyed the pitcher with hostility. Sam was absolutely furious at not

having had a hit in the first game, fearing for his reputation as the best athlete in the Rashi School. The Rocks'
pitcher threw one wide and then caught the corner with
a strike, but with the count one and one, he made a tremendous mistake, grooving a fastball right down the
middle. Sam's eyes widened in anticipation as he let
loose with a smooth swing, making solid contact. The
ball rocketed out into right center field, landing in the
gap and rolling to the wall.

Phil was on the move, and as he approached third
base, I frantically waved him in. He crossed home plate
to thunderous cheers from our fans, scoring the Rams'
first run of the tournament. He ran over to our dugout,
where he was greeted with a sea of slaps on the back
and helmet.

With Sam's double landing him on second, Gil
Slotnick walked to the plate. He still wore his shades despite the fact that the sun had basically set, and with
the glasses on, it couldn't have been possible for him to
see more than two feet in front of his face. Despite the
handicap, Gil was able to ground out to second while ad-
vancing Sam to third. And with two outs, Gabe came up
to hit. Before stepping in, he looked down the third baseline.

"All right, Gabey. Here we go. Wait for your pitch," I
called. He nodded and entered the box.

A minute later Gabe had worked the count to two and
two and was fighting with everything he had, desperately trying to get the run home. The Rocks' pitcher graciously assisted him, however, as the fifth pitch of the
encounter dropped into the dirt, scooting by the catcher

to the backstop. Gabe jumped from the plate, waving Sam home. The catcher grabbed the ball and flung it to the pitcher running in to cover, but Sam slid under the tag, scoring our second run of the game.

As Gabe swung and missed on strike three, I looked up at the scoreboard in disbelief. HOME: 0 VISITORS: 2, it read, and I blinked twice to make sure that it was not a dream. Running into the dugout from third base, I found the team in full-blown celebration mode.

"Dude, I can't freakin' believe it! We actually scored a run!" Jason Armon said, slamming his fist against the bench to emphasize his point.

"Two runs!" Rami screamed.

"We're up two to nothing! Do you believe it?" Robert said.

Charlie weaved in and out among the players, shaking his head back and forth while talking furiously. "Yeah, I had no idea that Phil was going to walk. And did you see how easily he stole second? It was a piece of cake. And I didn't know that Sam would be able to hit these pitchers. That's, like, unbelievable. And what about Gabe drawing a wild pitch like that. Did you know that was going to happen, Gabe?"

The team as a whole was ready to bring in the champagne and celebrate the night away. They likely would have just kept on going, but for Adam interrupting them.

"Excuse me, gentlemen, I agree that was a good *top half of the first inning*, but do you realize we have the rest of the game to play? Get out onto the field! Everyone's waiting for us!" He screamed the last as loud as he could.

"LET'S GO, A.J.! Let's go, A.J.!" the words of encouragement came from the Rocks' dugout as their leadoff hitter came to the plate. I had seen A.J. hanging around our bunk earlier in the day and noticed that he always had one or two of his teammates trailing after him. A small kid with the trademark Rocks' blond crew cut, it was clear that he was one of their leaders.

Sam Budd took to the mound for the first time, and he looked the part. His height and build made him an intimidating presence, and he threw with enough velocity that with his teammates focused, we actually looked, for a moment, as if we belonged. Sam wiped his right hand on his blue CDP uniform and went into his windup. The first pitch sped in at sixty miles per hour, and unfortunately sped out even faster. A.J. got hold of it, spanking it into left field for a base hit. Jason picked up the ball and threw it into second.

"Don't worry about it, Sam," Gabe called from third base. "Get the next one!"

Sam stomped his feet in anger and got back to work. As he went into his windup, A.J. took off for second. The jump was so good that Aaron didn't even throw down. The next pitch was grounded to Gabe at third. Picking it up cleanly, he looked back the runner and threw across the diamond for the out.

With one on and one out, a drive deep to center sent Ari running backward as fast as his legs would carry him. But there would be no replay of the first inning against the Extreme. This time, it flew over his head and rolled to the wall. A.J. scored easily from second on the stand up double.

I paced back and forth in the dugout, watching our lead rapidly dissolve. My mind turned to what type of pitch Sam might throw or how to position our fielders so as to maximize our chances of getting out of the inning quickly. The time to focus on baseball strategy was short-lived, however, as Adam elbowed me in the side and nodded out toward right field.

Jeff Goodman, who had started ahead of Charlie for this game, stood with his back to home plate. His cap sat askew upon his head, its brim cocked sideways at a thirty-degree angle. His shirt was not tucked in, having come loose while jumping up and down, twisting this way and that.

"Josh, what the heck is he doing?" Adam asked.

"How am I supposed to know?"

"I think there's a mosquito bothering him." Jeremy said, doing his best to enlighten us.

"Well, can you get him to stop?" Adam directed his question at me. "There is a chance the ball could be hit to him, you know."

Shaking my head in frustration, I walked over to the right side of the dugout and began calling out to Jeff. He did not respond, and if possible seemed to become even more focused on getting away from, or better yet, eliminating the threat posed by the mosquito. Jeremy joined me in screaming his name but to no avail, and the lack of response caused Adam to become increasingly irritated.

"Stan!" he called angrily to the guilty party's father, who was sitting quietly on the bench. "Can you do something about your son?"

"What's wrong?" he asked, rising slowly to his feet.

"There's a mosquito bothering him, but he's letting it distract him from the game."

Stan walked over to where we were standing at the edge of the dugout and called calmly to his son. "Jeffrey, please focus."

Despite all of our efforts, Jeff continued. The mosquito, oblivious to our concerns, would not leave him alone.

On the mound, Sam Budd, ignorant as to what was taking place behind him, had resumed pitching. As luck would have it, the next batter swung away, hitting a sharp line drive out toward right field. I figured that it would clearly fall in for a hit. There was little chance that any of our outfielders would catch such a ball even if they were paying attention to the game, but with Jeff's current distraction it simply wasn't possible. But, at the very last second, just as the ball was about to sail by him, Jeff turned, reached up with his glove, and snagged it out of the air. Casually throwing it in to the cutoff man, he immediately resumed hunting his flying adversary.

Stan watched the play with interest, then turned around and sat back down on the bench. "He's good at multitasking," he said to no one in particular.

Jeff's implausible catch was the final highlight of the game. Sam gave up a total of fourteen runs, and we were incapable of mustering any further offensive output after that glorious first inning. The Rams trudged off the field at nine o'clock weary and miserable. The only saving grace was that Aaron had been able to keep Sam's pitches away from his groin area for the duration of the game, and to the best of my knowledge, his future ability to procreate remained intact.

"DAD . . . THEY'RE . . . THEY'RE . . . they're . . . shaving Rami's head!" Charlie was breathless as he ran in from outside the bunk.

We were back in our cabin in the Baseball Village a half hour or so after having been soundly defeated by the Westfield Rocks. The team had returned in a sullen mood, but the activity taking place in and around the bunkhouse helped them move on and forget the game.

"What are you talking about, Charlie?" I asked.

"Well, after we got back, we heard the Rocks celebrating the win. So a bunch of us went around to their side of the bunk and they invited us to hang out with them. They're really nice, and we were really excited. They have some good junk food stored over there, and their coaches have cans of soda and stuff . . ."

"Charlie, spit it out," his father said.

"Right, well, it turns out that the Rocks celebrate their victories by having their coach shave their heads with a set of clippers and, well, they asked Rami if he wanted his head shaved, and he said yes, and now he's sitting in the Rocks' buzz chair!"

"Oh my God, first, no kosher food and now this? Melissa's going to have my balls in a sling!" I yelled, already halfway out the door and heading around the side of the bunk, Jeremy and Charlie close on my heels.

By the time I arrived, it was too late. Little Rami sat in a chair outside the front door of the Rocks' cabin, with both teams gathered around cheering and screaming. Westfield's head coach had a pair of clippers in his hand

and the dreadful deed had been done. Rami's precious brown hair, which had previously come down over his ears, now lay in a pile on the pavement at his feet. I had a vision of his mother, left hand on hip and right hand stabbing a stern finger in my face, lecturing me about the lessons of the biblical hero, Samson.

But the longer I looked at my little second baseman, the more I appreciated what I saw. Gone was the kid who looked as if he was born to study ancient Jewish texts, and in his place stood one that appeared as if he might actually be able to play some ball. He was more Rock than Ram now, and that made me smile.

"Rami, what do you think your mother is going to say about this?" I asked as he wiped the lingering hairs off the back of his neck.

"I'll probably have to spend the rest of the summer in my room, but it was worth it," he replied with a smile.

I rubbed my hand over the top of his now fuzzy head. "This one is going to be tough to hide," I said.

The Rocks and their coaches ended the night by coming over to our side of the cabin for a visit, and the boys from Westfield, Indiana, celebrated their victory with the very team that they had defeated. Adam had brought a portable television with him for the week, and he hooked up Ari's Nintendo GameCube. The Rams and Rocks sat around playing the video game MLB, cheering and laughing as if they had been friends forever. Jeremy snapped photos of the evening as I sat and watched the Rocks beat us up on the screen far worse than they had earlier that evening.

We just couldn't catch a break.

CHAPTER NINETEEN

CRISIS MANAGEMENT

"DUDES, WE ARE dead last," Jason announced to the bunk as we awoke in our beds on Monday morning.

The rankings of the entire tournament were posted twice a day in a few locations around the Baseball Village. Teams were ranked according to record and average runs allowed. Jason had gotten up early and ventured outside to see how we had faired against our competition on day one.

"Ninety-sixth," he reported. "We're ranked ninety-sixth!"

"How many teams are there?" Carlos asked from his bed above me.

"Dude, what do you think? There are ninety-six teams. That's why I said we're dead last."

"Well, look at the bright side," Gabe said. "We can't do any worse."

"They could kick us out of the park," Gil volunteered, already surveying his face closely in the portable mirror he had brought along for grooming purposes.

"They're not going to kick us out of the park," I said. "Gabe's right, we can only get better."

"We won't get better enough to win a game, that's for sure," Sam Budd volunteered as he rolled over in bed propping himself up on one elbow. "Let's face it, we stink."

"If that's your attitude, Sam, then you're right, you will never win a game," I countered.

Roused by our conversation, Adam stood up and inspected the cabin. Clothes were strewn everywhere. Dirty underwear covered the floor, and damp towels hung from the rafters. Our rank was the last thing he had on his mind.

"I don't know about how we're doing in the tournament," he said quietly. "But I do know that *I can't live in this stinking mess anymore!*" the ex-camp counselor finished the sentence with a thundering roar. "*Get out of bed you, lazy bastards, and clean up this cabin!*"

His yell woke the remainder of the bunk, and twenty-four feet hit the floor, fearing his wrath.

"Good idea," Jeremy chipped in. "And when you guys are done cleaning, get dressed in your blues. We have an eleven o'clock game this morning."

Jeremy was supportive of Adam's strict discipline, although not quite able to implement it himself. Both of them were neat freaks, and the sights, sounds, and smells of living in cramped quarters with a large group of ten-year-old boys was beginning to fray their nerves.

"All right, settle down, coaches," I said, trying to be the voice of reason. "Let's clean up a little, get dressed, and head down to breakfast. Phil, you're pitching this morning."

OUR FIRST GAME of the day was on Field No. 1. We were scheduled to face off against the Central Jersey Slammers. After getting dressed in our visiting blue uniforms and having a leisurely breakfast, we walked through the Baseball Village toward the front of the park, passing through the usual throngs of uniformed players and coaches.

We entered the field fifteen minutes before game time.

"Houston, we have a problem," Jeff Goodman, who was leading the way, announced to no one in particular.

I looked across the diamond, not sure what Jeff was referring to. Then I saw it—the Slammers were also dressed in their blues. We were wearing identical uniforms. Someone had screwed up. I prayed it wasn't us.

"Jeremy!" I called to my top administrative assistant. "What the heck is going on here? Are we at the wrong field?"

He looked over at the competition, then rummaged through the papers on his clipboard. Over the last couple of days, Jeremy had not only taken on the role of advance scout but also that of organizational supervisor. I had begun to rely on him for all scheduling issues, which included game times, locations, and getting us into the correct uniforms. His skills were particularly strong in that area, or so I had thought.

As he looked through his notes, I saw panic begin to set on his face. I recognized the look immediately as I had seen it many times before—young interns on rounds, flipping through their papers while doing their best to explain to me why they didn't have the patient's vital signs at hand.

"Josh, I am so sorry," Jeremy said. "I think I made a mistake. It looks like we're actually the home team. We're supposed to be in our red uniforms."

I shook my head in disappointment and frowned. "Listen, guys," I spoke to the coaches in an uncharacteristically stern voice. "Among the four of us, we have three MDs, and an MBA. We are board certified in four medical specialties. One of us buys and sells multimillion-dollar companies. I guarantee you, we have the highest collective coaching IQ in the park. Why is it that we can't figure out which uniform to get the team into?"

Jeremy, Adam, and Stan stared at the ground in silence.

"Well, it was my responsibility to double-check and I didn't," I admitted. "I'll take part of the blame. You guys stay here and stall while I take everyone back to change. Let's not have this happen again, shall we?"

I gathered up the team, and we ran back toward the bunkhouse as fast as we could. As we scampered away from the field, I could hear the Slammer's laughter chasing after us.

The boys were huffing, puffing, and sweating when we finally made it back to the Baseball Village and ultimately to our cabin. They had done a poor job cleaning up, and the mess that we walked into didn't help matters. It was utter chaos as the players combed through their areas, searching desperately for their red uniforms. Shirts were thrown everywhere, drops of perspiration flew through the air, and I was struck in the face with a smelly blue sock while monitoring the team's progress.

"Guys, you have three minutes, and then we're moving. If we don't show up on time, we forfeit the game!" I called.

"Would that be such a bad thing?" Sam yelled while pulling his shirt over his head.

"I can't find my red socks!" called Carlos as he began going through my trunk.

"Carlos, stay out of my clothes. Your socks aren't in there!" I informed him.

"Where the heck is my red stuff?" Gil launched himself from bed to bed in search of his missing uniform. Bounding near Phil's area, he slipped and landed with a crunch on the floor.

"What was that?" I asked.

"I don't know. I felt something under me," Gil responded.

"Arghhh!" Phil screamed. "You broke my glasses, you idiot! You broke them!" He held up his black sports glasses, the ones he used only for hitting and pitching. The glasses, or more accurately goggles, were utterly mangled. Half of the frame was hanging loose, having broken at the bridge that, under better circumstances, would have been able to rest upon his nose. The lenses were scratched beyond repair.

As Phil held them up and looked more closely, tears began to well in his eyes. "These were very expensive! Now, how am I supposed to pitch? I won't even be able to see home plate!"

"How do you see first base when you play shortstop?" Gil asked. "You don't wear them when you're in the field."

"That's different. You don't have to be as precise!"

"We'll come up with a plan as we go. Let's get out of

here!" I said as we hustled out of the cabin with shirt-
tails and shoelaces flying.

I spoke to Phil as we ran. "Phil, I know the glasses
are useless, but is there a chance you can pitch anyway?
We really need you."

He looked at me with tears in his eyes, shaking his
head and glaring at Gil, who ran in front of us. It was
apparent that not only could he not see, but he was in no
emotional state to take the mound.

With yet another game on tap for that evening, Gabe
and Sam were off limits, especially being that they had
both pitched the previous day. In desperation I turned to
my emergency backup plan—Jason Armon, the swear
master himself.

Jason had been a late addition to the staff, having
pitched some for his Little League team that spring. According to my scouting report he had performed well.
The only problem was that my scouting report consisted
of his mother's telling me how great he was while we
stood together on the Rashi playground after school.

"Jason," I called to him as we continued running toward the field. By now I was really out of breath. "We . . .
have . . . a bit . . . of a . . . problem here," I panted.
"Phil . . . was . . . supposed to . . . pitch but . . . he . . .
can't . . . see. Can . . . you . . . take the . . . start?"

"Son . . . of . . . a bitch . . . , you bet!" he answered,
gasping for air.

"I HAD TO do a little crisis management," I said to Adam and Jeremy as we ran into the dugout with less than
a minute to spare. Stan was standing at home plate,

schmoozing with the umpire about God knows what, doing his best to give the team cover until we got back. The Rams sat down on the bench, half of them looking as if they were ready to throw up from the long run.

"What type of crisis management?" Adam and Jeremy both questioned simultaneously.

"Well, Phil's a scratch," I explained.

"What do you mean he's a scratch?" They asked.

"Well, more precisely, his glasses are a scratch."

"He can't pitch?" they both said in unison.

"Nope, he can't."

"Who are we replacing him with?" They asked.

"Jason," I responded.

"Son of a bitch," they said.

FOR THE FEW brief moments before we took the field, the Central Jersey Slammers watched our dugout like hungry wolves sizing up a wounded rabbit. We were easy prey to begin with, but now breathless, exhausted, and with a last-minute change in our starting pitcher, the hunt was over before it had begun. And so, still huffing and puffing, the Rashi Rabbits hopped onto the field with Jason Armon on the hill.

"Carlos, get in there," I called, seeing that he had remained on the bench. "You're starting in right field today, remember?"

"I am?" he asked. "Are you sure about that?"

"Of course, I'm sure. I'm the coach, for crying out loud! Get in there!" He grabbed his glove and scampered out of the dugout for his first action of the tournament.

Having been ousted from his role as starting pitcher,

I placed Phil at third base to give Gabe a rest. Phil received a few warm-up grounders from Robert at first and immediately drew the attention of the opposing coaches.

"Third baseman's a lefty!" their first-base coach called out to the team.

"What's so important about that?" Jeremy asked as we stood inside the dugout looking over the field.

"The pivots are wrong," I responded while rubbing my chin. "The throw from third or short to first is not natural for a lefty." Coaching the Rams however, left me in no position to make decisions based on such fine details. Of course the opposing coaches didn't know that, so it made our staff look foolish.

"Maybe I should put Gabe back in at third," I thought out loud.

"Are you kidding me?" Adam chimed in. "That guy thinks he's a coaching genius because he picked up on some subtle weakness that our third baseman's a lefty? What a joke! He missed the fact that we're playing a lefty at third because he's one of our only players who can field the ball. A good coach would have just looked us over and told his team the obvious: 'They suck!'"

"GOD, THEY GROW them big in Jersey," Stan marveled as the Slammer's leadoff hitter stepped to the plate. He was a massive kid, large and strong, with greasy black hair that fell down to his shoulders.

"I can guess what he was doing this past winter while we were throwing baseballs off the walls of the Hyde Center," I whispered.

"Yeah, probably working out in the Slammers' state-of-the-art gym, pumping iron and doing position-specific drills under the tutelage of their strength and conditioning coach," Jeremy added. "My sources tell me that these guys have an intense off-season program."

I surveyed the rest of their team in the dugout. "We didn't need your sources to figure that one out."

Jason now settled in, his right foot touching the rubber. He didn't look bad out there as he felt for the seams of the ball and assumed the traditional pitcher's stance. Aaron crouched down behind home plate, signaling that he was ready, and the umpire pointed out to the mound.

Jason went into his windup. All looked well as he released the ball at a three-quarter angle, and it sailed toward home on an accurate trajectory. The problem was that it was thrown slowly, remarkably slowly considering that we were playing baseball and not softball.

The Slammer's leadoff hitter wasted no time taking a hack at Jason's meatball. His massive thighs rotated as he brought his hefty bat across the plate. A loud ringing sound echoed throughout the field. The ball shot out toward left, where Gil stood waiting.

I had been using Gil Slotnick as a utility fielder, and he had been performing well despite the fact that he played the game as if he were on national television. He had continued wearing his dark sunglasses, which likely hindered him as much as helped, and he had yet to master the art of being ready when the ball was pitched, continually using the opportunity to strike a pose, regardless of whether the opposition carried a female player on their roster. I had given up trying to fix the situation.

Nevertheless, despite his misguided priorities, Gil continued to make plays. Once again, he roused himself from his casual stance, reached up, and snared the sharply hit ball for out number one.

Looking over at the bench, he opened his mouth as he threw the ball into the infield. "We know, Gil," Adam hollered out to him. "*Oogah*. Forget the Hebrew and just focus on the game!"

Jason went right back to work, and although the Slammers made sharp contact on his slow offerings, the next two batters made the mistake of hitting them toward Sam Budd who patrolled shortstop. He made quick work of the ground balls, gobbling them up and throwing them down to Robert at first for the outs. The Rashi Rabbits hopped off the field temporarily unscathed.

"THAT GUY IS big," Phil said as he stepped out of the dugout bat in hand.

"Yeah, his arms are about as wide as my legs," Robert Matz concurred from the bench.

"Just do your best, guys. Let's try to make some contact. If you go down, go down swinging," I said. Unfortunately that is exactly what happened—three swinging strikeouts sandwiched around a base hit to left off the bat of Sam Budd.

"Let's go, guys. Hold 'em again," I called as they ran back onto the field. Jason picked the ball up off the dirt and continued to pitch. The results were different this go around. Two infield errors within the first three batters shook his confidence. Then a couple of pass balls resulted in a few runs.

With a runner on second and one out, a ball was hit high and shallow to right field. I watched with curiosity as Carlos searched the skies. Anxiously settling underneath it, he stood with both feet planted directly beneath him, sticking his glove straight up in the air. The ball plunged toward him, and my thoughts drifted back to the miraculous play in practice where Gil dove behind Carlos to scoop the ball on a very similar hit. I looked over to left field where Gil was playing, but salvation was nowhere in sight.

Ari was on the move from center, but the distance was too great. Regardless, Carlos was not interested in having the scenario repeat itself. He looked up toward the heavens, and at the very last possible moment, did the unthinkable—he caught it.

An overwhelming look of joy combined with tremendous relief swept over his face. He took the ball out of his glove, and examined it for a few seconds to make sure that it was real. Then with his right hand, he raised his trophy high overhead so that everyone could see it. Those of us in the dugout smiled, but Carlos's pose did not change and that brief moment turned into long seconds.

"He looks like a ten-year-old white version of Tommie Smith giving the Black Power salute in the 1968 Olympic Games," Jeremy said to me as we stood watching him.

"Good analogy, but more importantly, why isn't he throwing the ball in?" I asked.

"Beats me," he responded.

We were happy for Carlos, but we had a problem. The Slammer's runner on second base had thought there

were two outs. He was now halfway down the third baseline, heading home and had not tagged up. It was an unimaginable mental mistake, a gaffe that would not have
been considered unusual on our team, but I had seen
nothing like it from the competition at Dreams Park.

Our entire bench started screaming at Carlos to
throw the ball back to second for what would have been
the third and final out of the inning. Even Stan roused
himself from his seat to help out.

"Throw it, Carlos! Throw it!" he screamed.

The players on the field joined in, too, but fifteen people screaming at him made no impact. Carlos was just
too excited about his catch. He stood there holding the
ball high, waiting until every last person within viewing
distance had seen his accomplishment. Meanwhile, the
runner had backtracked around third and was heading
toward second, wondering what miracle had so far
spared him.

After what seemed an eternity, Rami who had run out
from the infield, was finally able to wrestle the ball out
of Carlos's hands. He threw it back in, but it was too late.
The runner had already made it back safely.

Knowing that he could have been out of the inning after giving up only a few runs, the scene was just too
much for Jason to bear. He voiced his familiar obscene
sentiment after receiving the ball back, then proceeded
to walk the next five batters before I mercifully yanked
him

WE WERE DOWN nine to nothing in the third, when
Carlos went back at it. With two outs, he stepped to the

plate. The hard-throwing right-hander on the mound led my thoughts to our batter's Styrofoam cooler resting in the nurse's freezer just a short walk down the path.

"That kid might as well be standing there with a loaded gun," I said. "Do you think Carlos's doctor had this situation in mind when he gave his fourth grade patient with a bleeding issue the thumbs-up to play?"

"Not sure," Adam responded. "Don't worry though. We're doctors aren't we?"

"Yeah, but I'd feel better if I were a hematologist and you were a trauma surgeon."

Despite my fears, the tension abated as Carlos walked on four pitches, but rose again as I realized that we had not manned the coach's boxes.

"Adam! Get over to first. We forgot we need base coaches!" The game continued as I ran to third, while Adam scrambled around the backstop.

I had no intention of giving Carlos the steal sign, but it was irrelevant, as he did not look over at me anyway. Whatever he had in mind he was doing on his own, and as the pitcher began coming toward home plate, off Carlos went. The team jumped off the bench, as it looked like it would be an easy steal and a notch in his belt. But then something inexplicable happened.

As the catcher stood up to throw down to second, Carlos looked at him—and froze. In the middle of the base path, Carlos simply stopped. He halted right then and there, the very embodiment of a deer caught in headlights. He looked at the catcher in abject fear, apparently not realizing that the other team was going to try to get him out. In his uncertainty, Carlos then began bouncing back and forth on the balls of his heels. He stood smack in between first and second while leaning toward the left and then the right and then back again.

The Slammers' catcher was totally bewildered. He had never seen anything quite like it. He stood there, not knowing whether to throw down to second or back to first, and so began pump faking in both directions. And that's how it stayed for a few very long moments— Carlos dancing around in the dirt and the catcher with ball in hand, faking the throw to second, then to first and then back to second.

Our entire team was on their feet screaming at Carlos once again, before he finally committed to getting back to where it all began. He slid into first base safely just as the throw finally came in over his head. Adam pulled him aside to review what had happened.

"Carlos," he fervently whispered, hoping that the other team would not overhear the need for such basic instruction. "You can't just stop in the middle of the base path! You have to make up your mind, either go for the steal or don't! Do you understand?"

"Yeah, got it, Coach," Carlos responded. But on the very next pitch, almost incomprehensibly, the exact same thing happened. Carlos took off for second and then, seeing the catcher stand up to throw, he froze yet again in his tracks, Adam's instructions already having left his mind.

Everyone on the field was now screaming and cheering. It was utter chaos. I yelled frantically across the diamond, trying desperately to get Adam's attention, while furiously pointing at the ground over and over again, signaling to keep him on the base. Yet, beyond all possible reason it happened a third and final time. This time, however, saw Carlos ultimately decide that, after doing his dance, he should move on to second instead of heading back to first. This completely blew the catcher's mind, and remarkably Carlos made it in safely.

Stan came out of the dugout to give me his opinion on the play. "That was without a doubt, the most humiliating, embarrassing, and thoroughly entertaining steal I have ever seen," he said.

"GAME OVER! MERCY rule in effect," the home plate umpire called with relief. It was the end of the fourth inning and we were down thirteen to nothing.

"What are you talking about?" I called, coming out from the dugout.

"They didn't tell you, Coach? If you're down by twelve or more after four innings, mercy rule takes effect. This game is over," he said definitively.

The dejected Rams, who had been heading out to the field, slumped back into the dugout, throwing their gloves on the ground in disgust.

"Hey, Gabe, that's three!" Sam Budd called. "You're running out of chances."

"Just play baseball, Sam. Let me worry about our record," Gabe responded.

AFTER THE GAME had been called, I made it my priority to deal with the Carlos situation. Despite our overall poor play, I felt that his base running gaffes made for a particularly uncomfortable situation that could not be allowed to repeat itself. Pulling him aside to discuss his in-game decisions, I began by asking about the play in right field. I never even got to his other mistakes.

"Carlos, that was a great catch in right. But why didn't you throw back to second? You could have doubled up the runner."

He thought for a moment, shrugged his shoulders and responded calmly.

"I don't know the rules, Coach," he said.

I thought that I had misheard him and asked for a clarification. "You . . . *what?*"

"I don't know the rules of baseball, Coach," he repeated, staring at me blankly.

The only thing in the world blanker than the stare on his face was the stare on mine.

CHAPTER TWENTY

BACK ON THE HILL

THE RAIN PELTED the ground with a nagging persistence, creating pockets of mud where the grass had refused to grow. By twos and threes, the Rams rolled in it, soiling their uniforms and destroying the remainder of the lawn that had been fortunate enough to take root.

It was Monday afternoon, just a scant few hours after our humiliating defeat at the hands of the Central Jersey Slammers. Our scheduled team barbecue at the rental home where Sheryl and Shani were staying had come close to being rained out. I stood on the sun porch of the Abner House, an antique white, colonial located just a quarter mile from the park entrance. Staring at the boys as they rolled over one another in the slop, I wondered how on earth we would get their uniforms clean. Their voices carried through the partially opened window.

"Let's have a mud wrestling competition," Sam Budd suggested.

"Good idea," Robert Matz agreed. "Let's break up into teams."

"Yeah, let's divide up. I'll be one captain, Gabe can be the other," Sam suggested forcefully.

"I know where this is heading," Gabe interjected.

"Oh, don't make such a big deal about it, man. I'll pick first," Sam said. I watched as the teams were chosen—Sam, Robert, Aaron, Rami, Gil, and Jason on one side and Gabe, Ari, Charlie, Phil, Jeff, and Carlos on the other. The two groups separated and, taking a moment to discuss strategy, proceeded to square off against each another.

"I'm not so sure I want to do this," Carlos said.

"C'mon, Carlos; without you, we're down a man," Gabe insisted. Carlos had no time to counter.

"If you get pinned, you're out. On three, we'll go," Sam announced the simple rules. "One, two, three . . . go!"

The two sides converged in a sea of arms, legs, and flying Dreams Park baseball caps. All twelve rolled, struggled, threw elbows, and did whatever they deemed necessary to get the upper hand. When the mud settled, they were all colored dark brown from head to toe. Sam sat proudly on top of Phil, pinning him to the ground with both hands. Robert had taken down Ari; the skinny centerfielder had not moved fast enough to escape. Jason had Gabe wrapped tightly between his legs, overcoming him with his extra height and girth. Gil had easily pinned Jeff, and Aaron had done the same with Carlos, albeit after being forced to chase him around in a circle a few times. Of the winning team only Rami found himself flat out on the ground, his wriggling and squirming having had little effect once Charlie got a hold of him.

"We win!" shouted Sam. "Five to one, not even close!"

"It would have been six to nothing if I had gotten to Charlie's legs," Rami said.

"Please. You would have been down a lot sooner if I wasn't worried about knocking my pump loose," Charlie explained as he fiddled with the device at his waist, ensuring that it still functioned properly.

"Doesn't matter. It was a solid victory," Sam said.

I shook my head in disappointment as I watched the scene. We were a team and yet perpetually divided.

Sheryl interrupted my thoughts.

"Hot dog?" she asked, holding out a plate.

"I don't think I can get enough saliva together to swallow it," I said. "I must be dehydrated."

"What's wrong?" she asked.

"What isn't? We're getting humiliated every time we take the field. The team is split in two. I can't get kosher food for my kosher player. One of my coaches and good friends is battling cancer. I'm physically and emotionally exhausted. And on top of everything else, we still have five more games to play."

"Maybe you'll get rained out this afternoon," she suggested hopefully.

"I wish. Didn't I tell you? Games never get rained out at Dreams Park. They make them up in the middle of the night if they have to."

"They do not."

"I'm not kidding. Sometimes they make you play at two in the morning if there's a rain delay. I heard it from some other coaches."

"Josh, go lie down in my bed upstairs for a little while. I think you need a break." She touched my hand gently.

I nodded in agreement and left her, making my way through the small crowd of family and friends clustered in the living room. I shook a few hands and heard words of encouragement as I went, but the faces and voices seemed distant. As if from far away, I saw my mother step in front of me and ask what was wrong, telling me how poorly I looked before I even had a chance to answer.

Pushing on, I found my way upstairs and lay down on Sheryl's bed. Flipping open my cell phone, I called the park's office and asked about our game. I was informed that it had been postponed from four o'clock until seven thirty that evening.

After hearing the news, I rested my head back on the pillow and listened to the rain softly pelting the roof. Rolling over, I was surprised to see Sandy Koufax lying on the bed next to me. His eyes were closed and he was snoring.

"Any thoughts?" I said to him. "Can you help me win a game? At least make a good stand?" Waiting for an answer that was not likely to come, I watched Sandy go right on sleeping. The brim of his Dodgers cap slipped down over his nose.

Whether I lost consciousness or finally fell asleep, I have no idea. One moment, I was curiously observing Sandy Koufax and listening to the rain rhythmically beat against the roof; the next, there was silence.

THE TEAM WAS tired from the long day, and I had low expectations that night. The game was to be played on Field No. 19 against the RBI Angels who hailed from Maryland. Jeremy had informed us that they were a well-established, highly competitive team in the tournament circuit.

At around seven o'clock, we traipsed down to the field under dark and overcast skies. The rain had finally relented but later than predicted, and we arrived to discover that things were delayed even more than we had been told.

The game taking place prior to ours was still in the second inning, and our first pitch likely wouldn't be thrown until after eight. Despite the late hour and the bleak weather, the park was still a beehive of activity as players, coaches, and fans meandered about, endeavoring to determine when their games would be played and trying to occupy their time in the meanwhile.

With nothing to do, I wandered into the stands of Field No. 19 to watch the game that was currently under way. The Long Island Playmakers were in the field, which immediately caught my attention. The Playmakers were one of the teams that I had researched while preparing for the tournament. I remembered their Website as one that had awakened the mind killer.

An overweight middle-aged man in a tight-fitting Play-makers T-shirt sat in front of me, his right knee bouncing up and down while his hands clung tightly to the railing in front of him. The image brought to mind what I must have looked like at the head coach's meeting that first night of the tournament.

"Way to go, Chuck!" he yelled over the fence. "Nice play out there!"

"Your son?" I asked.

"Yup, my pride and joy. He's playing first base," He looked up at me and recognized my attire. "Which team are you with, Coach?"

"The Rashi Rams."

"Oh, yeah? Where ya from?"

"Massachusetts."

"Oh, yeah? There are a few teams here from Mass. You guys any good?"

"Actually, it's our first time here. We're still learning the ropes."

"You got a son on the team?"

"Yeah, he's having a great time. This is his first time at a tournament like this."

"You know the Playmakers travel to tournaments year-round. We're fortunate that our son made the team."

"I'm sure he deserved it. It sounds like it's a great program," I said, silently thinking that playing on these teams year-round was probably as painful as it was pleasurable. "Does he like it?"

"Sure, he loves it. He wouldn't trade this for anything."

"That's good. Does he also play Little League?" I asked naively.

He looked at me like I had three heads. "They learn bad habits in Little League," he spit out, as if I had said something sacrilegious.

"Oh . . . of course," I stammered. He did a double take, looking at me as if it was beyond comprehension that I was unaware of that fact.

As we sat there, a bunt was laid down out on the field. The catcher picked it up to throw down to first, but not before my new friend screamed loudly to his son, "Outside target, Chuck!"

I saw Chuck lean into foul territory, holding his glove away from the first baseline, allowing the catcher a clear target out of the path of the runner. The ball was zipped cleanly down to first for the out. I made a mental note to teach that to the Rams when I had a chance. I was not too proud to acknowledge the obvious: The Playmakers had parents who knew more about baseball than I did.

I turned my back and made my way out of the stands. Chuck's father called after me. "Congratulations, Coach. Now that you've come to CDP, your program is really going to take off!"

"I'm sure it will," I called back. "I'm sure it will."

"COACH," JEFF GOODMAN said, tugging on my shirt-sleeve. "I'm getting bored with playing right field. Can I pitch now?"

It was just after eight p.m. and we had gathered in the first base dugout. The Rams sat on the bench in their mud-stained visiting blue uniforms. The sky was dark, although it might as well have been daytime out on the field. The artificial lights at the park were that good. The grass was still wet, but the grounds crew had raked the infield dirt over and over until the puddles had disappeared.

"No, you're not pitching, Jeff," I responded.

He looked perplexed and hurt. "I'm not sure how one can go from the starting pitching staff to not being allowed to pitch."

"Jeff, I'm not sure who told you that you were on the starting pitching staff, but it certainly wasn't me."

"Can I at least play second base then? I'm getting bored in right. I hardly get any balls."

"Jeff, you're an outfielder. You've never even practiced in the infield."

"I understand the position, Coach," he said. The look on his face made me think that he had calculated ideal angles for certain throws and the probability of a ball's being hit to one location or another based on pitch speed, bat size, and wind direction.

"All right, Jeff," I said. "You'll start at second base tonight." He smiled with satisfaction, but remained confused as to why he had been demoted from the pitching staff.

The RBI Angels took the field for warm-ups. They looked as big, as strong, and as fluid as our previous competition. The only difference that I could discern was with their coaches. They stood outside the dugout, dressed in matching tight white baseball pants, and surveyed their team. There were three of them, leaning casually with their backs to the screen, arms across their chests.

"They look ridiculous," Adam said as he walked up next to Jeremy and me in the dugout.

"Yeah," Jeremy agreed. "They would have been better served sticking with khaki shorts like the rest of us. They look like they take themselves a little too seriously, that's for sure."

"They're too cocky," Adam went on. "God, I'd like to wipe those smug smiles right off their faces."

"They have every right to be cocky," I countered. "I'm sure they've checked the rankings."

By now, every team in the park knew about us as we languished in last place on all the postings around the Baseball Village. Next to each team name was a number indicating average runs allowed per game. The gaudy 15.6 that was printed next to "Rashi Rams" not only put us squarely in last place, but also marked us as imposters.

I HAD JUGGLED the batting order in hopes of generating some runs. After taking a few swings in the on-deck circle, Gabe stepped calmly to the plate to lead us off. Digging into the batter's box, he looked to the mound and awaited the pitch. The Angels' pitcher was heavyset and used it to his advantage, putting all his weight behind each effort.

"Ball one!" called the umpire as the pitch ran inside, just below Gabe's knees. He stepped out and looked down the line at me as I stood in the third base coach's box.

"Be a hitter, Gabe!" I shouted the time-honored support for a batter at the plate. "Wait for your pitch, though!"

He took two more balls and then stepped out again to look down the line. I touched the brim of my cap and then wiped my hand across my mouth—our "take" sign. I was not sure who else on the team would have recognized it, but I had no doubt Gabe would understand the signal. As instructed, he did not swing, and the pitch went high and wide.

"Ball four!" hollered the ump. "Take your base!"

Gabe trotted down to first, immediately looking over at me for an indication as to how he should proceed. I touched my cap, rubbed my hands together and then touched my foot. As the pitcher went into his windup,

Gabe took off for second. The throw was late, and he slid into the bag smoothly.

"Safe!" yelled the infield umpire.

Feeling confident, and recognizing that we did not have much to lose, I repeated the "steal" sign to my son. He stared intently again, making sure that he had observed correctly. I caught his eyes in mine, nodding imperceptibly.

Gabe took a decent size lead, and as the next pitch was thrown, took off for third.

"Hit the deck, Gabe!" I screamed, both of my arms frantically motioning downward. He slid in as the ball arrived, and his right foot slammed against the bag just before the Angel's third baseman applied the tag to his upper thigh.

Both of the pitches had been balls and with no one out, I stepped close behind Gabe as he stood on the base.

"Not too shabby, kid," I said. It was the first time he had seen third base on offense all tournament. "Now take a good lead, and if it's on the ground, you're running."

"Okay, Coach," he said, taking a few steps off the bag.

"A little more . . . a little further . . . ," I encouraged him.

The third pitch came toward home. Gil, who was at bat, did his job, tapping a slow grounder toward the second baseman.

"Go, Gabe!" I shouted, and off he went. The Angels' second baseman went to first for the easy out, and Gabe scored standing up. For only the second time of the week, we had a lead—one to nothing, Rams over the vaunted

RBI Angels.

"GABE, YOU'RE BACK on the hill," I said before we took the field in the bottom of the first.

"I know, Dad," he said. "Just so you know—I'll do my best, but I'm really tired."

"I understand, buddy. It's not easy for a nine-year-old to start a game under the lights after staying up late the night before, playing four innings that morning, and competing in a team mud wrestling competition in the afternoon."

"Yeah, not to mention, I think it's my bedtime right now," he said with a small smile as he trotted out to the mound.

Sam Budd was again behind home plate. "You're looking good, Gabester!" he called after taking a few of his warm-up pitches.

"Feelin' good, Samster!" Gabe called back. He bent down and tightened the laces on his cleats before pulling his cap down low over his face and getting to work.

The Angels' leadoff hitter worked the count to one and one before hitting a hard ground ball toward second. I looked to see if Rami was in position, but as I turned my head it dawned on me that I had given Jeff the start. He was getting the action he was looking for.

Jeff's cap was back to being askew and already the left side of his shirt had come loose, hanging out over his pants. *Remember those angles, kid,* I thought to myself as the ball shot toward him. I watched in amazement as he scooped it up cleanly and threw over to first for the out.

"Way to go, Jeffrey!" Stan called from over my shoulder. He had stood up from his usual spot on the bench just in time to see the play.

"Stan, maybe we're not utilizing your son's talents appropriately," I said.

Gabe bore down on the second hitter in their lineup, and after two called strikes plus a swing and a miss, there were two outs with nobody on. The next batter drew a walk on four pitches and then was off in the blink of eye, stealing second easily.

With two down and a runner in scoring position, the Angels' heavyset pitcher stepped to the plate. This time his meaty hands grasped an oversize aluminum bat instead of a baseball. He stared down at the mound, looking for revenge.

Gabe delivered, and the kid stroked a sharp sinking line drive into left field. It was hit hard, and Jason charged the ball trying to make the catch. It landed on the ground just a few feet in front of him, but he reacted quickly, grabbing it on one hop and launching a bullet toward home.

The runner from second had been on the move, and his white-trousered third base coach gave him the green light in an attempt to tie the game. The kid rounded third and barreled into the plate just as the ball arrived. But Sam, deftly blocking him with his right leg, grabbed the throw and reached for the tag. The runner slid into Sam, and the two became entangled in a cloud of dust and mud.

For one long, agonizing moment, the umpire did not make the call as he stood and waited to see if Sam held on to the ball. But when Sam raised his arm to show that the ball remained inside his glove, the umpire lifted his right hand above his head and shouted at the top of his lungs. "OOOUT!" he screamed.

The Rams ran off the field jumping up and down while launching themselves into one another. It was our first outfield put out of the tournament as well as the first time that we had maintained a lead through an entire inning.

"Nice throw, Jason," Gabe said as he tousled his teammate's long, straight black hair with his hand.

"Yeah, I nailed that son of bitch, didn't I?" Jason responded.

"Great pitching, Gabe," Sam said, removing his catcher's mask.

"Sweet play at the plate, Sam," Gabe responded. "If you hadn't blocked that son of a bitch with your leg, we never would have gotten him."

"Teamwork, gentlemen," I said to all of them. "Teamwork is what you just witnessed out there. And Gabe—watch your mouth."

THE TEAMS PLAYED on, and no runs were scored in the second inning. As Gabe walked off the mound, the excitement and energy of the first inning had left him. His head was held low and his shoulders slumped. He was physically exhausted and emotionally drained. The endorphins naturally released at the start of the game were beginning to ebb. He slogged passed me into the dugout, not saying a word. I could see in his eyes that he wanted to be taken out. The game, however, was moving forward, and beyond all possible reason we were in it.

"Can you give me one more inning?" I pleaded. "We've got a chance here."

"One more, Dad," Gabe responded. "Just one more."

Adam walked over to me.

"He's wiped," he said.

"I know. He doesn't have much gas left in the tank."

"Time to put Sam out there."

"We need to save him," I argued. "Who's going to pitch tomorrow if we pitch Sam tonight?"

"Screw tomorrow. This may be our only chance to win a game!"

"Gabe can give us one more, and then we'll go with Sam."

IN THE TOP of the third, our first two batters struck out and Aaron Dines stepped from the on-deck circle.

Adam, who was coaching first base, called him over.

"Aaron, you need to use a lighter bat. You've been having a hard time getting around on this guy."

"No way, man," Aaron responded defiantly. "This is my favorite bat."

"Aaron, I'm your coach, and I'm telling you that you need a lighter bat." Adam's voice began to rise in anger.

"And I'm telling you that you're wrong," Aaron challenged, matching his coach's intensity.

"You haven't had a hit all tournament!"

"And you haven't coached a good game all tournament!"

They stood there facing each other in a classic stand-off. Each of them had one hand on Aaron's bat, which was suspended in the air between them. As I sat and watched, I knew that what I was seeing was destiny unfolding. Adam had been in full camp counselor mode all week, progressively tightening the disciplinary screws as the days went by. These two had gone at it before. During an earlier game, Aaron had complained about playing time. Hearing the gripe, Adam had launched into a stern and passionate lecture that included multiple references to his days of languishing on the end of the bench for the University of Rochester junior varsity basketball team. The scene that was playing out in front of me now was going to take place. It had only been a matter of time.

As Adam attempted to pull away the heavier bat, Aaron violently jerked it back. I immediately exited the dugout to disengage Adam from the confrontation.

"Let it go, Coach," I said. "Now's not the time."

However, Aaron beat us to it, dropping the heavy bat and picking up the lighter one, accepting the change but under protest. As he walked toward the plate, I heaved a great sigh of relief and looked around to see who might have witnessed the embarrassing display. All the RBI Angels, their white panted coaches, the umpires, and every single fan in the stands stared silently back at me.

OF COURSE, THE bat had no actual bearing on the play. Aaron grounded out to second for the third out of the inning, and slammed Adam's bat of choice to the ground in frustration as the Rams headed back out onto the field.

It was the bottom of the third, and I waited patiently

for the other shoe to drop. It was time that we gave up our usual six or seven runs. With fatigue working its way through every bone in his body, Gabe walked the first batter. The next two grounded out to the infield, and with a runner on third and two out, the first wild pitch of the game was thrown.

Gabe released it too high and it sailed over the top of Sam's outstretched glove all the way to the backstop. Gabe covered home and took the throw, but it was not in time. The game was tied at one.

My son went back to the mound and paced, shaking his head from side to side. He was weary to the core, and it showed over the next two batters as he walked them both. With two on and two out, the next hitter worked a full count.

"One more strike, Gabriel!" I called out to him. "One more strike and we are out of the inning! One more strike and you're done!"

He looked over at me and took a deep breath, nodding his head in acknowledgment.

"C'mon, Gabe, let's get this guy!" Sam called from behind home plate.

"This is it, Gabe!" Phil yelled from shortstop. "You can do this!" The rest of the team followed suit, each one directing words of encouragement toward the mound.

Gabe took off his cap and wiped the sweat from his brow. Then, feeling the strength flow from his teammates and giving them back the last bit of his remaining energy, he went into his windup, delivering a fastball low and inside. The batter swung over the top.

"Strike three!" hollered the ump while Gabe trotted

off the field, heaving a great sigh of relief.

"TAKE A LOOK at this," Jeremy said to me in the dugout, holding up his digital camera. It was the top of the fifth inning, and the score was still tied. I looked at the small screen on the camera to see an image of the scoreboard. It read: HOME: 1 VISITORS: 1 INNING: 5.

"I can't really believe this is happening," I said.

"Believe it," Jeremy responded. "Either we're better than we thought we were, or my scouting sources are worse."

Three up and three down in the top of the fifth, and we were unable to mount a threat. We took the field in the bottom half of the inning, and the fear was evident in the Rams' eyes. Since eyeballing the first game at Dreams Park, they had never expected to be this close to a win, and they were feeling the pressure.

"Keep pitching like you've been doing, and you're going to be saying 'sorry' to Phil before you go to bed tonight," Gabe said to Sam as he crossed the mound on the way to third base.

"Maybe I should throw up some meatballs," Sam responded.

"Your call," Gabe said.

Sam took a few warm-up pitches, all of which were outside the strike zone. He did not look sharp. I decided to make a trip to the mound and settle him down before the inning got under way. I called to Aaron, as he had taken over at catcher. Putting an arm around each of their shoulders, I spoke to them softly.

"Are you shitting me?" I said. "Are you guys shitting

me? We are tied with a great travel team in the fifth inning of one of the most prestigious youth baseball tournaments in the country. You guys are nervous. I can see that. I'd be nervous too. But let me tell you something—we have already won this game, boys. We have already won this game. Now have some fun this inning, okay?"

They nodded in response, and went back to their positions. As I walked back to the dugout, the home plate umpire stopped me.

"You guys have played a great game. This is a good team you're facing," he said.

"Thanks," I responded. "That means a lot to us."

THE BOTTOM OF the fifth inning against the RBI Angels will forever be burned into my memory. The sky was dark as the hour was late, but the bright lights illuminated the field brilliantly. The umpire called for play to begin, and the ball was thrown from Aaron down to Jeff at second base, then around the infield and back to Sam. The batter stepped into the box.

Before a single pitch could be thrown, however, we heard an unfamiliar sound. It began as a slow chant coming from the stands in right field. At first, we could not quite make it out, but it quickly became louder.

"Let's go, Rashi!" followed by the stomping of feet and the hitting of walls. "Boom, Boom . . . Boom, Boom, Boom." Then louder, *"Let's go, Rashi! Boom, Boom . . . Boom, Boom, Boom!"* Then working into a fever pitch, "LET'S GO, RASHI! BOOM, BOOM . . . BOOM, BOOM, BOOM!"

Adam, Jeremy, and I looked out toward right field,

wondering who could be cheering for us so loudly and with such enthusiasm. Stan stood up and craned his neck to see what was happening.

"Who is doing that—the parents?" Stan asked.

"Probably the younger siblings," Jeremy answered.

"No, they can't make that much noise," I said.

"LET'S GO RASHI! BOOM, BOOM . . . BOOM, BOOM, BOOM!"

Then finally I saw them, hanging over the low barricade along the right field foul line, standing on chairs to see the action, screaming with all their might, while banging loudly on the wooden fence below and behind. Our new friends and bunkmates, the Westfield Rocks, waiting to play their next game on our field, were the responsible party. The blond crew-cut kids from Indiana were swarming our bleachers, whipping the crowd into a frenzy and doing everything in their power to will their dark-haired Jewish friends to victory.

Unfortunately, victory was not to be ours. All magic must come to an end, and on that late night in Cooperstown, ours eventually did. Sam walked the first batter, who stole around and ended up scoring on an infield error. A walk and two hits later, we were down four to one. I knew it was over. We had no chance of scoring three runs to tie them in the sixth, and we did not. The upstart Rams were finally put down.

WE LINED UP to shake the Angels' hands, and the usual "good game" that the teams congratulated each other with was replaced with "great game." One of their coaches came over to Gabe afterward.

"Hey, kid, you pitched well. Not a tremendous amount of speed, but you've got some movement."

"Thanks, Coach," Gabe said.

"You got an extra pin on you?"

"A pin?"

"You know, one of your Rams pins. I'd like to wear it in honor of the fight you guys put up," he said.

"Sure, Coach, hang on." Gabe ran over to his equipment bag, and grabbed an extra Rashi pin that lay at the bottom. Running back, he handed it to the Angels' coach.

"Thanks, kid," he said as he fastened it onto his cap. "Good luck the rest of the week."

I smiled as I watched Gabe wave to him.

"Hey, Josh—thanks." I turned to see Stan Goodman standing next to me. He seemed tired and worn, the small bags that hung under his eyes had grown bigger. If possible, he looked a little thinner than he had just a day or two earlier.

"For what, Stan?" I asked.

"For letting Jeffrey play second base."

"Stan, it was my pleasure."

"And for helping the boys almost win a game."

"Anytime."

"Oh . . . and . . . thanks for giving me a chance to forget."

"Forget?" I said, momentarily forgetting myself.

"For the last two hours, I wasn't thinking about it. I wasn't thinking about the cancer. I wasn't thinking about the MRI. I was just enjoying the game. Thank you," he said, reaching over to hug me.

I hugged him back, and then stared not knowing how to respond.

"You're welcome, Stan," was all I could muster.

AS THE RAMS lay down in their bunk beds that night, I made the rounds, congratulating them on their remarkable performance. It was midnight, and most of them were sound asleep soon after I left their bedside.

In the dark, I walked over to Gabe, who was snuggled deep in his sleeping bag high on the top bunk. The room was unusually quiet as I stood by his side.

"You pitched an unbelievable game," I whispered in his ear while squeezing his hand. "I wish my father could have been there to see you. He would have been so proud."

He lifted up his head and kissed me, passing the compliment right back in his usual manner.

"You coached an unbelievable game, Dad. Abba would have been proud of *you*. I know I am." And with that, he put his head back down on the pillow, and drifted off to a well-deserved, peaceful night's sleep.

CHAPTER TWENTY-ONE

HECK IF I KNOW

WE AWOKE TUESDAY morning to bright sunshine and even brighter news.

"Dudes, we're ranked ninety-third! I can't freakin' believe it! We jumped three spots!" Jason Armon came rushing in after having checked the updated rankings which were posted just steps from the bunk.

"How did that happen if we lost?" Carlos asked as he jumped down from the bed above me.

"Carlos, we only lost four to one," Jeff explained. "Clearly our ranking was going to improve when we were giving up an average of fifteen runs a game. In fact, ninety-third is just about what I expected based on the calculations I made last night before going to bed."

"It's a great accomplishment," I said to the team. "As of this moment we are not the worst team in the park!" A smattering of self-congratulatory applause made its way around the cabin. "Now everyone get up, and let's get ready for breakfast and our first game of the day."

"Our first game—maybe," Adam said as he yawned and stretched inside his sleeping bag. "Breakfast—not likely."

"What are you talking about?" I asked.

"It's ten past eight. The game starts in twenty minutes."

"You're joking. Don't stress me out like that."

"I'm not joking, Josh. Your alarm must not have gone off."

"Oh my God, I was so exhausted last night I forgot to set it! Everybody out of bed *now*! Get into your uniforms—*hurry*!"

"Who are we playing this morning?" Charlie asked as he hung off the side of his bed, pricking his finger to check his morning glucose.

"The Steubenville Stars Baseball Club," Jeremy answered his son.

"Where are they from?"

"Ohio, I think."

"Let's hope they're still on Midwest time," I said.

"Sorry, Coach, Ohio is in the Eastern time zone," Jeff corrected me.

THANKFULLY, WE WERE able to get dressed and arrive at the field seven minutes before the game was scheduled to start. It's remarkable how much can take place in seven minutes.

"How could you not have given them breakfast?" Sheryl stood next to me outside the dugout, demanding an explanation. The boys had greeted their parents, and word had leaked out quickly. "The mothers are up in arms, Josh!"

"Up in arms? They're lucky their kids are alive!" I pointed out. "Do you have any idea what I'm dealing with here? Twelve boys, two long games every day, rain delays, not getting to bed until midnight, and then an eight thirty start the next morning! Breakfast? Are you kidding me?"

"Listen to me, Josh. These kids need something to eat before they play," she said.

"Okay, I'll just go out to the coaches' meeting and tell the umpire that we need to delay the start of the game so that we can go back to the village and sit down for breakfast. No, wait—I have a better idea! I'll just tell them that since we didn't eat this morning, we're going to forfeit the game. That should make your constituents happy!"

"Well, at least let me get a bunch of chocolate milks at the concession stand for the dugout," Sheryl compromised.

"Be my guest," I said. After everything that I had been through, I didn't appreciate being second-guessed on this one.

Within a minute, bottles of Nesquik chocolate milk were delivered and unloaded into the rack on the wall of the dugout while our bats played second fiddle, languishing on the ground. As I stood there questioning our priorities, Gil approached me with tears in his eyes. I turned to face him.

"Coach, I . . . chipped my tooth," he said as the tears started rolling down his cheeks.

"What are you talking about, Gil?"

He opened his mouth in explanation. Gil happened to have generously sized central incisors and when he bared them for me, a gaping hole was revealed in the center of his pearly whites. He was missing half of one large upper front tooth. A glance down at his open palm showed the missing piece.

"How did that happen?" I asked.

"I was . . . bouncing a bat . . . in front of me . . . ," he said between sobs, "and it jumped up . . . and hit me in the mouth!"

"All right, take it easy, Gil," I said, trying quickly to decide which way to go with this problem. The physician inside me tugged one way and the coach, the other. The coach won out. "Can you still play?" I asked.

"It depends what my dad says."

I sighed. Gil's father just so happened to be a dentist, and there was no way that he was going to allow his son to take the field missing half of a central incisor. Gil's parents had gone home after the first weekend, and with the game set to begin soon, I handed the whole situation over to Sheryl.

"Sher, since you insisted on purchasing chocolate milk for us, the bats were not in the bat rack where they should have been, and consequently one of them hit Gil in the mouth and knocked out his front tooth. Please take care of it. I have a game to coach."

"Take it easy, Josh. Calm down." She grabbed her cell phone, and within minutes, Sheryl and her new charge were on their way to Oneonta, New York, for a visit with a local dentist.

As I watched them walk away, it dawned on me why God had not seen fit to provide us with the huge-barreled bats that most of the other teams were using. If it weren't for a little divine intervention, Gil might have been looking at implants. I turned to watch the team prepare.

"GABE IS MY warm-up buddy!" Sam Budd called loudly across the field.

"But, Sam, you always warm up with me," Aaron complained.

"Go warm up with whoever Gabe usually warms up with," Sam commanded.

"Who does he usually warm up with?"

"Gabe, who do you normally warm up with?" Sam asked as he threw a ball down to him.

"Charlie, Phil, or Ari."

"Go warm up with Charlie, Phil, or Ari, then," Sam ordered, directing his comment at Aaron.

Aaron went over and started throwing with Charlie, and a domino effect ensued. Jason began tossing with Ari, Rami with Phil and Robert with Jeff. Carlos ran around looking for a pair to join up with.

The coaches stood together in the dugout, watching them. It was the first time that Sam's and Gabe's groups had cross-pollinated during warm-ups.

"Maybe we're making some progress after all," I said.

"Nice to see some teamwork," Jeremy agreed. "Perhaps it will translate into better play on the field."

"Josh, can you pass me a chocolate milk?" Stan asked, interrupting our brief moment of team harmony.

"Yeah, I'll take one, too," Adam joined in.

I grabbed four bottles of the Nesquik out of the rack and passed them down, keeping one for myself.

"To newfound teamwork," I said, raising my milk in a toast.

"To teamwork," they repeated.

We clicked the plastic bottles against one another and looked out over the field before simultaneously taking a swig.

IF NOT FOR the presence of an easy scapegoat, I'm sure I would have been sorely disappointed at our performance against the Steubenville Stars. But at least I had something to blame.

The Stars plated nine runs in the first inning alone and as the last one came around to score, I second-guessed the self-righteous attitude I had taken with Sheryl. Maybe I should have insisted on breakfast all along.

The Rams offensive highlight was a Rami Liebshutz walk. Minus his sports goggles, Phil Perlow pitched all four innings of the mercy-rule shortened game, and his final stat line was a crescendo of misery—two hit batters, three base-on-balls, nine hits, and sixteen runs allowed.

"Well, gentlemen," I said after the game as we gathered in the dugout. "That didn't work out quite the way we planned. Next time, maybe we'll get up a little earlier and have breakfast. But more importantly, I was glad to see that you guys mixed up the warm-up buddies today."

"Some good that did," Aaron Dines moaned.

"You're coming together as a team, and regardless of whether you win or lose that's something to be proud of." They heard my words, but I suspected they were not convinced.

THE BRICK FACADE of the Baseball Hall of Fame in

downtown Cooperstown rose up impressively before us. The multistoried building was divided into three attached sections, with a center entrance. Multiple large rectangular windows with white trim allowed warm sunlight to penetrate the hallowed halls. It reminded me of what a building at a New England prep school might look like, although the entrance exam to this particular institution was unlike any other.

The coaches, players, parents, and siblings stood on the steps leading to the front door, ready to explore the museum. After taking our beating at the hands of the Steubenville Stars, we had the afternoon off and had decided to use the time for a field trip. Dreams Park had provided each team with passes to the Hall, requesting that players remain in uniform while visiting.

Tourists, hauling bags overflowing with baseball mementos, strolled up and down Main Street, going in and out of stores. A multitude of souvenirs with the name "Cooperstown" printed on them would soon be making their way across the country.

"How are we going to do this?" Adam asked.

"I say we stick together," Jeremy suggested.

"Nah, small groups," I said. "That way we can go at our own pace."

"You're looking to take your time, huh?" Jeremy asked me.

"Exact opposite—I'm looking to get through quickly."

"Why is that?"

"Sorry but I'm in no mood to revel in the great history of our national pastime. In fact, despite all the pleasure it's given me over the years, at this point I think I wish the sport had never been created."

"You cutting down Abner Doubleday?" Adam jumped in.

"No, it's not his fault. I just wish he had discovered bowling or something. Actually, I don't think he even really invented baseball . . ."

"Noooooo! Oh my God!" Jeremy gasped out of the blue.

"What? You're disappointed Doubleday didn't invent baseball?"

"No . . . it's not that . . . I think Harvey has lice," he whispered, looking down at his younger son, who stood next to him.

"What are you talking about?"

"Take a look," he said frantically. Adam and I looked down at the top of Harvey's head to see a multitude of tiny eggs and a couple of crawling bugs.

"That's gross," escaped from my mouth before total chaos erupted. Those standing nearby had overheard our conversation, and it took about four seconds before the entire group was apprised of the situation.

Everyone bolted in the opposite direction of poor Harvey, leaving him standing alone. Within minutes, the poor seven-year-old had gone from sweet, lovable younger sibling to complete outcast, a pariah. He looked around in dismay and confusion, having no idea that his joyful and carefree week of vacation in upstate New York had come to a sudden and premature end.

"Oh, c'mon, Charlie!" Aaron Dines called out. "Your brother is disgusting, man."

"Yeah," Rami chimed in. "That is the nastiest thing I've ever seen."

"It's not his fault," Charlie did his best to defend his sibling.

"That's right, Charlie. It's not his fault," I said to the group. "Harvey's parents will deal with this. Let's get going. Before we do though, just find a partner and check each other's heads. Let me know if you see anything small, white, or moving. Adam—can you check me?"

A few tourists passed by with looks of confusion on their faces as they observed our sizable group bending over, picking through each other's hair. It was not what they had been expecting to see on the front steps of the legendary Baseball Hall of Fame.

JEREMY AND I wandered through the hallways, looking over the exhibits. Our sons lagged behind, calling to one another with enthusiasm as they pointed at this or that. A large staircase led from the first floor to the second. After having completed our overview of the bottom level, I wearily climbed to the top.

"Take a look at this," Jeremy called over to me. "Jim Palmer's cap!"

I looked behind the glass to see on old, beat-up Baltimore Orioles cap.

"Yawn," I said.

"How 'bout this—Lou Brock's shoes. Now, that's pretty cool," he persisted.

"Boring."

"Well come over here. You've got to find this interesting—Curt Schilling's bloody sock!" He pointed behind the glass at a dirty sock with red stains around the ankle.

"That's ketchup if I've ever seen it."

"Josh, what is wrong with you? This is good stuff. You'll be sorry that you didn't appreciate this later."

"Not likely. After this week, I think I'm done with baseball."

The group convened to watch a twenty-minute movie detailing the history of the game. Despite multiple elbows to the ribs from my fellow coaches, I fell asleep during the show.

Finally the Rams had gotten their fill, and we walked back down the stairs heading toward the exit. Just before leaving the building, however, we came across the final exhibit. In my foul mood I almost missed it.

Two doors opened to reveal a large, rectangular room with an arch at the far end and wooden benches cutting across the middle. Dark gray marble columns supported the ceiling on either side. Visitors milled about, pointing at the walls, which displayed a double row of plaques all along its length. Each nameplate was devoted to a unique and exceptional student of the game whose body of work had gained him admission to this most prestigious of prep schools. We looked out over the Hall of Fame Gallery.

"Cool!" Gabe said as he ran into the room with his friends.

I followed behind, walking slowly beside the walls, looking over the plaques. Each one contained a bronze relief of the player's face, along with a short paragraph detailing his particular accomplishments. As I scanned them, I suddenly felt an overwhelming feeling of shame for my earlier behavior.

"What about these?" Jeremy asked as he walked by my side.

I looked up at the walls and the faces that hung before me, row after row.

"You're right, Jeremy," I said. "Who am I not to appreciate this great sport? What have I ever done that gives me the right not to care about these players' achievements? I'm nothing. I'm nobody."

Jeremy looked at me and shook his head in bewilderment.

I wandered up one side of the room and down the other, trying to decide whether I loved baseball intensely or hated it with a passion. As the war in my schizophrenic mind raged back and forth, something about one of the plaques caught my attention, distracting me from my internal debate.

I moved over for a closer inspection. Looking up at the engraving, I recognized a familiar face. Then scanning down to the paragraph written beneath it, I read the following:

Set all time record with 4 no-hitters in 4 years, capped by 1965 perfect game, and by capturing earned run title 5 seasons in a row, 1962–1966. Won 25 or more games three times. Had 11 shutouts in 1963. Strikeout leader four times, with record 382 in 1965. Fanned 18 in a game twice. Most valuable player 1963. Cy Young award winner 1963–65–66.

It was my old friend Sandy Koufax, the greatest Jewish baseball player of all time. His bronzed image was staring down at me. He had found me for a reason. I stood there in front of him in my Cooperstown Dreams Park windbreaker, my Cooperstown Dreams Park cap perched upon my head. The world went silent. Gone were the screaming boys, complaining parents, and opposing coaches giving me the once-over. My eyes were heavy with fatigue and I was tired to the core.

I suddenly saw myself for the fool that I was, an adult trying to live out a childhood fantasy. I was every father I had sat in judgment of, trying to live vicariously through my son. I began to second-guess everything that I had done. Doubt and fear plagued my mind once again. I had only one question for the great Mr. Koufax, and something deep inside me knew that this time he had an answer.

"What in God's name am I doing here?" I asked.

There was silence for a moment and then ever so subtly, I saw his bronzed lips move under his cap. His dimple disappeared for just a moment. I heard his voice loudly and clearly, but he spoke only to me.

"Heck if I know," he said.

Touching his plaque, I kissed my hand. Turning around, I gathered the boys and left the building.

CHAPTER TWENTY-TWO

AWKWARD DELIVERY

"SHOW ME HOW it looks," I said to Gil. It was four thirty in the afternoon, and we had returned from the Hall of Fame for our game against the North Wake Mustangs, who had traveled all the way from North Carolina to play us. Sheryl had brought Gil back from Oneonta just in time. We stood in the dugout along the first baseline, the sun's rays warm on our faces as it descended toward the horizon.

"It'll never be the same," he said, baring his teeth. The broken piece had been replaced, but there was a faint fault line visible that stretched horizontally from one side of the tooth to the other.

"Can't even tell," I said.

"Yeah, right. The girls will never like me now."

"You'll be fine, Gil. Go warm up."

I looked out onto the field to see that our team's two groups had remained intermingled. Once again, Sam and Gabe were tossing the ball back and forth to each other, and the rest had fallen in line.

"You're running out of time, Gabe," Sam was saying. "You've only got three games left."

"I'll take my chances," Gabe responded.

THE TOP OF the first inning against the North Carolinians felt very familiar, three up and three down without even a chance to muster a run. In the bottom half, Jason Armon took the mound. Overall, his performance against the Central Jersey Slammers had not been that bad, and if Carlos had somehow been able to educate himself on the rules of baseball prior to the tournament, it might have been dramatically better. I had hopes that Jason might somehow be able to keep us in the game, but it was not to be.

The Mustangs came to the plate and refused to leave. The first inning saw five hits, two errors, and a total of six runs scored. The lone highlight was a diving stop by Gabe at third, which while not resulting in an out, kept two additional runs from crossing the plate. In the second inning, the team from North Wake went right back to work, putting up a five spot and making it eleven to nothing.

"Time to get out the hook, Coach."

I looked behind me to see Jeffrey, who was sitting next to his father on the bench.

"Is that so, Jeff?" I asked.

"He's right," Stan said, while perusing a Hall of Fame brochure that he had brought back from our field trip.

I called time and walked slowly to the mound where Jason was standing. When both Goodmans agreed on something, it was best to follow suit.

"That's it, buddy," I said, holding out my hand to receive the ball. Jason took off his cap and ran his hand through his long straight black hair.

"Who're you putting in, Coach?" he asked.

"I thought I would give Robert another shot at it," I said.

"Robert? Are you freakin' kidding me, dude? I can do better than Robert."

"Jason, I hate to tell you, but you just gave up eleven runs in less than two innings."

"Yeah, well, Matz will give up more," he said.

"Maybe. Now give me the ball, please."

He handed it over and walked slowly back to the dugout. "Son of a bitch," he whispered under his breath as he took a seat on the bench.

ROBERT TOOK OVER, and Jason was proved correct. Matz was worse. When the lead swelled to fifteen, the Mustangs coach decided that we had had enough.

"Switch 'em around!" he called from his location in the third base coach's box. I winced when I heard the words.

"Well, that hurts," I said aloud in the dugout.

"It was inevitable," Adam said.

"Yeah, but it still hurts."

"Not as much as this," Jeremy said, pointing out at the field.

The Mustang players had received their instructions, but were refusing to listen to their head coach. He was signaling for them to switch to the opposite side of the plate, and yet they all shook their heads no.

While the opposing coach and players were arguing over whether to put an end to their batting practice or not, one of the umpires stopped by the mound to pay Robert a visit. She was a female umpire, the first we had seen that week. With mouth agape, I watched as she began to give Robert some pointers, her motherly instincts overriding her umpire's. She put her back foot on the mound, and then in slow motion simulated the release of the ball, walking him through his mechanics.

"What is she doing?" Adam questioned. "She's supposed to be impartially judging the game!"

"She feels sorry for him," Jeremy said.

"Well, this is just ridiculous! This type of thing might be appropriate in a seven-year-old neighborhood tee ball game, but not here. This is downright humiliating!" Adam was not happy.

Some of the umpire's pitching advice must have conflicted with what we had taught Robert, because he looked over at me and began making questioning hand motions. He didn't know whom to listen to.

"Do what she says, Robert!" I called out to the mound. Clearly, the instructions that I had given him over the last six months weren't doing him any good.

Robert went back to the hill, and when the score reached seventeen to nothing, I heard a familiar voice.

"Time to pull him, Coach," Jeff said from the bench.

"Stan?" I asked.

"Yup," he said.

I walked out to the mound.

"Sorry, Robert, time's up," I said.

"But I can do this, Coach," he pleaded.

"I'm sure you can, but you've just given up six runs without recording a single out." I took the ball from his hand and he walked to the bench, shaking his head in identical fashion to his predecessor but without the profanities.

I called to Phil to come in from shortstop and take over. He took the ball from my hand.

"Can I use my change-up, Coach?" he asked.

Phil believed that he had two pitches, a fastball and a change-up. The latter was delivered in a bizarre fashion with arms and legs flying in four different directions. He had yet to unleash it in the tournament.

"I don't care if you pitch underhand, just get some outs," I said. The umpire called for the resumption of play.

Phil went into his windup. Immediately after releasing the ball, his left arm flew toward the sky while his right whipped out at a ninety-degree angle. Then one leg hammered the ground while the other extended behind him in a maneuver the average human body would not be able to execute.

The batter was so distracted by the awkward delivery that he let the ball float slowly by him for strike one. Aaron returned the ball to Phil, and by the time he had thrown his second so-called change-up, we began to hear loud heckling from the stands.

"Come on, Coach! Pull him out! He's clearly hurt! What are you doing, Coach? Pull him! This is ridiculous!"

"Who the heck is that?" I said, extending my neck from the dugout to get a better look.

"Whoever it is, they're yelling at you," Jeremy said.

"Yeah, I got that. But who is it? It's coming from our stands!"

"David Perlow," Adam said, looking down the foul line.

"You've got to be kidding me."

"Nope, it's him."

"He's yelling at me to pull his own son?" I asked.

"Looks like it," Adam said. "He thinks Phil's hurt."

I looked down the line to see David Perlow, Phil's father, standing in front of the fence and screaming with every ounce of strength he had.

"Josh, his face is redder than your grandfather's during his verbal tirade against the Tustin Extreme," Stan said, standing up from the bench to get a look.

"Well, I guess I can't blame him for being confused. Phil's form is certainly unorthodox," I said while walking out to the mound. David settled down and the heckling stopped.

"Phil, your pitch delivery looks weird. Are you injured?" I asked as I arrived at his side.

"No, not at all, Coach. That's just my change-up."

"That's what I thought. Unfortunately, your father thinks you're hurt, and he wants you out of the game. I think you're done."

"But you're the coach," he said.

"And he's your father."

"I'll go explain to him what's happening," Phil tried.

"I don't think we have time for that right now," I responded, taking the ball from his glove as the home plate umpire began to walk toward us.

Phil left the mound shaking his head, a mirror image of Jason and Robert.

I had Gabe mop up the game, and we finally walked off the field, the recipients of a twenty-six to nothing thrashing at the hands of the North Wake Mustangs. The mercy rule dictated that we complete a minimum of four innings, regardless of how bad it got during the first three.

"No wins, six losses," Sam Budd said to Gabe afterward. "Two to go."

"Two to go," Gabe agreed sullenly.

"CARLOS! YOU JERK!" Gil screamed as the two returned to the cabin from the shower house, towels wrapped tightly around their respective waist. It was nine thirty at night, and the other coaches were doing their best to get the boys to bed after an exhausting day.

"Settle down, Gil," I said. "What's wrong?"

"Carlos threw a shampoo cap in the shower, and broke my tooth again!" he cried, pointing an accusatory finger at the alleged guilty party.

"It was an accident," Carlos said.

"Wait a minute," I intervened. "Are you guys trying to tell me that Carlos threw a shampoo cap, and it happened to hit you right in the same spot that was repaired this morning?"

"That's exactly what happened!" Gil said.

"Let me see."

Gil opened his mouth, and sure enough, half of the lower piece that had been reattached that morning was gone. Gil held out his outstretched hand to reveal the broken quarter-tooth in exactly the same manner as he had done some twelve hours earlier.

"Carlos, since when is your arm that good?" I asked.

"I've been practicing, Coach."

"Hmm . . . maybe we need to get you a little more playing time . . ."

"More playing time?" Gil was furious. "What about

my tooth?"

I shook my head to clear my thoughts. "I'll call your dentist."

"My dentist is my father."

"I know, Gil. Give me the tooth." He handed over the chip.

After a few phone calls, a plan was set in place. Sheryl would take Gil back to Oneonta in the morning. Meanwhile, it was my responsibility to get some milk in which the tooth could be stored. Apparently, milk preserved teeth, something I had not been taught in medical school. I left Adam, Jeremy, and Stan in charge and walked to the parking lot. I hopped into my car and drove down the road to the local convenience store outside the park.

Thankfully, despite the late hour, it was open. I paused in front of the refrigerated section, struggling to decide what type of milk to get. Gil's father had not specified whole versus skim, so I split the difference and bought a small container of 2%.

Upon my return, I found the bunkhouse quiet. Everyone was asleep. I dug out a small plastic bag I had purchased at the store and poured the milk inside, tossing the chip in afterward. I placed the bag on the floor by the alarm clock next to my bed and changed into sweats. Climbing onto the cot, I lay my head on the pillow, awaiting the blessing of unconsciousness that came with sleep. But I was not so fortunate.

For a time, I tossed and turned wondering how the milk would protect the tooth. I reviewed our games from that day and my experience at the Hall of Fame. Sleep still eluded me, and so I tried to place my mind outside of the park, thinking of work and of home. But no matter what I tried, I was unsuccessful.

For a long while I couldn't understand why I remained awake. I was completely exhausted and should have been asleep hours ago. Was it Gil's tooth? No, his father was a dentist. He'd be all right. Was it David Perlow's questioning my coaching? No, he was just a concerned father. It wasn't personal.

Then it came to me. I finally realized what had brought on the sudden bout of insomnia. In a few hours, the sun would rise in Cooperstown, bringing with it something that I had been dreading for days. It would bring with it a team that had been ranked number one based on runs allowed and runs scored for the entire week of the tournament. It would bring a team that our boys had been hearing every player in the park speak of with the utmost fear and respect. It would bring a team that would make us want to throw our bats and gloves out the windows of the cabin and cower under our cots in terror.

The rising of the sun would bring the Central Florida Sting.

CHAPTER TWENTY-THREE

JUST ONE K

ASIDE FROM THAT one aberrant morning after the RBI Angels game, all week long when we checked the tournament rankings, there were but two constants. The Rashi Rams were ranked last, and the Central Florida Sting was ranked first. It was just rotten luck that we had drawn them in our final scheduled game of the week. The contests were put together randomly prior to the event, and there was no way for the schedulers to foresee that they would be forcing number ninety-six to play number one. There was no doubt, however, that the Sting's head coach was pleased to see our name crop up on his schedule. The Sting was at Dreams Park for one reason and one reason only—to win the tournament. Its players were not going to complain about the Powers That Be granting them an easy W.

After the seven-game "regular season" was complete, a new list of ranks was to be posted, with every team participating in a sudden-death play-off that would begin that afternoon. If the Sting could hold us scoreless on Wednesday morning, it would go a long way toward helping them keep their top ranking.

I WAS HOLDING back Sam Budd to pitch our play-off game later that afternoon, so Gabriel was to get the start against the all-mighty Sting. We awoke that morning to bright sunshine streaming through the windows of our bunkhouse, but the usual lighthearted chatter among the boys was subdued. The pall of our upcoming date with one of Dreams Park's great bullies weighed heavily on the team.

After breakfast we got dressed in our visiting blues and headed down to Field No. 12. Despite the early hour, the park was bustling as teams moved about preparing for the upcoming play-offs that afternoon. Baseball chatter could be heard coming from the diamonds as we walked past, everyone expressing an opinion on how the rankings might fall.

Gabe walked slowly by my side, the duffel bag containing our bats swinging back and forth from his shoulder. He had been steadfast and brave all week long, but when it came to the Sting, even he was not immune to the mind killer.

"Dad, I'm scared," he said.

"You'll be fine, honey," I responded, placing a hand on his shoulder as we walked.

"But, Dad, it's the Sting. Everyone says they're the best, and you know how badly the teams in the middle of the pack have beaten us. Imagine what this is going to be like."

"Gabriel, you have performed so well this week, doing everything I've asked of you and more. I agree. There is no way we're going to win this game. But look at the opportunity that you've been given. You have a chance to be the starting pitcher against one of the best ten and under teams in the country, if not the world."

"Wonderful," he said sarcastically.

"Gabe, no one expects anything of you against this team—not a thing. But think of the chance you now have. It doesn't matter if the score ends up being thirty to nothing. Just think about it. What if, just what if, you had one strikeout? Just one K! You would always know that you probably struck out one of the top one hundred ten-year-old baseball players in the country, possibly someone who will one day play in the majors. Think about that!"

"I guess," he said with minimal enthusiasm.

"Gabe, you'll probably never get a chance to face a team like this again. If you can, I want you to do one thing for me."

"What's that, Dad?"

"Go out there on the mound and enjoy this game. Most likely, it will never come again."

"Okay, I'll try," he said. "Dad, can I ask you something?"

"Shoot."

"Were you ever in a situation like this, where you were pitching against such a dominant team?"

"Never—unless you count playing Camp Bauercrest every summer." We laughed together. "Besides, you know that I was much more of a third baseman than a pitcher."

"I feel like I'm more of a third baseman, too."

"And a good one at that."

WE FINALLY MADE it down to the field and walked into the visitor's dugout, dropping our equipment on the ground. The Sting was already there warming up, and we stood for a moment watching the team. Every throw was hard, crisp, and sharp. Not a single ball was dropped. The players moved with a grace and skill that even our prior competition had not possessed.

"They look like professional ballplayers in ten-year-old bodies," I said, staring at them in bewilderment.

"Automatons," Jeremy informed us. "That's what they are, automatons."

"What's an automaton?" Rami asked.

"It's from the Latin, meaning 'self-operating machine,'" Jeff Goodman explained. "It's like a robot."

"Yeah, they do look like robots—baseball-playing robots," Charlie added.

We watched in silence, not even daring to begin warming up ourselves.

"It's a shame we have to face them," Adam lamented. "In another life I probably would have paid money to watch these guys play."

"You did pay money," I said.

"Yeah, but usually when I buy a ticket to the zoo, it's so I can look at the lions through the bars. We now have to climb into the cage."

I WALKED OUT to the third base coach's box praying for an earthquake, tornado, or any natural disaster that might cancel the game. As none was forthcoming, I went back to watching the Sting's infield warming up. And there, to my great surprise, I saw Goliath. The same Goliath I had introduced during my pep talk before our opening game against the Extreme. At the time of the speech I thought I was relying on a clever metaphor, but no longer. The Sting's first baseman was the biggest ten-year-old kid that I had ever seen. He must have been at least my height and was carrying around a good-size beer belly. I considered asking to see his birth certificate, but the grizzled sixty-something-year-old head coach of the Sting seemed to be in no mood for a joke.

Central Florida's pitcher was warming up by throwing fastballs in the seventy-mile-per-hour range. He looked better than any pitcher we had previously seen. I sauntered over near one of the opposition's assistant coaches, fishing for a little information.

"Your pitcher seems to be throwing some serious heat. Is he your ace?" I asked.

"No offense, Coach," he said. "But why would we throw our ace for this game? He's our eighth or ninth guy."

Unbelievable, I thought. Then the umpire uttered the words that everyone on our bench had been dreading.

"Play ball!"

Aaron Dines led off, and this time he did not need to be cajoled into using a lighter bat. He stepped to the plate, settling in warily. The first pitch blew by, nearly causing him to topple over.

"Strike one!" yelled the ump. The next two pitches were duplicates of the first, and Aaron returned to the bench shaking his head.

"Good luck," he said to Phil as they crossed paths near the on-deck circle. "Be careful up there."

Phil dug in from the left side of the plate, cautiously eyeing the pitcher.

"His shoulder, Phil, remember to look at the shoulder!" I called.

Although he had yet to have a hit, Phil had been playing with increasing confidence as the week wore on. He watched the next pitch rapidly approach the strike zone. Swinging quickly, Phil made enough contact to lift the ball over the third baseman's head into left field for a base hit. He ran down to first, and the Rams' bench went wild.

"Way to go, Phil. Great hit!" I called over to him, while watching Sam Budd drop one of his two bats in the on-deck circle and step to the plate. If we were going down, then we were going down swinging, and with that mentality in mind, I immediately gave Phil the "steal" sign.

As the pitcher delivered the ball toward the plate, Phil, easily our fastest player, cut loose, darting toward second. But the Sting's catcher had his own tool to call upon in situations like this, namely a cannon attached to his right shoulder. He gunned it down to second faster than I thought possible. But when the dust settled, Phil was lying with his left foot touching the bag, and the umpire had his arms spread wide, signaling that he was safe.

Sam worked the count to one and two before lining a pitch into the gap in right center. It was the first time the Rams had back to back hits, and although momentarily paralyzed, I shook off the surprise to scream at Phil who was standing on second base in disbelief.

"Run, Phil, run!"

He rounded third, but the right fielder scooped up the baseball and fired it toward home. By the time I could even think about sending him, the ball was rocketing over the pitcher's mound. I quickly held up both hands. Phil put on the brakes and scampered back to third. Sam trotted into second with a stand-up double.

And just like that, there we were, second and third with one out in the first inning against one of the top teams in the country. I looked over at our bench and saw the entire squad on their feet, including Stan Goodman.

Over at the Sting's bench, the head coach was pacing back and forth wringing his hands. The gray-haired, seasoned veteran of the ten and under baseball circuit was in complete shock at the possibility that we might score. Knowing our reputation and our record, he had been confident that they would keep us from plating even a single run. The Sting had only given up a handful in its previous six games, and even one run here could drop the team in the rankings.

For an instant, I felt pity for him. He was a paid professional hired to win tournaments, and here he was at risk of losing his precious top seed due to a team that put the *rec* in *park and rec*.

But the Sting's fears proved groundless. First Gil and then Gabe struck out. The inning ended with us squandering an immense opportunity.

As I walked into the dugout, Jeremy approached me.

"Do you realize we were just sixty feet away from scoring?" he asked.

"Yeah, well, after Phil and Sam, they could have given us seven outs and it wouldn't have mattered."

"Sixty feet, Josh, sixty feet, against one of the best teams in the country," Jeremy said almost to himself. "If you had told me back at that first practice at Pierce that we would be sixty feet away from scoring on the best team in the country, I'd have taken it."

GABE APPEARED SMALL on the mound as he warmed up. There was not a single shadow on the field as the sun climbed toward its zenith. The heat, along with the stress, caused rivulets of sweat to trickle down the side of his face. He glanced over at me as I stood in the dugout.

"Just one K, Gabe," I called. "Remember—an opportunity!"

He nodded seriously and turned to focus on the Sting's leadoff hitter, a small kid with a quick bat. He let Gabe's first pitch go by, low and outside, for ball one.

"Just throw strikes, Gabe!" I called. "You can do it!"

The batter stood nonchalantly at the plate without the usual sense of vigilance that typically accompanied a leadoff hitter.

"He's taking," Jeff Goodman said, standing at my side. I looked down at him and then back at the batter.

"Are you sure?"

"One hundred percent."

I looked over at the batter again, examining his stance and demeanor closely.

"You're right," I said to Jeff.

It was a sound strategy for a leadoff hitter. Let the pitcher throw a few to see what he had. It also allowed the batter's teammates a chance to get a look at what they were up against. It was a completely rational approach, considering the talent level of the teams that the Sting typically faced. But under the current circumstances, when up against the mediocre velocity and pinpoint accuracy of Gabriel Berkowitz, it was a huge mistake.

"Just throw strikes, Gabe!" I called again from the dugout, and he did. Two in a row actually, and before we knew it, he was ahead in the count.

"One more!" I hollered out to my son. "One more and you've got your K!"

Gabe took off his cap and with his forearm wiped a few beads of sweat from his brow. Pitching from the stretch, he delivered his patented forty-five-mile-per-hour "fastball." The Sting's leadoff hitter knew that he was down in the count and that he must protect the plate. Yet his monumental error of taking too many pitches was now compounded by the fact that he had been unable to get his timing down. He was used to facing seventy- to eighty-mile-per-hour fastballs, and what came at him now was unlike anything his coaches had ever prepared him for.

Gabe threw it straight toward home with the look and feel of an elite pitch but so much slower. The batter swung too early, and his bat crossed the plate well before the ball did.

"Strike three!" hollered the umpire.

Cheers erupted from the field and the stands. Sheryl grabbed Shani and swung her in a circle. I ran over to the bench, grabbed Jeff's face, and kissed him on the cheek. Just that quickly, Gabe had a memory to last a lifetime. He had struck out the all-powerful, completely dominant, number one ranked, Central Florida Sting's leadoff hitter.

GABE WENT ON to pitch a stellar game against the Sting that was called after three and a half innings due to the mercy rule. Before our last at bat, their head coach pulled me aside. It was the first time he had spoken to me the entire game.

"Sorry," he said, nodding out toward the pitcher's mound. "Can't let you guys score."

I looked out onto the field to see what was apparently their closer, warming up on the mound. He was throwing significantly harder than their starter, which in my mind put him into the eighties. I nodded at my counterpart.

"We're flattered," I said. He gave me a quizzical look. We had put enough of a scare into the old man to warrant his calling out his closer from the bullpen despite the pressing immediacy of the play-offs. I was proud of my Rams even though the Sting's closer polished us off on nine pitches, bat never touching ball.

Yet Gabriel had again kept us from being humiliated, giving up a measly thirteen runs on eight hits and no base on balls. According to Jeremy's calculations, Gabe's fielders had let him down with nine errors, and as a result only one of his runs was earned.

"Get me the name of their leadoff hitter," I said to my statistician in the dugout after the game.

Jeremy scanned through their lineup card. "Lopez,"

he said. "It says his name is Lopez."

"Thanks," I said, making a mental note.

"Why do you want to know?"

"Because he fanned against my son, and if Mr. Lopez ever plays in the majors one day, I want to know. I'll be watching for him."

CHAPTER TWENTY-FOUR

HOLD MY CALLS

"WELL, IT'S OVER. The regular season, that is," Jeremy said as we sat in the mess hall, having lunch after our loss to the Sting.

"Yeah, no wins, seven losses, but at least it's behind us," I responded.

The open-air tent was crowded with teams that had come in after their morning games. Coaches called out to one another, players demanded more food, and the kitchen staff hustled up and down the buffet table, filling empty trays.

"Coach, who do you think we'll play in the play-offs?" Rami said from the seat next to me, while shoving yet another peanut butter and jelly sandwich into his mouth.

"Probably the Concord-Carlisle Minutemen. They've been fighting us all week long for the rights to be the worst team in the tournament."

As their coaches had expected, the Minutemen had indeed experienced a rough go of it, and most of the week they had been ranked ninety-fifth, just one slot above their neighbors fifteen minutes south on Route 128. The Rams and the Minutemen were two of only five teams in the tournament that had gone winless.

"Yeah, but even they can't match our complete incompetence," Sam Budd said from across the table.

"We fought hard," I countered. "We'll see how it turns out. Hey, Rami, are you sick of those peanut butter and jellies?"

"I was sick of them before the week even started, Coach. But I gotta keep kosher. I'm gonna have enough explaining to do about this haircut." Rami's parents had returned home at the beginning of the week, not having seen the dramatic change that had come over their son. He rubbed his small hand over the fuzz on the top of his head.

The team resumed eating, and it was not long before we got the news that we had been waiting for.

"Dudes, it's official!" Jason said breathlessly as he came running up to us from outside the tent. "We're ranked ninety-sixth going into the play-offs. They just posted the list."

"Who are we playing?" Carlos asked.

"That team from Concord. You know, the sons of bitches that suck almost as much as us."

I stood up from the table, clearing my tray. "Well, that's it, gentlemen. Now we know. Let's finish up and get back to the bunk. Next game starts in two hours."

WE STAYED IN our visiting blue uniforms as was befitting the lowest ranked team in the tournament, and walked down to Field No. 7. It was located in the front half of the park but farthest from the entrance. Ninety-fifth versus ninety-sixth did not merit prime real estate. I had spoken to Sheryl on the phone as soon as we knew where we would be playing, and as we approached the field, I saw that she had already arrived.

"Hail the conquering heroes!" she called, giving Gabe a squeeze. "One more game and you're through."

"Thanks," I said, giving her a kiss. "But don't rush us. We actually might have a shot at this one."

"How so?"

"We're playing the Minutemen. They're not quite as sorry as us, but they only recruited from two towns' worth of Little League players. Plus I've been saving Sam's arm for just this occasion. We've got a fighting chance."

"Well, good luck, guys," she called to the team as she made her way toward the stands. "Everyone's pulling for you!"

We entered the visitors' dugout, looking across the diamond at the competition. The Minutemen, decked out in their red uniforms, were already out in left field, warming up. For once I saw a team that seemed less than formidable. I walked across to reintroduce myself to their coaches.

"So we meet again," I said to the tall one.

"As we thought might happen," he replied. "How was your week?"

"Well, we learned our limitations; let's put it that way."

"And we learned that this place is a far cry from Little League back home."

"Amen to that," I said. "Well, despite everything, one of us is going to leave this tournament with a win, that's for sure."

"That's true and may it go to the best team."

"To the best team," I said. Turning on my heel, I headed back to our dugout. Before I could get inside however, Jeremy approached me. His facial expression revealed both shame and tension.

"Aaron is not playing," he reported.

"What are you talking about?" I asked, the now-familiar sick feeling beginning to rise in my stomach.

"He was acting up, and I yelled at him. Now he says he won't play. He says there's nothing that anyone can do about it."

"Stay here," I told him.

The biggest game of the week was moments away from starting, and our catcher had decided to call it quits. I entered the dugout to see Aaron sitting in the dirt, his back leaning against the far wall. I sat down on the ground facing him.

"I'm not playing," he said calmly and with great conviction. "Jeremy is a jerk and I'm not playing."

"That's what I heard," I whispered to him. "Do you know something?"

"What?" he asked, his head hanging low.

"You're right," I said.

"Right about what?"

"Jeremy is a jerk. Everyone knows that."

"You think so?"

"Of course," I said, pulling my head back as if I was surprised he hadn't heard what the general consensus was. "But I have to tell you something, Aaron. This is our play-off game. Sam is pitching, which means that you're the only catcher we have. The team needs you. I need you."

"You really think Jeremy is a jerk?" he asked.

"Yes, I do."

"Okay, I'll play,"

"Thank you, Aaron."

I got up and left the dugout, passing by Jeremy on the way to home plate for the head coaches' meeting.

"All set," I said.

"Thanks," he replied.

"No problem, big guy."

THE MINUTEMEN TOOK the field, and we watched them continue to warm up.

"These guys aren't auto mechanics or whatever those Sting guys were," Jason said as he witnessed a few balls being dropped.

"Automatons," Jeff said from his seat on the bench. "The word is *automatons*."

"Whatever, these guys aren't them," Jason responded.

Their pitcher, however, was intimidating. He had a large frame, and seemed to be throwing fairly hard.

"Let's go, Phil; start us off!" I called, clapping my hands together as I walked out to the third base coach's box.

"C'mon, Phil, base hit now, buddy!" Sam Budd yelled as he stood in the dugout. Gabe looked over at him and smiled.

"What?" Sam said. "We're on the same team, for crying out loud."

Phil stepped to the plate and dug in from the left side. After working the count to one and one, he launched a fly ball to deep center. The Minuteman centerfielder backtracked and caught it at the warning track.

"Nice try, Phil," Sam said as he returned to the dugout. "You got good wood on it." Gabe looked at him again questioningly.

"What? He made good contact," Sam said.

WE TOOK THE field in the bottom of the first after coming up empty handed in the top half of the inning. Sam bent his long torso to the ground, picking up the baseball as it lay near the rubber. I had used him relatively sparingly during the week, with just this occasion in mind. The plan was to pitch him all six innings.

"Let's go, Sam. Throw strikes now!" Phil returned the support he had received as he slammed his right fist into his glove, while getting into the ready position at shortstop.

"Here we go, Sam!" Gabe called from third, where he flexed his knees and dropped his own glove down in front of him.

"Throw strikes now, Sammy!" Rami called from second, spitting into the dirt by his side.

The leadoff hitter took Sam's first offering and hit a slow grounder down the third baseline. Gabe scooped it up and threw it accurately across the diamond to Gil, who was manning first base. Gil, losing focus for an instant, dropped the ball as the runner ran across the bag safely.

"That's okay, Sam!" I heard come from behind me in the dugout. "Just focus on the next one!"

I turned and saw Stan on his feet, watching the game

intently.

"Stan," I said. "What are you doing? It's only the first inning and nothing's happened yet."

"It's the play-offs," he responded. Turning his attention back to the field, he continued. "C'mon, Sam, let's get this guy!"

Frustration over the error was plainly evident on Sam's face, but he held his tongue and went back to work. After wiping his hand on the side of his pants, he went into his windup and came toward the plate. The runner on first read the delivery well, and getting a great jump, took off for second. The pitch was grounded toward the right side of the infield. Rami picked it up, throwing over to first for out number one. The runner scooted down to third. After making the play, Rami again spit on the ground.

"Nice play, Rami," I called to him.

"Thanks, Coach," he responded.

The third batter in their lineup took Sam's next offering and launched it deep into centerfield. Ari scampered backward and, reaching over his shoulder, grabbed the ball in midflight. He took a second to shake the long hair from his eyes before making the throw back to the infield. The runner on third tagged up and scored easily. There was no way to stop him. With bases empty, the final out was made, and the Rams ran off the field down one to nothing.

"Good job, guys," I said to them as they plopped down in the dugout. "We're only down one."

"Yeah; nice pitching, Sam," Gabe said.

"Not nice enough. I can't let up runs. We're not exactly an offensive juggernaut."

"You pitched well, Sam. We'll be okay." It was Ari who had spoken and everyone in the dugout looked at him in surprise. I had barely heard him say anything since the drive up to Cooperstown.

The game proceeded, and we found ourselves down five to nothing after two innings. Things were starting to have an all-too-familiar feeling.

"Maybe this isn't going to be different from our other efforts, after all," I said to Jeremy.

"It's only the second inning," he said. "Have some faith."

His words were prophetic. In the top of the third, we finally made some noise. Gil led off with a walk. Sam singled to left, and a subsequent double steal put runners at second and third with no outs. Aaron Dines stepped to the plate.

"Here we go, Aaron. Get a hit now!" Ari called from the dugout, his small smile suddenly replaced with a large one. He had found his voice.

"Let's knock in some runs now, Aaron. Here we go!" Gabe called and the rest of the team picked up the chorus.

Aaron leveled his bat over the plate, waiting for the pitch. The ball came in fast, but his swing was faster. Making solid contact, he drove a sharp single to right, bringing both runners home.

Cheers erupted from the bench.

"Nice stroke, Aaron!"

"Way to go, man!"

"Thank you, Lord," the last comment coming from

Stan.

Aaron followed up his heroics by stealing around to third and ultimately scoring on a wild pitch. It was Minutemen five, Rams three, and we were back in the game.

The parents were screaming from the stands and unbeknownst to me, at that very moment, my sister, Jody, was pacing up and down the length of her small office back in downtown Boston.

Our game was being broadcast via a small webcam placed behind home plate. Jody had reluctantly returned home earlier in the week to get back to work. She was now desperately trying to follow along, while for the most part only being able to see the backside of the home plate umpire. She could barely make out the scoreboard as she burned a hole in the computer with her eyes while frantically attempting to control her shaking legs.

"Hold my calls!" she yelled out to her secretary.

REVITALIZED BY THE three runs, our team played inspired ball, and over the next two innings, the game seesawed back and forth, with first the opposition from Concord having the lead, then us. In the fourth inning, we were up seven to six when, with two runners on, one of the Minutemen hit a rocket over the head of Charlie in right.

As we watched, Charlie chased after it, but then stopped and stood like a statue with his back to us, not moving a muscle. The runner kept rounding the bases.

"Jeremy, what is he doing?" Adam asked.

"No idea," Charlie's father replied.

We all began screaming at Charlie to throw the ball

in. There was no response.

"Throw the ball back, Charlie!"

"Move, Charlie!"

"What is going on out there?" Stan hollered.

After what seemed like an eternity, Charlie finally turned around and began yelling back at us. He stood with his back to the outfield fence with his arms raised high over his head. His mouth was moving, but he was so deep in right field that we couldn't hear a word he was saying.

"What's happening now?" I asked.

"Why doesn't he throw the ball in?" Adam voiced everyone's thoughts.

"He looks like he's in a silent movie from the 1920s," his father chipped in.

"Maybe the ball is stuck under the fence," Jeff Goodman suggested. We all turned and looked at him as he continued. "CDP rules state that a ball stuck under the fence is a ground rule double. Of course, that's only if the umpire sees it where it lies."

"How do you know the CDP rules?" I asked.

"I read the rule book," he said.

That was enough for us, and we all turned back toward right field and began screaming at Charlie not to touch the ball. But Charlie knew the rules better than any of us, and hadn't gone near it.

The umpire went out to confirm, and we waited anxiously as he ran all the way to the fence. What he saw out there only Charlie knew, but he quickly signaled that it was a ground rule double, and the runners were forced to return to their bases.

"Good job not touching the ball, Charlie!" Adam screamed out to him.

"My son, the genius," Jeremy said.

THE GAME CONTINUED back and forth, and we found ourselves knotted up at nine after six innings. The pressure was mounting with both teams desperate for their sole win. The Rams gathered in the dugout before the top of the seventh.

"We need base runners," I said to them. "Get on base, no matter what it takes."

Ari did as he was told and led off the inning with a walk. Gabe stepped to the plate next, looking for his first hit of the tournament. He dug his right foot into the dirt, and as the pitch came in, he swung, popping the ball up toward right field. It looked as if it might drop, but the hustling right fielder came in to make the catch. Ari had guessed incorrectly and started for second. He now found himself in no-man's land and was doubled off easily. Gabe slammed his bat into the turf and ripped off his helmet as he headed back toward the dugout.

With two outs, Phil was up. After a called strike, he knocked a solid single into left field. Gil followed that with a walk, putting runners on first and second for Sam Budd, who came from the on-deck circle. Taking a moment, he knocked the dirt from his cleats with his bat.

Sam was first pitch swinging, and he lined the ball into right center for a hit. Phil had a full head of steam as he rounded third, and I waved him in. He stumbled slightly before sliding into home. The catcher took the throw and reached for the tag, but Phil hooked his leg around him, touching the plate just in time.

"Safe!" screamed the umpire.

IT WAS TEN to nine, our lead, going into the bottom of the seventh. There was silence in the dugout as each player and coach seemed lost in his own thoughts.

"Three more outs, guys," I told the team. "Just three more outs and you will have won a game at the best youth baseball tournament in the country."

"Three more outs!" Gabe encouraged his teammates. "We can do this."

"Three more, dudes!" Jason called as he grabbed his glove and headed out toward left field.

"I can't stand the tension," I said to the other coaches after the team had filed out of the dugout.

"It all comes down to this," Jeremy said. "All we need is three."

Sam went back to the hill to pitch the final inning. He looked exhausted out there on the mound, and it showed in his performance. The leadoff hitter knocked a sharp single to left, and then stole second. I could tell that Sam did not have the same velocity as at the beginning of the game, and the hitters were getting on top of him. I briefly considered pulling him and putting in Gabe, but for better or for worse decided to stick with my original plan.

The next batter hit one sharply to left, and the runner on second came around to score, dashing our hopes of ending it then. Our rivals from Concord had tied the game.

Things continued in the same vein. A subsequent walk and another steal put runners at second and third with no one out.

"Infield in!" I called from the dugout. "We can't let the run score."

Gabe stepped up on the grass at third and Phil, Rami, and Gil did the same at short, second, and first, respectively. The batter made contact with the next pitch, grounding it toward shortstop. Phil fielded it cleanly and threw home, but this final time when the dust settled the results were not in our favor.

"Safe!" called the umpire, and the game was over. We had lost eleven to ten in extra innings.

For the Rashi Rams, the tournament was complete. We had finished with no wins and eight losses, placing dead last among all ninety-six teams. The boys slumped off the field with their chins resting on their chests as the Minutemen celebrated their well-deserved victory.

Gabe put his arm around Sam's shoulder as the two walked off the field side by side.

"You win, Sam," Gabe said.

"For once in my life I wish I hadn't," Sam replied with a tear in his eye.

CHAPTER TWENTY-FIVE

TOKEN OF THANKS

THAT NIGHT I had a dream. I was sitting in the stands at Fenway Park along the first baseline, being peppered with questions by my grandfather. I felt the roughness of the leather glove on my left hand as I watched Butch Hobson step into the batter's box. I could smell the hot popcorn and hear the chatter of the fans surrounding me. I reached down for just a moment, trying to find my Coke, which lay on the ground. My hand brushed against a wad of sticky pink gum.

Suddenly I heard a loud "*CRACK!*" Looking up, I saw Hobson's sharply hit line drive coming directly at me. The ball was hit like a rocket and was on top of me before I knew it. As it flew just inches from my face, I had but a split second to react. What should I do? Stick my glove out and risk getting hurt, but possibly come away with the prize that I had prayed for all these years? Or watch it go by, not risking anything but never knowing what could have been?

I squeezed Papa's arm for support, closed my eyes, and reached up with my left hand. The roar of the crowd was loud in my ears as I brought the glove down into my lap and opened it slowly. Inside lay a baseball, but not an ordinary one. It was a ball that I had received earlier in the day, a ball that contained a very special message from my son.

AFTER BEING DEFEATED by the Minutemen, the Rams walked off the field and into the dugout. The boys slouched on the bench, discouraged by our final loss and the realization that they would have no more chances. Along with the other coaches, I stood inside the dugout with my back to the screen, facing them.

There was silence for a minute or two. No one wanted to speak.

"Rams," I said. "I want to tell all of you something. It's not something I'm proud to admit but I feel I should."

They remained quiet, staring at the ground.

"I was afraid to come here," I said. "I was afraid to bring you guys to this tournament."

"Why?" Charlie asked.

"I was scared, Charlie—scared to fail, scared that we would be embarrassed, scared that I wouldn't measure up."

"It's okay, Coach. I was scared, too," Charlie said. "I was scared that my blood sugar would drop in the middle of an inning, and that I wouldn't be able to get to the bench."

Everyone smiled half-heartedly at Charlie.

"I was scared too, Charlie, scared about starting the game against the Sting," Gabe offered.

"I was scared that I would make too many errors," Jeff Goodman admitted.

"I was scared that I didn't know the rules of baseball,"

Carlos muttered.

"I was scared that I would forget my father's hitting instructions," Phil announced.

"I was scared that I wouldn't fit in with the team," Ari confessed.

"I was scared that you guys were relying on me, and that I wouldn't come through," Sam disclosed.

And on and on they went, listing every fear that had plagued them over the last six months.

"Listen to yourselves, guys," I said. "So many fears, and yet none of them stopped you from going forward. Each and every fear was faced head on, if not entirely conquered. Whatever our record was or wasn't simply does not matter. I am proud of this team and what we accomplished. Mazel tov, boys. We did it!"

WE LEFT THE dugout and walked out of the stadium, into the warm embrace of family and friends.

"Congratulations," Sheryl said, squeezing me tightly. "You did it! You made it through. It's over!"

"Yeah, I can't believe it. I feel as if we must have another game coming up, or something. I guess I need to come to grips with it, though. As you said, it's over."

"It was worth all the anxiety and hard work, Josh. Every time I looked at Gabe's face this week and every time I looked at him looking at you, I knew it was worth it. I'm so proud of both of you."

"Thanks, honey. I couldn't have done it without you."

"What do you think? Should you bring them back for the twelve and under tournament in a couple of years?" she joked.

That brought a chuckle to my throat. "Stranger things have happened," I said.

Jason and Charlie's mothers came around and handed each of the coaches a small token of thanks for the work we had done. It was a Cooperstown Dreams Park baseball that the players had signed in secret. Each ball was held in a square cardboard box.

I praised the parents for their support, and looked around meaning to congratulate the team once more. Fathers and sons were locked in embraces; I saw Adam and Ari holding each other, Jeremy and Charlie hugging, David walking with his arm tightly around Phil, and Stan with his hands on both sides of Jeff's face as he kissed him. Then all the Rams picked up their gloves and began throwing the ball around in a small grassy area outside of the field where we had just played. At first it was just two or three of them, then a few more, and before I knew it, the entire team had formed a large circle, zipping the baseball back and forth one to the other. Nothing could have made me happier.

"How do you feel?" Adam walked up to me, followed closely by Jeremy and Stan.

"Exhausted."

"You should be proud," he said.

"As should you, all three of you . . . even though we finished dead last."

"Jeff did the math," Stan volunteered. "We gave up a hundred and seventeen runs and scored thirteen. That might be some kind of Dreams Park record."

"Gabe played well, huh?" Jeremy asked.

"He's given me more joy in six days than any father

could expect in a lifetime."

"And how about that 'mind killer' thing you're always talking about? Are you over that yet?" Jeremy had not been able to put my behavior at the Hall of Fame behind him.

"I'm sure it'll still rear its ugly head every once in a while, but something tells me I'll be able to fight it off better than before. Taking twelve Jewish boys to play at Cooperstown Dreams Park for a week will give you some perspective."

He agreed.

AS THE TEAM and parents began to disperse, I looked around for Gabriel. He wasn't playing catch with the others, and I realized that I hadn't seen him at all since we had walked out of the dugout. He was nowhere to be found.

Then I caught a glimpse of him sitting alone on the grass with his back to the outside of the stadium fence, head hung low between his knees. I walked over, and sat down next to him, putting my arm over his shoulders. Tears streamed down his face.

"It's been an emotional week, huh, kiddo?" I said.

He did not respond, so we sat together in silence for a while as he rested his head against my shoulder, his tears dampening my shirt. Minutes passed and watching him, I began to cry as well. Then he looked up at me and spoke softly.

"Did you look at your ball, Dad?" he asked, nodding toward the box that was resting in my hand.

"No, I didn't get a chance yet."

"Take a look," he said.

I removed the gleaming white ball from the cardboard box and examined it. The signatures of all twelve Rashi Rams players were scattered along the surface. But when I came to Gabriel's signature, I saw that underneath his name he had written something else.

Throughout the week my son had received praise for his remarkable pitching performance. But it was not his pitching of which he was most proud. I guess following in his father's footsteps, however small they may be, was far more important to him. Tears welled in my eyes anew as I turned the ball over in my hand.

"Gabe," it read. "Third base for life."

EPILOGUE

ON WEDNESDAY NIGHT after tucking the boys into bed, we announced their stats for the week. Nine of our twelve players had batting averages of .000, and the team batting average was a measly .100. Remarkably, Sam Budd hit .381 over the eight-game span. Phil Perlow led the team with ten stolen bases, but unfortunately also matched that with a team high ten strikeouts. Rami Liebshutz was happy to hear that he placed second in on base percentage at .364. It was tough for the opposition not to walk a player whose strike zone was about the size of the baseball.

Charlie Finkelstein tied for the team lead by being hit by a pitch once, but I also granted him the award for making the most intelligent play of the week—resisting the temptation to pick up that ball stuck under the fence in our final game. Jeff Goodman had two assists to his credit, and a pat on the back for being the only player to start in the infield who had never practiced there. Carlos Garcia-Feinstein had an on-base percentage of .333 and of course provided us with some of the most thrilling moments in the tournament.

Jason Armon was third on the team with an earned run average of 18.00, but in addition was the only player to have an outfield assist. Aaron Dines saved us over and over by catching masterful games behind the plate, and his knees took more abuse during the week than anyone had a right to ask of them. Gil's tooth however, inched out Aaron's knees for the "body part that saw the most damage award," and he was congratulated on taking one (or two) for the team. As our youngest member, Ari placed third with four stolen bases and had eight put-outs, more than any of our outfielders. Having played the majority of his time at first base, Robert Matz overwhelmingly led the team with thirty-three put-outs. He was also the proud owner of one of my favorite stats of the week, a whopping ERA of 36.00.

I still keep the stat sheet in my office, and every time I glance at it, one number always stands out. The team leader in ERA was none other than my Gabriel, allowing a stingy 2.65 earned runs per six innings against some of the best talent in the country.

THE AWARD FOR our most dedicated fan came down to two unlikely contestants—my daughter, Shani, and the overly passionate but devoted David Perlow. With apologies to David, Shani won, hands down. She was present at nearly every practice and every game, never complaining, always willing to help out when asked, and supportive of her brother to the very end.

Behind the scenes, team mom Sheryl was constantly working to make it all happen. In retrospect, she was right about so many things that we disagreed upon—the additional teammates, the early practices (done at her insistence), and even the Nesquik, just to name a few. But that so often seems to be the case. She inspires me each and every day to stretch myself, to try for more and never to fear. I could not have done it without her.

I cannot say enough about our coaches who donated much more than a week of their time and energy to help me make Gabe's dream a reality. Adam was a rock all week long. There is no better anchor in a storm. Jeremy and I created a friendship that will last a lifetime. I cannot overstate how lucky I was to have him there with me. And Stan? In all my years as a physician, I have never seen someone fight so hard. The strength and devotion that he showed to his son and to each member of our team should be an inspiration to us all.

WE STAYED ON at Dreams Park until Friday morning, to watch the remainder of the play-offs and to participate in the closing ceremonies. We again marched with our banner, which by now had taken some abuse; part of the ink from our logo had started to run. Oddly enough, the RBI Angels marched in front of us, and the two teams got into some good-natured taunting about their game. Gabe found me to report that the Angels were saying our starting pitcher had been throwing up meatballs, but I gave him a straightforward response.

"Ask them, if you were throwing up so many meatballs, why they scored only one run off you?" He liked that, and returned quickly to the fray.

During the closing ceremonies, the head coaches called their players and assistants individually to run onto the field through a waiting arch, where each was handed a special CDP ring by none other than Lou Presutti, the owner of the park.

The rings were unique, made of sterling silver with

the words "American Youth Baseball Hall of Fame" surrounding a green stone. The boys received them with
pride, and ran off to show them to parents and friends.

THE PARK MADE an announcement that they were
planning to build a youth baseball Hall of Fame, and
were seeking any team paraphernalia associated with
broken records. We certainly had not broken any ourselves, unless it was most runs allowed or least runs
scored, but I felt that I should leave a memento of our
stay. So I had the team sign one of our Rashi practice
balls and handed it in, notifying the park that we were
the first all-Jewish team to compete there. The ball had
the word *rashi* written on it in lowercase letters in pur-
ple marker. The teenage boy collecting the souvenirs did
not seem to grasp the significance of the keepsake, but
no matter; hopefully, someday it will be displayed in the
Hall.

The final game of the week was played on Thursday
night under the lights, in a mild drizzle. The vaunted
San Diego Stars North defeated the Viper Baseball
Academy from Alabama for the championship. We were
pulling hard for the Vipers, keeping allegiance with un-
derdogs everywhere. When the Viper's centerfielder
dropped a routine fly ball, resulting in two critical runs,
I was reminded that these were just kids and not automatons after all.

Somewhere along the line, the Sting had been
knocked out of the play-offs. Gabe reported to me that he
had overheard its coach giving his postgame talk. He
told his team that they now knew what they needed to

work on to accomplish their real goal—the AAU National Championship. Having only beaten a team thrown together from a small Jewish day school thirteen to nothing, I would say that they had a ways to go. Reportedly, the Sting voted to leave the park and return home prior to the closing ceremonies. *What a shame,* I thought.

For our part, the week ended quietly as we packed up on Friday morning and went our separate ways. Some of the boys were going home, others directly to overnight camp. I'm sure the cars were filled with nonstop stories that day.

Early that next week, Gabe, Shani, and Ari went on to spend a month at Yavneh in Northwood, New Hampshire, where they had the time of their lives. Dominating on their camp softball team was easy for the boys after what they had been through. Not surprisingly, Gabe wrote home that they notched their first win over Bauercrest that summer. I wrote back that he should savor the victory, and not expect another.

WHEN WE RETURNED to school that fall, none other than my idol, Milton Schwartz, approached me. He wanted to know about our experiences in Cooperstown, as he was interested in taking another Rashi team there the following summer. I filled him in on the details and advised that he tread cautiously. Despite the mixed reviews, Milt forged ahead, attempting to organize another school team to return to the park. The families in the new fourth grade were far more focused on potential conflicts with Little League play-offs, having witnessed Aaron Dine's dilemma. Consequently, a new team to carry the Cooperstown torch never materialized. When I heard, I was saddened by the news.

OVER THE NEXT few years, Sam Budd worked diligently on his baseball skills. He went on to play for a highly competitive Massachusetts travel team, competing in tournaments up and down the East Coast.

Phil Perlow played two years of Little League, and after shifting to centerfield, became one of the best players on his team. Ultimately, he gave up on baseball, realizing that his tremendous athletic gifts translated more naturally to the basketball hard court.

Throughout their remaining years at Rashi, Phil and Sam treated each other with compassion and respect, each having earned it from the other during their week in Cooperstown.

Aaron Dines transferred to a secular independent school, but still kept in touch with his old cronies. He forever regretted missing that first day at Dreams Park and the resulting damage it had done to his pin collection. With age, Aaron's focus turned toward entrepreneurship. He went on to open a local hip-hop clothing store while still in his early teens.

Rami Liebshutz stayed to complete his years at Rashi. He never allowed his hair to grow back, deciding that the Rocks' look suited him just fine. Although he enjoyed his time at second base, he never picked up a glove again, recognizing that he could spit on a soccer field just as easily as on a baseball diamond.

A year after our return from Cooperstown, Robert Matz transferred to his local public school. Whenever I

saw him, he always exuded the same, happy-go-lucky
optimistic spirit. Years later, he still insisted that his
frightening Dreams Park ERA was an aberration. He
was sure if he could do it again, things would be different.

Carlos Garcia-Feinstein matured rapidly, finding a
comfortable place at school and within his grade. He
could be seen walking the hallways, joking and laughing
with friends at his side, but it's doubtful that baseball
was ever one of the subjects under discussion. He never
did bother to learn the rules.

Jason Armon's foul mouth did not improve, and his
repertoire of profanities expanded considerably with age.
He continued to fine-tune his timing, however, and kept
up his incredible knack of putting a smile on everyone's
face. Similar to his good friend, Rami, Jason quickly put
the world of competitive baseball behind him. A year or
so after we got back, he discovered ice hockey, which
suited his personality far better.

Gil Slotnick and his family returned to Israel, where
his combination of good looks and American *joie de vivre*
made him the envy of every boy at his new school. His
repaired tooth remained intact, and despite his concerns,
did not affect his ability to attract the opposite sex.

Adam returned to his quiet surgery practice at the local community hospital, deciding to focus on lap-band
obesity surgery. It was never clear whether his patients
lost weight due to the procedure or for fear of not following his strict orders to keep from eating.

After Cooperstown, Ari began to speak and speak
some more, making up for lost time. My quiet nephew

blossomed into a social butterfly. He could often be heard loudly calling to his friends down the hallway at school, and never missed a party.

Jeremy Finkelstein continued flying around the world, buying and selling companies. Meanwhile, he burned holes in countless pairs of sneakers as he logged hour after hour on the treadmill. Jeremy went on to make significant donations to the Rashi School for its new building. The facilities included Rashi's first baseball diamond.

Charlie continued to grow at a rapid pace, his height demanding that basketball be his primary sport. Over the ensuing years, Charlie and Gabe spent endless hours arguing over whether their time was better spent shooting hoops or playing catch.

Tragically, Stan Goodman had, come home from Cooperstown to discover that his tumor had not been completely eradicated. Repeat surgery was performed in an attempt to remove more of the cancer, but to no avail. Stan continued to fight. When we saw each other, I did my best to raise his spirits by reminiscing about our week at Dreams Park, and on occasion I would elicit a smile or even a chuckle.

Two years after his diagnosis, Stan passed away, outliving his original life expectancy by a full twelve months. His funeral took place on a cool, rainy spring afternoon, and as I stood outside under an umbrella at the cemetery, I was reminded of a similar day two years prior when Stan had run the bases at our first practice with the uninhibited joy of a young boy.

It is Jewish tradition for family and friends to shovel

a small amount of dirt onto the grave, and while watching Jeffrey Goodman do so, I prayed that he would live a life in a manner akin to his dad. I had little doubt. When you see a superior father, a similar son is not far behind.

Gabriel completed his years at Rashi, spending plenty of time catching footballs on the playground and participating in games of pickle. He continues to play baseball, last year pitching a seven-inning shutout in the opening game of his Babe Ruth season. We still play catch in the yard, where I work with him on his delivery, cousin Jordan's lessons echoing in my head.

The memories of that week in Cooperstown still linger in our home. Gabriel's pin collection hangs on a bulletin board in his room, the Rams' pin in the center surrounded by those of the eight teams that we competed against. My cap and coach's shirt lay in the closet, gathering dust.

I continue to make the long drive to and from work each day, at times dreaming about coaching the Rams once again. But that piece of my life is over and baseball is now mostly about watching the Red Sox with the kids by my side. Occasionally, when the Sox aren't playing well, Sandy Koufax will pay me a visit, but he has yet to utter a word since that fateful day at the Hall of Fame.

ACKNOWLEDGMENTS

THERE ARE TWO very important people without whom this book would never have come to be: editor Joseph Pittman and literary agent Andy Zack. Joe, you took a chance on our story when launching a new imprint. I cannot thank you enough. Andy, after working with you for over two years, I guarantee that you are the Central Florida Sting of agents, one of the very best.

A special thanks to Sam at SLGWORKS for creating our website. Your personal touch goes a long way.

Thanks to all of the families who participated and supported us. We talk about *kehillah* where I come from, the Hebrew word for "community." I could not ask for a better one.

Thanks to my brother, Jonathan, and his wife, Ellen. Your unbridled enthusiasm for this project and all things is contagious.

My gratitude goes out to my brother-in-law, Kenny, his wife, Carlana, and their kids, for opening up a window to a world I never knew existed. It's not your fault I climbed through.

To the rest of my family down south: Lynn, Allen, Paula, Jerome, and their children, thanks for all your encouragement.

To my sister-in-law, Karen, and her husband, Freddy, I say support comes in all shapes and sizes. "This deserves to be published," is a big one, especially when you're the very first to say so.

To Jody, your secret worked after all. As Gabe and Phil discovered, "A good friend . . . is ever a useful thing," and how much more true that is when it's your sister. For Adam, thank you for your friendship, generosity, and, of course, your ability to discipline.

To Mom, thank you for showing your children and grandchildren the beauties of family, culture, and tradition. Your hand is in every page of this book. To my late father who I miss desperately, I wish you could have been there. I hope this book appeals to you, Dad.

Shani and Gabe, a father could not ask for more special children. Thanks for allowing me to tell the world that I'm your dad.

To Sheryl, thank you for sharing your life with me. I am blessed to have you as a partner in all things. I love you more than words allow.

And finally, a word of thanks goes out to my dear friend Nora, who spent countless hours lying at my feet while I slaved away at the computer. For all you struggling authors fearful of the never-ending late nights when it's just you and the screen, a parting word of advice—get a Newfoundland.

ABOUT THE AUTHOR

BORN AND RAISED in Boston, Joshua Berkowitz is an avid Red Sox fan. He currently practices internal medicine on the North Shore of Boston and enjoys spending time with his wife, Sheryl, and their two children, Gabriel and Shoshana. www.thirdbaseforlife.com